Symphony of Flavors

Best Wishes,
Debbie Caswell

compiled by
Christine Askew
Debbie Caswell
Sirita Inklebarger

cover sketch by
Betty L. Askew

calligraphy by
Carol Measures

A Classic Collection of Recipes

First Printing   September 1991   10,000 copies

Library of Congress Catalog Card Number: 90-064430

International Standard Book Number: 0-9629059-0-9

Introduction

There are a few things in life that bring a person a sense of well being and satisfaction. Some of these are a loving family, good friends, beautiful music, and flavorful food. In SYMPHONY OF FLAVORS we have tried to bring together recipes that are delicious, enjoyable to eat, and fun to prepare. As we have prepared and served these recipes, we have made many memories of good times with family and friends. Just as the various instruments and notes in an orchestra blend to create distinctive and exquisite sounds, the various combinations in our recipes blend to create distinctive and exquisite flavors.

Our recipes range from the simple, such as a common tune, to the elegant, such as a complex symphony. We've included a variety of recipes from popular to classical, many being traditional dishes with new variations.

We appreciate all of our friends, both old and new, who have so generously shared their favorite recipes with us. We realize there are a very few truly "original" recipes, but we also realize that we each put our personal touch to the dishes that we create. Keeping this in mind as you follow our recipes, add your own personal touch to create your own masterpieces.

Christine, Debbie, and Sirita

Table of Contents

Hors d'Oeuvres 7

Brunch 29

Beverages 37

Breads 43

Salads 59

Entrées 83

Casseroles 135

Vegetables and Side Dishes 145

Cakes, Candies, and Cookies 167

Pies, Puddings, and Ice Cream 223

Potpourri 247

Hints 253

Index 257

Hors d'Oeuvres

Olive Nut Sandwiches
A hit at any party

1 (6 oz.) package softened
   cream cheese
1/2 c. mayonnaise
1/2 c. chopped pecans
1 c. salad olives, chopped
2 Tbsp. olive juice
Dash pepper

Mash cream cheese with a fork, then add mayonnaise. Blend well. Stir in pecans, olives, olive juice, and pepper. Do not add salt. Mix well. This will be slightly mushy, but after it is refrigerated for a few hours, it will be firmer and of spreading consistency.

Besides making a delicious sandwich, this is great on toast or lettuce leaves, or both.

Should you have any left over, the spread also keeps well in the refrigerator for a week or two.

Cheese Cookies by John Fisher
A very popular, often requested recipe

1 stick oleo
2 cups grated cheese
   (Cracker Barrel sharp)
1 c. flour
1 tsp. salt
Tabasco or red pepper to
   taste
1/2 c. pecans, finely
   chopped

Blend ingredients together. Divide mixture in half and roll in long roll about one inch thick. Wrap in wax paper and chill. Slice very thin. Place on ungreased baking sheet and bake at 350° for 10 to 15 minutes.

Tortilla Rollups
Quick and easy

1 lb. cream cheese,
    softened
1 small carton sour cream
1 (4 oz.) can green chilies,
    drained and chopped
2 Tbsp. picante sauce
1 Tbsp. finely chopped
    onion
1/2 c. chopped black olives
1/8 tsp. garlic powder
10 (8") flour tortillas
Additional picante sauce

Use mixer to beat the first 5 ingredients until blended. Add olives and garlic powder. Spread mixture on tortillas and roll up. Wrap in plastic wrap. Refrigerate several hours. Cut in 1/2" slices. Serve with additional picante sauce.

Cocktail Crackers

1 large pkg. oyster crackers
3/4 c. vegetable oil
1 pkg. Hidden Valley
    Ranch salad mix
1-1/2 tsp. garlic powder

Pour oil over crackers and toss. Let set awhile then sprinkle powders over and toss more. Enjoy!!!

Sandwich Spread
JoAnn Brown serves this at children's parties and they love it.

1 lb. Velveeta, grated
1 small jar pimientos,
    drained
1 small can crushed
    pineapple, drained
1/2 small jar pickle relish
4 boiled eggs, grated
1 c. chopped pecans,
    optional
Onion powder to taste
Mayonnaise to spreading
    consistency

Blend all ingredients. This will keep in refrigerator up to one week. HINT: Freeze the Velveeta and it will grate easily.

T V Trash

1 box Cheerios
1 box Rice Chex
1 box Wheat Chex
1 box Corn Chex
1 pkg. pretzel sticks
1 can peanuts
1 c. pecan halves
1 stick butter
1/2 c. bacon grease
1 Tbsp. garlic salt
1 Tbsp. Tabasco sauce
2 Tbsp. Accent

Mix cereals, pretzel sticks, peanuts, and pecans. In a saucepan, melt butter and bacon fat. Add garlic salt, Tabasco, and Accent. Blend completely and pour over mixed cereals. Fill a large roasting pan full of mixture and roast in oven at 225° for 1 to 2 hours. Stir every 15 minutes. Repeat as often as necessary until all mixture is roasted.

Bourbon Wieners

Thanks to Susan Guinn for this unusual and delicious hors d'oeuvre.

1 c. brown sugar
1 c. catsup
1/4 c. bourbon
1 - 2 pkg. wieners (Little Smokies)

Combine brown sugar, catsup, and bourbon and blend thoroughly. Add wieners and simmer. The longer — the better!

Bacon and Chicken Liver

Christine enjoys serving these when unexpected company pops in.

1 box chicken livers
1 lb. bacon

Preheat oven to 375°. Cut bacon strips in half. Cut livers in small pieces about the size of a pecan. Wrap each piece of liver with a strip of bacon, secure with toothpick, and place on a large cookie sheet. Bake until bacon is crisp. (These freeze well).

Spinach Quiche

1/2 c. oleo, melted
10 eggs
1/2 c. unsifted flour
1 tsp. baking powder
1 tsp. salt
1 (10 oz.) pkg. frozen
  chopped spinach,
  thawed
1 (8 oz.) can green chilies,
  chopped
2 c. cottage cheese
1/2 lb. Cheddar cheese,
  shredded
1/2 lb. Monterey Jack
  cheese, shredded

Preheat oven to 400°. Place oleo in 9″ × 13″ pan in oven, just long enough to melt butter. Beat eggs in a large bowl, then mix in flour, baking powder, and salt. Squeeze thawed spinach very dry and add to egg mixture, along with melted butter, chilies and cheeses. Pour mixture into pan and bake 15 minutes. Reduce heat to 350° and bake an additional 35 to 40 minutes. Let stand 5 minutes to set. Cut into 60 squares for hors d'oeuvres.

Little Smokies in a Blanket

Ben and his friends can't get enough of these.

1 can Crescent Rolls
1 sm. pkg. Little Smokies
  (16 count)

Roll out each roll and cut it into four triangles. This will give you 32 triangles. Cut each of the Little Smokies in half, and this will give you 32 smokies. Roll each smokie with one triangle. Bake on a greased cookie sheet at 375° until lightly browned.

Crabby Mushrooms
From Rick Talley of Hewitt

1/2 lb. fresh or thawed
   frozen crab meat, rinsed
   and drained
2 tsp. fresh lemon juice
1/3 c. chopped black olives
1/4 c. mayonnaise
2 Tbsp. chopped fresh
   parsley
1/4 tsp. garlic powder
1/4 tsp. onion powder
24 medium mushrooms,
   washed, dried and stems
   removed
Grated Parmesan cheese

Preheat oven to 400°. In a bowl, combine crab meat with lemon juice. Add next 5 ingredients and mix well. Fill mushroom caps with mixture. Sprinkle with Parmesan cheese. Arrange mushrooms on a baking sheet. Cover with foil and bake 12 to 15 minutes. Remove foil and continue baking until tops are golden brown, about 5 minutes. Makes 24 appetizers.

Cheese Logs

1 lb. sharp Cheddar
   cheese, grated
1 lb. Philadelphia Cream
   Cheese
1 clove garlic, crushed
1 Tbsp. grated onion
1 Tbsp. Worcestershire
   sauce
1/4 c. chili powder
1/4 c. paprika
1 c. pecans, finely chopped

Mix Cheddar cheese, cream cheese, garlic, onion, and Worcestershire. Mix well and roll into logs about 1-1/2″ diameter and 8″ long. Roll in a mixture of equal parts chili powder and paprika. Roll in pecans, then wrap in wax paper. Refrigerate until ready to use. Cut in 1/4″ slices to serve.

Alpine Appetizers

Easy to make and so, so good!

2 c. shredded Casino
   Monterey Jack cheese
   (8 oz.)
2 c. shredded Casino Swiss
   cheese (8 oz.)
4 bacon slices, crisply
   cooked and crumbled
1/4 c. green onion slices
3 eggs, beaten
1/4 c. milk
Stone ground wheat
   crackers

Combine cheeses, bacon, and onion. Add combined eggs and milk, mix lightly. Spoon into 8″ square baking dish. Bake at 325° for 25 to 30 minutes, or until knife inserted in center comes out clean. Cut into squares and serve on crackers.

Stillwater, Oklahoma Beef Jerky

From Charles Headrick, Truitt and Lucille Smith's son-in-law

4 to 5 flank steaks (about 3
   pounds)
1 c. Worcestershire sauce
1 c. soy sauce
1/2 tsp. garlic powder
1/2 tsp. red pepper
2 tsp. Lawry's season salt
2 tsp. Cavender's Greek
   seasoning
Mesquite chips
Hickory chips

Partially freeze so meat will be easy to slice. Slice across the grain into 1/4″ slices. Make sauce from Worcestershire sauce, soy sauce, garlic powder, red pepper, Lawry's salt, and Cavender's seasoning. Cover meat in sauce and marinate for 24 hours. Cook in a smoker about 2-1/2 to 3 hours. Soak chips in water before placing in smoker.

Hint: Charles marinates the meat in freezer bags.

Beef Jerky

1 beef flank steak
1/2 c. soy sauce
1/2 tsp. garlic salt
1/2 tsp. lemon pepper
1/2 tsp. red pepper

Trim fat from meat. Cut with grain into strips 1/8″ thick. Easier to cut if frozen. Mix soy sauce, garlic salt, lemon pepper, and red pepper. Cover meat with mixture. Place meat strips close together on rack over a cookie sheet. Bake in slow oven (150° to 175°) overnight for 10 to 12 hours. Store at room temperature in air-tight containers.

Spinach Cheese Triangles

1 (17-1/4 oz.) pkg.
  Pepperidge Farm Frozen
  Puff Pastry Sheets
1/2 c. minced onion
2 Tbsp. butter
1 (10 oz.) pkg. frozen
  chopped spinach,
  thawed and squeezed
  dry
1/2 c. finely chopped
  parsley
2 Tbsp. minced green
  onion
1/4 lb. feta cheese,
  crumbled
2 eggs, beaten
1 egg, beaten with 1 tsp.
  water

Preheat oven to 375°. Thaw pastry according to package directions. Sauté onion in butter in large frying-pan until transparent; remove from heat. Add spinach, parsley, green onion, cheese, and 2 eggs, mixing thoroughly. On a lightly floured board, unfold pastry and roll to a 15″ square. Cut each sheet into 25 3″-squares. Place about 2 teaspoons spinach mixture in center of each square. Brush edges with egg-water mixture and fold pastry over to form a triangle. Pinch edges with tines of a fork to seal. Brush tops with egg mixture and bake for 12 to 15 minutes. Makes 50 hors d'oeuvres.

Water Chestnut Appetizers

Linda McCutcheon of Brownfield delights her guests with these.

1 (5 oz.) can water
  chestnuts, drained
1/4 c. soy sauce
1/4 c. sugar
4 slices bacon, each cut in
  half

Marinate water chestnuts in soy sauce for 30 minutes. Roll each chestnut in sugar, then wrap with a strip of bacon and secure with a toothpick. Arrange on a baking pan. Bake at 400° for 20 minutes. Drain on paper towels.

Cheese Squares

A snappy little dish to throw together for an impromptu party

4 eggs, beaten
2 Tbsp. minced onion
4 c. grated Cheddar cheese
3 Tbsp. chopped jalapenos
  (or green chilies)

Mix together and put into an 8″ square Pyrex dish. Bake at 350° for 30 minutes.

Party Sandwiches

Pepperidge Farm very thin
    White Bread
Pepperidge Farm very thin
    Whole Wheat Bread

Use cookie cutters to cut desired shapes or use a sharp knife and cut desired shapes. Choose toppings from the recipes that follow.

Spread with cream cheese and top with a thin slice of smoked salmon and a sprig of dill.

Spread with butter and top with thin slices of cucumber and/or tomato; sprinkle with salt and pepper.

Spread with Jalapeno Cheez Whiz and top with crumbled bacon.

BLUE CHEESE BUTTER:
1/2 c. butter, softened
4 oz. crumbled blue cheese

Mix butter with cheese until smooth. Spread on bread and top with thin-sliced red radishes and capers.

STRAWBERRY CREAM CHEESE:
1/4 c. strawberry preserves
6 oz. softened cream cheese

Mix until completely blended. Spread on bread and top with fresh strawberries.

HAM AND ALMOND PATE:
1/4 c. chopped almonds
1/4 lb. boiled ham
3 oz. softened cream cheese
1/4 tsp. dry mustard
1/8 tsp. paprika
1/8 tsp. pepper
1/2 tsp. Worcestershire
    sauce
2 drops Tabasco sauce
2-3 Tbsp. sour cream

Put all ingredients in food processor and process until smooth. Spread on bread and top with sliced black olives.

GINGERED CREAM CHEESE:
3 oz. cream cheese,
    softened
1-1/2 Tbsp. finely chopped
    preserved ginger
1 Tbsp. ginger syrup

Mix until blended. Spread on bread and top with kiwi slices.

Fried Cheese

8 slices mozzarella cheese,
  3/4" thick
1/2 tsp. salt
1 c. flour
2 eggs, beaten
1-1/2 c. bread crumbs
1 c. shortening

Sprinkle cheese with salt. Dip slices in flour, then in egg, and finally in bread crumbs. Fry quickly in hot shortening until golden brown.

Prize Mushrooms

2 (6 oz.) cans mushroom
  crowns
1 (8 oz.) carton cottage
  cheese
2 Tbsp. minced chives
Dash of hot pepper sauce
1/4 tsp. Worcestershire
  sauce
1/2 tsp. celery salt
1/2 tsp. powdered mustard

Drain mushrooms and hollow out stem. Mix remaining ingredients and beat well. Top each mushroom with mixture. Makes 2 dozen.

Sausage-Cheese Balls

1/2 lb. hot sausage
2 c. Cheddar cheese, grated
  (8 oz.)
1/8 tsp. cayenne pepper
2 c. Bisquick
2 Tbsp. water

Fry sausage, stirring until crumbly and completely browned. Drain on paper towels. Combine sausage, cheese, pepper, and Bisquick. Add water and mix well. Form into 1" balls. Bake on greased cookie sheet at 375° for 15 minutes, or until lightly browned. Makes about 5 dozen.

Cheese Crackers
Great to serve with dips

1 stick butter
1 c. flour
1 small jar English cheese
1/8 tsp. red pepper

Cut butter into flour with pastry cutter. Add other ingredients and mix well. Refrigerate at least 2 hours, or until easy to work with. Form small balls and press with thumb to make a wafer. Bake at 400° for 15 minutes. Serve while hot. These can be made and frozen to cook later.

Ham And Cheese Appetizers
Veta Ford's fantastic appetizers

2 c. Bisquick
3/4 c. ham, cooked and
   finely chopped
1 c. Cheddar cheese,
   shredded
1/2 c. onion, chopped
1/2 c. Parmesan cheese,
   grated
1/4 c. sour cream
2 Tbsp. parsley, snipped
1/2 tsp. salt
1/2 tsp. garlic powder
2/3 c. milk
1 egg

Heat oven to 350°. Grease 9" × 13" baking dish. Mix all ingredients, spread in pan. Bake until golden brown, 25 to 30 minutes. Cut into rectangles, about 2" × 1". Makes 36 appetizers.

Sausage-Onion Squares

1 lb. hot sausage
1 large onion, chopped
2 c. Bisquick
2 eggs
3/4 c. milk
2 tsp. caraway seeds
1-1/2 c. sour cream
1/4 tsp. salt
1/4 tsp. paprika

Cook sausage and onion until sausage is brown and onion is tender, then drain and set aside. Combine Bisquick, 1 egg, and milk, and mix well. Spread mixture in 9" × 13" pan. Sprinkle with caraway seeds. Mix sour cream, salt, and remaining egg into sausage mixture, and mix well. Spread on top of biscuit mixture. Sprinkle with paprika. Bake at 350° for 40 minutes. Cool and cut into squares. Serves 12.

Bacon Crunchies

1 egg, beaten
1/4 tsp. chili powder
3 - 4 drops Tabasco
1 Tbsp. water
3/4 c. Parmesan cheese
8 slices bacon, cut into
    thirds

Mix egg with seasonings and water in a small shallow dish. Place Parmesan cheese on wax paper. Dip bacon in egg mixture, then coat with cheese. Cover completely. Place on a broiler pan. Bake at 350° for 15 to 20 minutes, or until golden. Serve immediately.

Cheese Straws

A crowd-pleasing snack from Louise Barrett

1 glass Kraft Old English
    Cheese
1 stick butter
1-1/2 c. flour
1/4 tsp. salt
1/4 tsp. red pepper

Let cheese and butter softened. Add flour and seasonings. Beat with mixer. Use cookie press and press out to desired length. Bake at 400° for about 7 minutes on cookie sheet. Do not brown.

Sausage Pinwheels

Louise Barrett's delightful hors d'oeuvres are great for showers.

2 c. flour
1/2 tsp. salt
3 tsp. baking powder
5 Tbsp. shortening
2/3 c. milk
1 lb. sausage

Mix all ingredients except sausage and blend into a dough. Divide dough into 2 parts. Roll out each part until 1/4" thick. Spread sausage evenly and roll up into roll and refrigerate. Cut pinwheels and bake at 350° until toasty.

Shrimp Dip

Easy and delicious

3/4 c. Catsup
1 Tbsp. Worcestershire
    sauce
1/4 tsp. Tabasco sauce
1/4 tsp. horseradish
1/4 tsp. dry mustard
1 c. miniature shrimp

Mix catsup, Worcestershire sauce, Tabasco sauce, horseradish, and mustard well. Stir in shrimp. Chill and serve with crackers. This can be doubled and tripled easily.

Zesty Meatballs And Dip

MEATBALLS:
2 eggs, beaten
1/3 c. milk
2/3 c. mashed potato
  flakes
2 Tbsp. instant minced
  onions
1 tsp. salt
1/8 tsp. pepper
1/8 tsp. garlic powder
1 tsp. Worcestershire sauce
1 lb. ground beef

Combine eggs, milk, and potato flakes and set aside. Mix onions, salt, pepper, garlic powder, Worcestershire sauce, and beef. Blend the two mixtures together and shape into 1″ meatballs. In large skillet, cook meatballs until done and well browned. Keep warm until ready to serve. Serve with toothpicks.

DIP:
1/2 c. chives
1/2 c. onion flakes
1 c. sour cream
1 Tbsp. brown gravy mix
2 tsp. milk

Mix chives, onion, sour cream, gravy mix, and milk. Cook, stirring constantly, over low heat for 5 to 10 minutes. (Do not boil.)

Prairie Fire Dip
One of Oleta Smith's tasty dishes

1/2 lb. Cheddar cheese,
  grated
1 clove garlic, chopped
  fine
2 Tbsp. minced onion
6 jalapenos, chopped
1/2 lb. butter
1 qt. red beans (drained)

Mix cheese, garlic, onion, jalapenos, and butter in a food processor or blender until smooth. Add beans and again process until smooth. Place mixture in an oven-to-table dish, top with cheese and heat until cheese has melted. Serve hot with tortilla chips.

Pineapple-Cheese Spread

1 (3 oz.) pkg. cream
  cheese, softened
1/2 c. crushed pineapple,
  drained
1/4 c. finely chopped
  pecans
1/2 tsp. ground ginger

Beat cream cheese until light and fluffy. Stir in remaining ingredients. Serve with fruit, vegetables, or on crackers.

Ham Spread

1 (3 oz.) pkg. cream
   cheese, softened
3/4 c. finely chopped,
   cooked ham
1 Tbsp. mayonnaise
1/2 tsp. dry mustard
1/8 tsp. red pepper

Beat cream cheese until light and fluffy. Stir in the remaining ingredients. Serve with crackers and chips.

Mexican Dip

You can't get any easier than this!

1 small pkg. Mexican
   Velveeta
1/4 c. milk

Cube cheese and put into microwave dish. Add milk and microwave on medium setting for 2 minutes. Stir with a wire whisk. Keep heating and stirring until cheese is completely melted. Serve with Tostitos.

Quick and Easy Dip

1 (10-1/2 oz.) can cream of
   onion soup
1 (8 oz.) pkg. cream cheese
1 (4 oz.) can chopped
   green chilies

Heat, stir, and serve with chips or raw vegetables.

Curried Shrimp Cheese Ball

1/2 c. coconut
1/4 tsp. curry powder
2 (8 oz.) pkg. cream
   cheese, softened
2 (4-1/2 oz.) cans shrimp,
   rinsed, drained, and
   chopped
2 Tbsp. minced onion

Combine coconut and curry powder and mix well. Spread mixture on a baking sheet. Bake at 350° for 7 minutes, stirring every 2 minutes. Cool and set aside.

Combine remaining ingredients and mix well. Shape into ball. Mixture will be sticky. Roll in coconut. Chill 1 to 2 hours. Serve with crackers.

Seafood Spread

1 (8 oz.) pkg. cream cheese
1 (6-1/2 oz.) can crabmeat, rinsed, drained, and flaked
1/2 c. sour cream
1/2 c. chopped celery
1/4 c. chopped green onion
1/4 c. chili sauce
1/4 tsp. garlic powder
1/4 tsp. onion powder
1/4 c. sliced almonds
Paprika
1 Tbsp. chopped fresh parsley (opt.)

Place cream cheese in a 9″ pie plate. Microwave at high setting for 45 seconds or until soft. Stir until cream cheese is smooth and creamy. Stir in crabmeat, sour cream, celery, green onions, chili sauce, garlic powder, and onion powder. Mix well. Spread mixture evenly in pie plate. Sprinkle with almonds and paprika. Microwave uncovered for 4 minutes. Sprinkle top evenly with chopped parsley and serve spread with crackers. Makes about 3 cups.

Artichoke Dip

1 (8-1/2 oz.) can artichoke hearts, drained
1/2 c. mayonnaise
1/2 c. Parmesan cheese
1 tsp. minced garlic
1 pt. sour cream

Drain artichokes, saving juice. Blend artichokes, mayonnaise, cheese, and garlic in blender. Fold in sour cream. Use reserved juice, if needed, for thinning. Refrigerate for several hours before serving.

Chili Con Queso X

1 large onion, chopped
2 Tbsp. margarine
1/2 c. tomato puree
4 canned green chilies
8 oz. American cheese
1 c. cream
Salt and pepper to taste

Simmer onion in margarine until lightly browned. Add tomato puree and chopped chilies. Simmer 15 minutes. Add cut up cheese and cream and heat until cheese is melted. Keep heat as low as possible so cheese does not boil. Serve at once with chips.

Shrimp Spread

An easy, make-ahead party dish from Louise Barrett

1 (8 oz.) pkg. cream
   cheese, softened
1/2 c. salad dressing
1 (4-1/4 oz.) can tiny
   cocktail shrimp, drained
   and rinsed
1/3 c. finely chopped
   onion
1/8 tsp. garlic salt

Combine cream cheese and salad dressing, mixing until well blended. Stir in remaining ingredients. Cover and chill. Serve with assorted crackers. Makes 2 cups.

Black-Eyed Pea Dip

A real humdinger dish from Louise Barrett

2 c. cooked black-eyed peas
1 stick oleo, melted
1 jalapeno pepper
1/2 tsp. juice of peppers
1 medium onion, chopped
1 clove garlic
4 oz. grated Cheddar
   cheese
3/4 to 1 c. milk (if needed
   for consistency)

Mix first six ingredients in blender, then place in saucepan. Add cheese and milk as needed for consistency. Stir over heat until cheese melts. Serve hot or cold.

Layer Dip

The Xi Pi Phi girls in Lamesa love this!

1 can refried beans
1 pkg. dry Taco mix
1 can green chilies, diced
   and drained
1 small carton sour cream
1 small onion, chopped
1/2 c. chopped ripe olives
1/2 c. diced tomatoes
4 oz. grated Cheddar
   cheese
4 oz. grated Mozzarella
   cheese

Mix refried beans and Taco mix, and pour into a large Pyrex or Corning Ware dish. Layer other ingredients in order.

Russian Sauce

We enjoyed this at the ASCS open house.

1 c. real mayonnaise
1 Tbsp. chopped bell
   pepper
1 Tbsp. chopped green
   onion
(or 1 tsp. onion flakes)
1 Tbsp. chili powder
1 Tbsp. red wine vinegar
Salt and pepper to taste

Mix and use as a dip for chips or veggies. DO NOT use Miracle Whip for the mayonnaise.

Sausage Cheese Dip

Tracy's family loves this.

1 lb. hamburger meat
1 lb. sausage (reg. or hot)
1 onion, diced
2 lb. Velveeta cheese
1 can cream of mushroom
   soup
1 can Rotel diced green
   chilies and tomatoes
1/2 tsp. garlic salt
Salt and pepper to taste.

Cook meat and onion, then drain. Melt cheese and stir in soup and Rotel tomatoes. Add soup and cheese mixture to meat. Add seasonings, mix well, and serve hot.

Fresh Vegetable Dip

1/4 c. shredded cabbage
1/3 c. shredded carrot
2 Tbsp. finely chopped
   green pepper
1 Tbsp. finely chopped
   onion
1 (8 oz.) carton sour cream
2 Tbsp. mayonnaise
1 tsp. tarragon vinegar
3/4 tsp. garlic salt
1 tsp. bacon bits

Mix together and serve with relish plate of fresh vegetables.

Hot Broccoli Dip

Mildred LeMond gave this delicious recipe to us.

1 pkg. frozen chopped
   broccoli
1 minced onion
2 Tbsp. butter
1 roll garlic cheese
1 can mushroom soup
1 (4 oz.) can mushrooms,
   drained
3/4 c. chopped almonds
1 tsp. Accent
1/2 tsp. salt
1/8 tsp. black pepper
1 tsp. Worcestershire sauce
1/8 tsp. Tabasco sauce

Cook broccoli according to package directions. Drain. Cook onion in butter then add cheese and soup. Add broccoli then cook 1 minute. Add remaining ingredients and serve with chips. Keep dip hot by serving in a fondue dish.

Shoepeg Dip

1 (12 oz.) can shoepeg
   corn, drained
1 c. shredded Cheddar
   cheese
1/4 c. grated Parmesan
   cheese
1 (8 oz.) carton sour cream
1/2 c. mayonnaise
1 to 2 Tbsp. grated onion

Mix all ingredients; stir well. Chill several hours or overnight. Serve with taco chips or a variety of crackers.

Mozzarella Cheese Dip

1 pt. mayonnaise
1 c. sour cream
8 oz. grated Mozzarella
   cheese
1 tsp. garlic salt
2 Tbsp. sugar
1 tsp. Accent
1 Tbsp. Parmesan cheese

Mix all ingredients and chill. Dip or spread for vegetables and crackers.

Bacon and Cheese Surprise

2 c. grated sharp cheese
1 small can chopped ripe
 olives
2 Tbsp. chopped onion
1 c. Hellmann's
 mayonnaise
1 loaf rye or wheat rounds
Bacon bits

Combine all ingredients, spread on 1 loaf party rounds. Sprinkle with bacon bits. (Too many will make it greasy.) Bake at 300° for 15 minutes. Can be made ahead and refrigerated or frozen until baked. Serve on heated tray or right from oven.

Potato Dip

2 c. sour cream
1 (1.5 oz.) pkg. potato
 toppers

Mix well. Refrigerate 2 hours or overnight, before serving. Serve with chips.

Cream Cheese Dip

2 (8 oz.) pkg. cream cheese
1 small can crushed
 pineapple, drained
1/4 c. finely diced bell
 pepper
1 Tbsp. Morton Nature's
 Seasons salt
1/4 c. chopped pecans
1/4 c. finely diced onion

Blend in blender, roll into a ball and chill. You may want to roll ball in additional crushed pecans.

Artichoke Delight

1 large can artichokes
1 c. grated Parmesan
 cheese
3/4 c. mayonnaise

Drain artichokes and mash, add Parmesan cheese and mayonnaise. Bake in 350° oven until bubbly. Serve with crackers or chips.

Fruit Dressing

1 (3 oz.) pkg. cream
   cheese, softened
1/2 c. packed brown sugar
1-1/2 c. sour cream
2 Tbsp. Triple Sec

Beat cream cheese at medium speed with an electric mixer until smooth. Add next 3 ingredients, and beat 1 minute or until smooth. Cover and chill. Serve as a dip with fruit.

Spinach Dip
Good for bridge parties or any party

1 c. mayonnaise
1-1/2 c. sour cream
1 small can chopped water
   chestnuts
1 onion, chopped
1 pkg. frozen chopped
   spinach, thawed,
   drained
1 pkg. dry vegetable soup
   mix

Blend mayonnaise and sour cream. Mix in remaining ingredients, chill. Use round loaf of Hawaiian bread. Cut 1/4" off the top of bread and make a bowl with the bread. Fill bread with spinach dip. Use the bread taken out of loaf and slice into bite-size pieces. Place bowl in large dish and add bread pieces around bowl.

Fruit Dip
Wanda Price of Lubbock serves this at her bridge parties.

1 c. sour cream
3 to 4 tsp. brown sugar

Mix brown sugar in sour cream in small amount, and beat well. Serve small size fruit with toothpicks to dip. Easy to double. Good with any kind of fruit.

Flamboyant Fondue

This makes a fun party dish.

Fondue Sauce (recipes
  follow)
1 pt. strawberries
1 banana, cut into chunks
Seedless grape clusters
1 c. fresh or canned
  pineapple chunks,
  drained
1/2 frozen pound cake,
  thawed and cubed

Pour sauce of your choice into fondue pot. Set over candle warmer or on hot tray. Arrange fruits and cake on small platter or serving plate. Use picks or skewers to dip fruits and cake into warm sauce.

KIRSCH SAUCE:
3/4 c. whipping cream
3/4 c. powdered sugar
1 to 2 Tbsp. Kirsch

Mix cream and sugar in small saucepan. Bring to a boil, stirring constantly. Cook 1 minute. Remove from heat and add Kirsch.

BUTTERSCOTCH
SAUCE:
3/4 c. whipping cream
1/3 c. brown sugar
1 to 2 Tbsp. rum (opt.)

In small saucepan, blend whipping cream and brown sugar. Bring to a boil, stirring constantly. Cook 1 minute. Remove from heat and add rum, if desired.

CHOCOLATE SAUCE:
3 squares semisweet
  chocolate
1/3 c. sugar
3/4 c. half and half

In heavy pan, over low heat, melt chocolate. Stir in sugar and half and half. Cook and stir over medium heat until thickened and smooth.

Cheese Ball

Betty Merrick of Lamesa and Linda Givens of Lubbock give these as Christmas gifts.

2 (8 oz.) pkg. cream
  cheese, softened
1 (8 oz.) can crushed
  pineapple, drained
1/4 c. green pepper,
  chopped fine
2 Tbsp. onion (grated)
1 Tbsp. seasoned salt
2 c. chopped pecans

Mix cheese with fork. Add other ingredients and 1 cup of the pecans. Put plastic wrap in bottom of small bowl. Add mixture and refrigerate overnight. Shape and roll in remaining cup of pecans. Serve with crackers.

Cheese Ball

Nancy Stockstill of Lamesa serves this to family and friends.

2 (8 oz.) pkg. cream
   cheese, softened
1 bunch green onions
1 (4 oz.) can chopped
   green chilies
1 small jar dried beef

Mix all ingredients and form into ball. Serve with crackers.

Cheese Ball

1 Tbsp. Worcestershire
1/2 tsp. dry mustard
1 (2-1/4 oz.) can deviled
   ham
Dash of cayenne pepper
3/4 lb. Cheddar cheese,
   cubed
1/2 c. milk
1 c. chopped pecans (opt.)
1 c. parsley flakes (opt.)

Blend Worcestershire sauce, mustard, ham, and pepper until smooth. Alternately add cheese cubes and milk. Blend until smooth. Mixture may be served as a spread or formed into a ball and chilled several hours before rolling in chopped pecans or parsley.

Olive and Pimiento Cheese Ball

2 (8 oz.) pkg. cream cheese
2 jars Kraft olive-pimiento
   spread
1 envelope Lipton onion
   soup

Mix well, shape into ball. Refrigerate overnight. Serve with crackers.

Tuna Ball

1 (8 oz.) pkg. cream
   cheese, softened
2 Tbsp. chili sauce
1/4 c. minced onion
1 Tbsp. Worcestershire
   sauce
1/2 tsp. Tabasco sauce
2 (6 oz.) cans white tuna
   with oil

Soften cream cheese before mixing. Beat ingredients except tuna with electric mixer. Drain tuna and add to mixture, beat well. Chill for 3 hours, then form into ball. Serve with crackers or chips.

Brunch

Bake-Ahead Breakfast

1 lb. sausage, regular or
  hot
2 slices day-old bread, cut
  into 1/2" cubes
1 c. grated Cheddar cheese
6 eggs
2 c. milk
1/2 tsp. salt
1/2 tsp. dry mustard

Crumble sausage in skillet, cook over medium heat until browned, drain well. Spread bread cubes in buttered 9" × 13" dish, top with sausage and cheese. Mix eggs, milk, and seasonings and pour over mixture. Cover and refrigerate overnight. Bake at 350° for 30 to 40 minutes. Serves 6 to 8. Can be doubled easily.

Breakfast Egg and Cheese Souffle

Watch out Waco, Wey has another winner with this one.

1 stick butter or
  margarine, melted
12 slices bread, crusts
  trimmed
3 c. grated sharp Cheddar
  cheese
1 (4 oz.) can chopped
  green chilies
6 to 8 fresh mushrooms,
  sliced
1/4 c. chopped onion
1/2 c. cooked, crumbled
  sausage, diced ham,
  cooked bacon, shrimp,
  or crab.
4 eggs, beaten
3 c. milk
1 tsp. salt
1/2 tsp. pepper

Melt butter in 9" × 13" Pyrex dish. Slosh both sides of bread in butter and set aside. Line dish with 6 slices bread. (Both sides of bread need to be buttered.) Cover bread with 1-1/2 cups grated cheese, chilies, mushrooms, onions, and meat of your choice. Cover with next 6 slices bread. Top with remaining grated cheese. Mix eggs, milk, salt, and pepper. Pour over whole casserole. Cover and refrigerate overnight. Bake at 350° for 1 hour or until puffy, brown and bubbling. Should not be runny in center. (Check by inserting knife.) Serve immediately. Cut in squares. Serves 6 to 8.

Buttermilk Hot Cakes

A great breakfast recipe from Lee Moore of New Home

2 eggs
2 c. buttermilk
1 tsp. soda
2-1/4 c. flour
2 tsp. baking powder
1 tsp. salt
2 tsp. sugar
4 Tbsp. vegetable oil

Beat eggs well, then beat in buttermilk and soda. Add sifted dry ingredients and oil. Cook on hot griddle. Any unused portion may be refrigerated and used the next morning.

Cheese Javelina

Nancy Askew Warren brought this to the family reunion.

2 lb. grated cheese
1 (7 oz.) can chopped
   green chilies, drained
   and reserve juice
1 lb. cooked, crumbled
   bacon
1 large onion, chopped
1 doz. eggs
3 to 4 Tbsp. chili juice
   (opt.)

Mix cheese, green chilies, bacon, and onion. Pour into 9″ × 13″ pan. Beat eggs and add chili juice. Pour eggs over cheese mixture. Bake at 350° for 45 minutes to 1 hour.

Cheese Quiche

2 bacon slices
1 c. thinly sliced onion
3 eggs, slightly beaten
1-3/4 c. milk
3/4 c. shredded Swiss
   cheese (3 oz.)
1 tsp. salt
Dash of pepper
1/3 c. Post Grape-Nuts
   Brand Cereal
1 lightly baked 9″ pie shell

Fry bacon until crisp; drain and crumble, reserving 1 tablespoon drippings. Sauté onion in bacon drippings until tender and lightly browned. Combine eggs, milk, cheese, salt, pepper, and cereal. Stir in onion and bacon. Pour into pie shell. Bake at 450° for 15 minutes. Reduce oven temperature to 350° and bake 10 to 15 minutes longer. Makes 4 servings.

Cheeseburger Quiche

1 (9") unbaked pastry shell
1/2 lb. lean ground beef
1/4 c. chopped onion
2 tsp. instant bouillon or
   two bouillon cubes
3 eggs
1/2 c. light cream or milk
1/4 c. catsup
1 c. shredded Cheddar
   cheese (4 oz.)

Preheat oven to 425°. Bake pastry shell 8 minutes; remove from oven. Reduce oven temperature to 350°. In medium skillet, brown beef; pour off fat. Stir in onion and bouillon; cook and stir until onion is tender and bouillon dissolves. In medium bowl, beat together eggs, cream, and catsup. Stir in meat mixture and cheese. Pour into prepared shell. Bake 25 to 30 minutes or until set. Let stand 10 minutes before serving. Garnish as desired. Refrigerate leftovers.

Cheesy Egg Casserole

1/4 c. flour
1/4 tsp. salt
1/4 c. margarine, melted
4 eggs, beaten
1 c. cottage cheese
1 (4 oz.) can chopped
   green chilies, drained
2 c. shredded Monterey
   Jack cheese (8 oz.)
1 (4 oz.) jar whole
   pimientos
1 green pepper, chopped

Combine flour, salt, and margarine in a large bowl. Add eggs, cottage cheese, chilies, and cheese. Mix well. Pour mixture into a lightly greased 10" × 6" × 2" baking dish. Garnish casserole with pimientos and green pepper. Bake uncovered at 375° for 30 minutes. Makes 6 to 8 servings.

Puffed Eggs
Dot's Party Dish

6 eggs
1/2 c. milk
1 tsp. salt
1/2 tsp. pepper
2 Tbsp. chopped green
   chilies
3 oz. shredded Monterey
   Jack cheese
2 Tbsp. butter
4 slices white bread

Mix first 4 ingredients completely. Stir in chilies and cheese. Spread butter over one side of each bread slice, cut each slice into 4 triangles. Arrange half of the bread triangles, buttered side out and cut side down, around the edge of dish. Arrange remaining bread triangles, buttered side down, in bottom of dish. Pour egg mixture over bread. Bake at 350° for 30 minutes. Easy to double and triple for large parties.

Cream Cheese Breakfast Bread
One of Bryan's breakfast favorites

2 pkg. crescent rolls
2 (8 oz.) pkg. cream
  cheese, softened
2 eggs
3/4 c. sugar
1 tsp. vanilla
1 tsp. lemon juice

Use one package crescent rolls as a crust in an 8"square baking dish. Completely seal all edges. Blend remaining ingredients, beating until smooth. Spread blended mixture over crust. Place other package of rolls on top. Bake at 350° for 20 minutes or until lightly browned. Cool before cutting.

GLAZE:
1 c. powdered sugar
1 tsp. vanilla
3 Tbsp. milk

Mix ingredients and drizzle over slightly cooled bread.

Fruit Pizza

1 roll refrigerated sugar
  cookie dough
1 (16 oz.) cream cheese,
  softened
3/4 c. sugar
1 tsp. lemon juice
Any three or more of the
  following fruits:
Strawberries
Bananas
Kiwi
Grapes
Mandarin oranges
3 oz. apricot preserves
2 Tbsp. fruit juice

Pat cookie dough into 12" pizza pan, forming rim. Bake according to package directions and cool. Remove to a pretty platter. Combine cream cheese, sugar, and lemon juice in bowl, mix well. Spread on crust. Arrange fruit over top. Mix apricot preserves with fruit juice. Drizzle over fruit. Refrigerate.

Grit Casserole

This great dish is from Mary Louise Louder.

4 c. water
1 c. grits
1 stick oleo
2 eggs, beaten
2 tsp. salt
2 c. grated Cheddar cheese
1 can chopped green
   chilies
Savory salt to taste

Bring water to boil and add grits. Turn heat down and cook, stirring occasionally for 4 minutes. Add oleo, eggs, salt, cheese,and green chilies. Put in greased casserole dish. Bake 1-1/2 hours at 250°.

Hot Cheese Grits

2 c. quick grits
8 c. boiling water
1 tsp. salt
1-1/2 sticks margarine
8 oz. hot jalapeno cheese
16 oz. garlic cheese
2 eggs, beaten
2 Tbsp. sherry, (opt.)
1 tsp. Worcestershire sauce
1 tsp. Tabasco sauce
2 (12 oz.) cans green
   chilies, chopped

Slowly stir grits into boiling salted water. Turn heat off. Add margarine and cheese to grits mixture. Cool. Add eggs, sherry, Worcestershire, Tabasco, and chilies. Spoon mixture into greased baking dish and bake 1 hour at 300°. This freezes well. Water will appear on top, but just remix and reheat. Superb with ham or chicken.

Jalapeno Quiche

1 c. drained, seeded
   jalapeno peppers, cut in
   strips or rings
1/2 lb. Cheddar cheese,
   grated
1/2 lb. Monterey Jack
   cheese, grated
8 eggs, beaten
Salt and pepper to taste
1/4 tsp. Worcestershire
   sauce

Layer bottom of a 9″ × 9″ Pyrex dish with peppers. Cover with cheese, pat down. Add salt, pepper, and Worcestershire sauce to well beaten eggs. Pour mixture over cheese. Bake at 275° for 40 minutes, or until bubbly. Cool 15 minutes. Cut into small squares for appetizers or large servings for brunch.

Party Brunch

6 c. shredded Monterey
   Jack cheese
1/2 lb. fresh mushrooms,
   sliced
3/4 c. chopped onion
1/4 c. melted margarine
1 c. cubed cooked ham or
   cooked Canadian bacon
8 eggs, beaten
1-3/4 c. milk
1/2 c. flour
1 Tbsp. seasoned salt

Place half of cheese in a buttered 9" × 13" baking dish. Sauté mushrooms and onion in margarine in a large skillet until tender; spoon vegetable mixture over cheese. Sprinkle meat over mixture; top with remaining cheese. Beat eggs, milk, flour, and seasoned salt. Pour egg mixture over cheese. Bake at 350° for 40 to 50 minutes. Recipe is easy to double for large party.

Super Duper Quiche

10 eggs, beaten
1-1/2 tsp. sugar
1-1/2 tsp. salt
1/8 tsp. red pepper
3 (8 oz.) pkg. Monterey
   Jack cheese, cubed
2 (8 oz,) cartons cream
   cheese, cubed
1 (12 oz.) carton cottage
   cheese
1 Tbsp. margarine
3/4 c. flour
1-1/2 tsp. baking powder
1 (4 oz.) can chopped
   green chilies, drained

Mix eggs, sugar, salt, and pepper in a mixing bowl. Mix cheeses in a large dish and mix margarine into cheese mixture. Mix flour and baking powder in a small bowl. Add flour and egg mixtures to cheese, stirring gently. Add green chilies. Pour mixture into a greased 9" × 13" baking dish. Bake at 350° 40 to 50 minutes. This will serve around 16 people.

Quiche

2 c. milk (or half and half)
1/2 c. Bisquick
4 eggs
1/4 tsp. salt
Dash of pepper
12 slices crisp fried bacon
    (or 1-1/2 c. other meat)
1/2 c. finely chopped
    onion
1 to 2 c. grated Swiss
    cheese

Blend milk, Bisquick, eggs, salt, and pepper together in a blender. If using bacon, crumble crisp bacon in bottom of greased casserole dish. Add chopped onion and grated cheese. Pour blended mixture over ingredients in dish and bake in pre-heated oven at 350° for 50 to 55 minutes.

If using other meats such as cubed ham, spam, or boned chicken, etc., take blended mixture out of blender and stir into your meat, onion, and cheese. Then pour into well-greased casserole dish. Bake in pre-heated oven at 350° for 50 to 55 minutes.

Quiche Delight

10 eggs
1/2 tsp. salt
1 pt. small curd cottage
    cheese
1/2 lb. sharp Cheddar
    cheese, grated
1/3 c. margarine
1 (8 oz.) can chopped
    green chilies
1/2 c. flour
1 tsp. baking powder
1 lb. Monterey Jack cheese,
    grated

Beat eggs until light and fluffy. Add remaining ingredients. Bake in a greased 9" × 13" dish at 350° for 25 to 30 minutes.

Beverages

Celebration Punch

6 large bottles cranberry
  juice
1 qt. ginger ale
1 (48 oz.) can pineapple
  juice
1 (48 oz.) can orange juice
1 qt. club soda

Mix all ingredients and serve over ice ring.

Cranberry Perk

The Inklebargers love this on cold winter nights.

1/2 c. brown sugar
1 c. water
2 c. unsweetened pineapple
  juice
2 c. cranberry juice
2 sticks cinnamon
1/2 Tbsp. whole cloves
1/2 tsp. salt

Mix brown sugar, water, and juices and pour into percolator. Place cinnamon sticks, cloves, and salt in filter basket.

Frozen Fruit Punch

This makes a tart and tangy slush.

1 pkg. cherry Kool-Aid
1 pkg. orange Kool-Aid
2 c. sugar
3 bananas, mashed
3 lemons, juice and pulp
1 small can crushed
  pineapple
3-3/4 quarts water
30 oz. 7-Up

Mix all ingredients except 7-Up and freeze in shallow pans. Pour 7-Up over and make slush.

Fruit Punch

Patsy Edens gave this to me when we both lived in Colorado City.

1 c. sugar
1 c. hot water
1 (12 oz.) can frozen
    orange juice
1 (6 oz.) can frozen
    lemonade
1 (46 oz.) can pineapple
    juice
Water called for on each
    frozen juice can
2 qt. ginger ale

Dissolve sugar in 1 cup hot water. Add orange juice, lemonade, and pineapple juice and correct amount of water (according to juice can directions). Mix well and freeze in 1/2 gallon milk cartons. Remove from freezer and thaw just enough to be slushy when you add ginger ale. Makes an icy, slushy punch. This makes about 25 servings.

Golden Punch

Arbie Brumit told us this had become known as O'Donnell punch.

6 c. sugar
1 qt. water
2 large cans frozen orange
    juice
1 large can pineapple juice
1 small can frozen lemon
    juice
1/4 oz. almond extract
1/4 oz. vanilla extract
2 gal. water

Boil sugar and 1 quart water until sugar dissolves. Cool. Add remaining ingredients. If another color is needed, use food coloring. Makes 4 gallons. Serves 125.

Hot Cranberry Punch

1 (32 oz.) bottle cranberry
    juice cocktail
2 c. orange juice
1/2 c. ReaLemon juice
1/2 c. honey
1/4 c. ReaLime juice
3 whole cloves
2 cinnamon sticks
1 (32 oz.) bottle ginger ale
Additional cinnamon
    sticks (opt.)

Combine all ingredients except ginger ale. Simmer over medium heat about 15 minutes. Remove spices. Just before serving, add ginger ale and heat through.

Instant Hot Chocolate
Easy to make and handy to have around

1 (8 oz.) box instant milk,
   (3-1/3 c.)
1 (8 oz.) jar Coffee Mate
1 lb. Nestles Quick
   Chocolate
1 c. powdered sugar

Combine all ingredients and store in an airtight container. Use approximately 1 tablespoon of mix for each cup of hot water. Adjust amounts according to size of cup and personal tastes.

Instant Spice Tea
Makes a nice gift

1 c. Tang (Start)
2 c. sugar
1 pkg. Lemonade Mix
   (Twist)
1 c. instant tea
1-1/2 tsp. cinnamon
3/4 tsp. cloves
3/4 tsp. allspice

Mix together and use 2 to 3 teaspoonfuls to a cup of hot water. Add a few red hots to each cup if desired.

Tomato Juice Cocktail

4 bruised celery ribs
1 (46 oz.) can tomato juice
1/3 c. vinegar
1/4 c. sugar
4 bay leaves
2 Tbsp. grated onion
1/3 c. lemon juice
1/8 tsp. red pepper
1 Tbsp. salt
2 tsp. Worcestershire sauce

With handle of knife, bruise the celery ribs. Then mix all ingredients. Let stand overnight, or longer, in refrigerator. Strain through colander before serving.

Versatile Punch

This Brownfield Punch is from Sharon Hensley.

1 pkg. Jello (flavor to
   determine color)
3 cans frozen lemonade
1/2 large can pineapple
   juice
1/2 c. sugar

Combine ingredients and fill rest of a 1 gallon container with water.

Wassil Cider

This refreshing wassil is great for holiday entertaining and the recipe is from Doris Ashcraft.

4 qt. apple cider
4 (6 oz.) cans lemonade
4 sticks crushed cinnamon
3 Tbsp. whole cloves
1 tsp. allspice

Mix all ingredients and heat and enjoy.

Breads

Angel Flake Biscuits
Thanks to Patsy Sanders for this delicious recipe

1 pkg. dry yeast
2 Tbsp. lukewarm water
2 c. buttermilk
5 c. flour
1 tsp. soda
4 Tbsp. sugar
1 tsp. salt
3 tsp. baking powder
1 c. shortening

Dissolve yeast in warm water and mix in buttermilk. Mix dry ingredients and cut in shortening. Add dry ingredients to yeast mixture. Roll dough about 1/2" thick and cut into biscuits. Bake at 400° for 20 minutes. This is a large recipe and can be kept in refrigerator for future use.

Beer Rolls
Thanks to Brenda Smith, a Mississippi friend, for this quick and easy recipe

4 c. Bisquick
2 Tbsp. sugar
1 (12 oz.) can of beer

Mix all ingredients and drop by spoonfuls into greased muffin tins. Cook immediately or let rise. Cook at 350° until browned, about 15 minutes.

Broccoli Cornbread
We all enjoyed this when Nadine brought it to the lake.

5 eggs
1-1/2 sticks margarine
2 c. cottage cheese
1 box frozen chopped
 broccoli, thawed and
 drained
2 boxes Jiffy cornbread
 mix

Mix eggs, margarine, cottage cheese, and broccoli. Add cornbread mix and bake at 350° for 50 minutes in greased 9" × 13" pan.

Flour Tortillas
This is from Fern Barnes of Draw.

3 c. flour
2 Tbsp. baking powder
1 tsp. salt
1 c. shortening

Mix ingredients with enough warm water to mix, but remain very stiff. Roll dough thin and cook in iron skillet without any grease.

Cheese Biscuits Red Lobster Style

Delight your friends and family with these fancy little biscuits.

2 c. Bisquick mix
1 c. Cheddar cheese, grated
2/3 c. water
Parsley flakes to taste
Butter to taste
Garlic salt to taste

Preheat oven to 450°. In a large mixing bowl, dredge cheese in Bisquick. Add water and stir until blended. Drop by spoonfuls onto greased cookie sheet. Sprinkle parsley flakes on top. Bake until browned. After removing from oven, spread butter over top and sprinkle with garlic salt. Makes 10 large biscuits.

Cornbread

Truett says Lucille's cornbread is the best ever.

1 c. yellow cornmeal
1/2 c. flour
1 Tbsp. baking powder
1/2 tsp. soda
1 tsp. salt
1 tsp. sugar
1 c. buttermilk
1/2 milk
1 egg
1/4 c. melted oleo

Preheat oven to 425° and oil muffin pan. Sift first 6 ingredients together. Mix next 4 ingredients and add to dry mixture. This makes 18 small cornbread muffins. Bake 20 to 25 minutes.

Cornbread Plus

1 c. yellow cornmeal
1 c. flour
4 tsp. baking powder
1 tsp. salt
1 Tbsp. sugar
1 egg
1 can chopped green
   chilies
1/2 c. shredded Longhorn
   cheese

Mix all ingredients and pour into a greased cookie sheet. Bake at 400° until brown.

Fresh Apple Bread by Carolyn Dorning

2 c. sifted flour
2 tsp. baking powder
1 tsp. salt
1/2 tsp. cinnamon
1/4 tsp. nutmeg
1/2 c. butter
1 1/4 c. sugar
2 eggs
1-1/2 c. peeled grated
  apple
1/2 c. chopped walnuts or
  pecans

Sift together first 5 ingredients and set aside. Cream butter and sugar until light and fluffy. Beat in eggs, one at a time, beat well after each. Stir in apples and dry ingredients, half at a time. Fold in nuts. Pour into greased and floured loaf pan. Bake at 350° for 1 hour. Cool in pan for 1 hour then turn onto wire rack. Cool completely before slicing. Makes 1 loaf.

Gingerbread

1/2 c. shortening
1/2 c. sugar
1 egg
2-1/2 c. sifted flour
1-1/2 tsp. baking soda
1 tsp. cinnamon
1 tsp. ginger
1/2 tsp. cloves
1/2 tsp. salt
1 c. molasses
1 c. hot water

Cream together shortening and sugar. Add egg and beat well. Sift together flour, soda, cinnamon, ginger, cloves, and salt. Set aside. Combine molasses and water. Add alternately with flour mixture to creamed mixture. Pour into greased and floured square pan. Bake at 350° for 50 to 60 minutes.

Lemon Bread

1/2 c. shortening
1-1/4 c. sugar
Rind of 1 lemon, grated
2 eggs
1/2 c. milk
1-1/2 c. sifted flour
1 tsp. baking powder
1/4 tsp. salt
Juice of 1 lemon

Cream shortening and 1 cup sugar. Add lemon rind, eggs, and milk. Sift together flour, baking powder, and salt; add to creamed mixture. Place in greased loaf pan. Bake 50 to 60 minutes at 350°. Remove from pan. Mix remaining sugar and lemon juice; spoon over loaf while warm.

Poppy Seed Cheese Bread

1 c. milk
2 eggs
2 Tbsp. poppy seeds
1/2 tsp. dry onions
6 oz. grated Cheddar
   cheese
3 c. Bisquick
1/2 c. Crisco oil

Combine milk, eggs, poppy seeds, onion, and cheese. Add Bisquick. Then add oil. Pat into a well-greased 7″ × 11″ Pyrex dish. Bake at 325° for 25 to 35 minutes.

Rolls in a Flash

Impress your guests with these quickies.

1 pkg. RapidRise yeast
1 c. warm water
1/4 c. sugar
3/4 tsp. salt
2 Tbsp. Crisco oil
1 egg
2 c. flour
3/4 c. whole wheat flour

Mix yeast in water and let set for 5 minutes. Blend in sugar, salt, and oil, then add egg. Add flour all at once and stir until completely blended. Drop by spoonfuls into muffin tins sprayed with Pam. Let stand for 30 to 45 minutes. Bake at 375° until browned. Makes 12 rolls.

Zucchini Bread

Thanks to Linda Womack

3 eggs
3 c. sugar
1 c. oil
3 c. zucchini (peeled and
   grated)
2 tsp. vanilla
3 c. flour
1/4 tsp. baking powder
1 tsp. soda
1 tsp. salt
3 tsp. cinnamon
1 c. chopped pecans

Combine first five ingredients. Add flour, baking powder, soda, salt, cinnamon, and pecans. Stir all until well blended. Pour into greased and floured loaf pans. Bake at 350° for 1 hour or until toothpick inserted comes out clean. Makes 2 or 3 small loaves.

Ranch Biscuits

Rachel Huffaker makes these for her boys.

4-1/2 c. flour
4 tsp. baking powder
1/2 tsp. soda
1 tsp. salt
1/4 c. sugar
1/4 c. melted shortening
   or oil
1 pkg. dry yeast dissolved
   in 1/2 c. warm water
2 c. buttermilk

Mix all ingredients and keep refrigerated. Use as needed.

Vegetable Bread

Jo Ella Rash surprises her family by serving this.

1-1/2 sticks oleo, melted
   and cooled
1 bell pepper, chopped
1 onion, chopped
1/2 c. grated Cheddar
   cheese
1/2 c. celery, chopped
4 or more slices bacon,
   cooked crisp and
   crumbled
2 cans biscuits, cut into
   fourths

Mix all ingredients in bowl except biscuits. Add biscuits last and stir gently. Pour into bundt pan and bake at 350° for 20 to 30 minutes. Let cool enough for oleo to absorb before removing from pan.

Whole Wheat Biscuits

1 c. whole-wheat flour
1 c. all-purpose flour
2 tsp. baking powder
1/4 tsp. baking soda
1/2 tsp. salt
1/3 c. shortening
1 egg beaten
1 Tbsp. honey
3/4 c. buttermilk

Mix first 5 ingredients, cut in shortening with a pastry blender until mixture resembles coarse meal. Mix egg, honey, and buttermilk, add to flour mixture, stirring until dry ingredients are moistened. Turn dough out onto a lightly floured surface, and knead. Roll dough to 1/2" thickness, cut with a 2" diameter biscuit cutter. Place on greased baking sheet. Bake at 450°for 8 to 10 minutes.

Zucchini Bread
From Shirley Draper of Tahoka

3 eggs
1 c. oil
2 c. sugar
2 c. grated zucchini
2 tsp. vanilla
3 c. flour, sifted
1 tsp. soda
1/2 tsp. baking powder
1/4 tsp. salt
1 tsp. cinnamon
1/2 c. chopped pecans

Preheat oven to 325°. Grease and flour large loaf pan or two small loaf pans. Beat eggs. Add oil, sugar, zucchini, and vanilla. Cream together. Combine flour, soda, baking powder, salt, and cinnamon. Add to creamed mixture. Mix until thoroughly blended. Add pecans. Bake 1 hour.

Bucket Bread
Mac Edwards' famous bread

2 pkg. dry yeast
2 Tbsp. sugar
1 c. warm water
4 Tbsp. sugar
2-1/2 tsp. salt
4 Tbsp. oil
2 tall cans Pet milk
8 c. flour
5 (1 lb.) coffee cans

Mix first three ingredients and set aside until it bubbles. In mixer, mix sugar, salt, oil, and milk. Add yeast mixture. Add 1 cup of flour at a time until 6 cups have been added. Remove bowl from mixer and add remaining flour and mix with a wooden spoon.

Grease cans and lids. This recipe makes 4-1/2 cans. Fill can 1/2 full, put lid on and let rise. Gently remove lid. Cook on bottom rack at 350° for 45 minutes. Remove from can immediately.

Yeast Biscuits

1 pkg. dry yeast
2 Tbsp. warm water
5 c. flour
1 tsp. soda
1 tsp. salt
3 tsp. baking powder
4 Tbsp. sugar
1 c. Crisco
2 c. buttermilk

Mix yeast and warm water and set aside. Sift flour, soda, salt, baking powder, and sugar. Cut in Crisco. Add buttermilk to yeast mixture, then blend into dry ingredients. Grease pan, do not let rise. Cut out size biscuit you desire. Bake at 400° until golden brown.

Coffee Cake

Do the work the night before, enjoy the treat the next morning.

3/4 c. packed brown sugar
3/4 tsp. cinnamon
1 stick oleo
1 pkg. Bridgeford frozen
   rolls (24)
1/2 - 3/4 c. pecans,
   chopped
1 box butterscotch
   pudding and pie filling
   (not instant)

Melt brown sugar, cinnamon, and oleo until it bubbles. Put frozen rolls in bundt pan sprayed with Pam. Add pecans between rolls. Sprinkle dry pudding over and pour sugar mixture on top. Add more pecans. Cover with foil and leave out on cabinet overnight. Cook at 350° the next morning for 30 minutes. Let set for 5 minutes and turn over on plate.

Onion Bread

1 pkg. RapidRise yeast
1 tsp. salt
2 c. flour
4 Tbsp. olive oil
1 c. water
1 c. whole wheat flour
1 Tbsp. cornmeal
1 medium red onion,
   sliced
2 Tbsp. grated Parmesan
   cheese
1 tsp. dried rosemary
1/4 tsp. pepper
Salt to taste

In large bowl, combine yeast, salt, and 1 cup flour. In 1-quart saucepan, over medium heat, heat 2 tablespoons olive oil and 1 cup water until very warm (125°-130°). With mixer at low speed, beat liquid into dry ingredients just until blended. Increase to medium speed and beat for 2 minutes. Add 1/2 cup flour and beat 2 more minutes. Stir in whole-wheat flour.

Knead dough about 8 minutes, working in about 1/2 cup flour. Cover and let rise 15 minutes. Grease a 9″ × 13″ pan and sprinkle with cornmeal. Pat dough into pan, pushing dough well into corners. Cover and let rise in a warm place until doubled, about 30 minutes.

In 2-quart saucepan over medium setting, heat 1 tablespoon olive oil and cook onion until tender. Drain and set aside.

Preheat oven to 400°. With finger, make deep indentations over entire surface of dough. Drizzle with 1 tablespoon olive oil and top with onion, Parmesan cheese, rosemary, pepper, and salt. Bake 20 to 25 minutes until golden brown. Makes 8 servings.

Cream Cheese Braids

Julia Paske's favorite to make and give as gifts at Christmas.

1 (8 oz.) carton sour
   cream, scalded
1/2 c. sugar
1/2 c. butter or margarine,
   melted
1 tsp. salt
2 pkg. dry yeast
1/2 c. warm (105° to 115°)
   water
2 eggs, beaten
4 c. all-purpose flour
Filling (recipe follows)
Glaze (recipe follows)

Combine scalded sour cream, sugar, butter, and salt; mix well, and let cool to lukewarm. Dissolve yeast in warm water in a large mixing bowl; stir in sour cream mixture, then eggs. Gradually stir in flour (dough will be soft). Cover tightly, and chill overnight.

Divide dough into 4 equal portions. Turn each portion out on a heavily floured surface, and knead 4 or 5 times. Roll each into an 8″ × 12″ rectangle. Spread 1/4 of filling over each rectangle, leaving a 1/2″ margin all around edges. Carefully roll up jelly roll fashion, beginning at long side. Firmly pinch edge and ends to seal. Carefully place rolls, seam side down, on greased baking sheets.

Make 6 equally spaced X-shaped cuts across top of each loaf. Cover and let rise in a warm (85°) place, free of drafts, until doubled in bulk, about an hour. Bake at 375° for 15 to 20 minutes. Spread loaves with glaze while warm.

FILLING:
2 (8 oz.) pkg. cream
   cheese, softened
3/4 c. sugar
1 egg, beaten
1/8 tsp. salt
2 tsp. vanilla extract

Combine all ingredients. Process in food processor or electric mixer until well blended.

GLAZE:
2 c. sifted powdered sugar
1/4 c. milk
2 tsp. vanilla extract

Combine all ingredients, mixing well.

Dilly Bread
One of Little Mother's DILLicious recipes

1 pkg. yeast
1/4 c. warm water
2 Tbsp. sugar
1 Tbsp. instant onion
   flakes
1 Tbsp. butter
2 rounded tsp. dill seed
1 tsp. salt
1/4 tsp. soda
1 egg
1 c. cottage cheese,
   creamed
2-1/2 to 3 c. flour
Onion salt (opt.)

Soften yeast in warm water in a mixing bowl. Combine all ingredients except cottage cheese and flour. Beat well. Add cottage cheese and mix. Fold in flour and knead until completely blended. Cover and let rise until double in bulk. Stir down and knead, then place in a buttered round casserole dish. Let rise until double in bulk. Bake at 350° for 40 to 50 minutes. After baking, brush with butter and sprinkle with onion salt.

Easy Rolls
From Wey McNeil of Waco

1 c. cold water
2 yeast cakes
2/3 c. sugar (3/4 c. for
   sweet rolls)
1 c. shortening
1-1/2 tsp. salt
1 c. boiling water
2 eggs, beaten
6 c. sifted flour
1 stick butter, melted

Crumble yeast cakes and add to 1 cup cold water and let stand 5 minutes. Place sugar, shortening, salt in large mixing bowl. Add boiling water, mix until shortening is dissolved. When lukewarm, add eggs and yeast. Add 2 cups flour at a time mixing with wooden spoon. Mix will be sticky. Cover and refrigerate at least 6 hours. Roll out on floured board 1/2" thick. Cut desired shape. (Calumet baking powder can is good size). Roll in melted butter and fold over and place in greased pan. Cover with Saran Wrap and let rise about 2 hours. Bake 375°for 10 to 15 minutes, or until brown. Dough will keep 7 to 10 days in refrigerator. Can bake and freeze, or freeze unbaked, or bake and warm up later. (I take a measuring cup and fill with hot water, add shortening to this until 2-cups level and place in microwave to melt, then add to sugar and salt. Saves a cup to wash.)

Holiday Wreath Bread
A breakfast ring favorite of the Caswell family

1 pkg. dry yeast
1/2 c. warm water
1/2 c. lukewarm milk
1/3 c. sugar
1/3 c. Crisco oil
1 tsp. salt
1 egg
3-1/2 to 4 c. flour
2 Tbsp. squeeze butter
3/4 c. sugar
1 Tbsp. cinnamon
1/2 c. chopped pecans
Maraschino cherries
Pecan halves

Dissolve yeast in warm water in large bowl. Stir in milk, sugar, oil, salt, egg, and 2-1/2 cups of the flour. Beat until completely mixed. Mix in enough remaining flour to make dough easy to handle. Work on a floured surface and knead in remaining flour until dough is smooth and elastic. Place dough in a greased bowl then turn the greased side up. Cover with a damp cloth and let rise in a warm place until double, about 1-1/2 hours.

Punch down dough and divide into two equal portions. Place one portion back into the bowl and cover. Roll the other portion into a 9″ × 15″ rectangle. Cover top with squeeze butter, sugar, cinnamon, and chopped pecans. Roll up jelly-roll fashion, beginning with the long side. Pinch edge of dough to seal. Stretch roll to make it even. Turning the seal down, shape into ring and place on a greased pizza pan. Pinch the ends together to seal. With scissors, make cuts 3/4 of the way through ring at 1″ intervals. Turn each section on its side. Let rise until double, about 35 minutes. While this is rising, repeat procedure with the reserved portion.

Preheat oven to 375°. Bake until lightly browned, about 25 minutes. While cake is warm, decorate with glaze (recipe below), Maraschino cherries cut in half, and pecan halves.

GLAZE:
1 c. powdered sugar
1 Tbsp. milk
1/2 tsp. vanilla
1 tsp. squeeze butter

Blend all ingredients with wire whisk until completely smooth. To attain desired consistency, add additional milk or additional sugar.

Kolache

1/3 c. warm water
2 pkg. dry yeast
1 c. warm milk
1/2 c. sugar
3/4 tsp. salt
3/4 c. oleo, softened
4 eggs, at room
    temperature
1 Tbsp. orange juice
6-1/4 c. flour
1-1/2 c. seedless raisins
2 Tbsp. milk
2 Tbsp. slivered almonds,
    chopped

In a large mixing bowl, sprinkle yeast into warm water. Stir until dissolved and let set for 5 minutes. Add warm milk, sugar, salt, oleo, 3 eggs, orange juice, and 2 cups of flour. Beat until smooth. Stir in raisins and enough remaining flour to make a stiff dough. Knead on a floured surface for 8 to 10 minutes. Place in a greased bowl and grease top. Cover and let rise until doubled, about 1 hour.

Punch down and divide into 3 equal portions. Roll each portion into a 24" rope. Braid the ropes together and place in a greased tube pan, bringing the ends together to seal. Beat remaining egg and milk and brush on loaf. Sprinkle with almonds. Cover and let rise until doubled, about 1 hour. Bake at 350° for 45 minutes or until done. Remove from pan and cool.

Linda's Hot Rolls

Linda Givens has used this recipe for her family for 45 years.

2 pkg. dry yeast
2 c. warm water
4 Tbsp. shortening
8 Tbsp. sugar
1/4 tsp. salt
2 eggs
6 c. sifted flour

Dissolve yeast in 1/2 cup of the warm water, set aside. Blend shortening, sugar, and salt until fluffy. Add eggs, one at a time. Add yeast water and mix well. Alternate remaining water with flour, until all is used. Put in greased large bowl, grease top with shortening and cover with damp cloth. Put in refrigerator overnight before using. This will keep a week in the refrigerator, just take out what you need for rolls or loaf. Remember to keep cover cloth moist.

You can also make cheese rolls by using 7 ounces grated mild Cheddar cheese. Dredge cheese in flour and then mix into dough.

Potato Hot Rolls

Little Mother's wonderful recipe

1 yeast cake
1/2 c. warm water
1 c. scalded milk
2/3 c. shortening
1 tsp. salt
1/2 c. sugar
1 c. creamed potatoes
2 well beaten eggs
6 to 8 c. flour

Dissolve yeast cake in warm water. Pour scaled milk over shortening, add salt and sugar, potatoes, and eggs. When cool, add dissolved yeast, then add flour. Let rise twice and punch down, then put in refrigerator. When ready to use, make the size rolls you want and let rise 1 to 1-1/2 hours before baking. Bake at 450° for 15 to 20 minutes.

Refrigerator Bread Dough

Jean Warren makes this up in lots of different ways, from rolls to Christmas trees.

1 c. Crisco
3/4 c. sugar
2 tsp. salt
1 c. boiling water
2 pkg. dry yeast
1 c. warm water
2 beaten eggs
6 c. unsifted flour

Cream Crisco, sugar, and salt, then add water. Dissolve yeast in 1 cup very slightly-warmish water. When first mixture is lukewarm, add water with yeast and 2 beaten eggs. Beat in flour (with the mixer). Before baking, put in refrigerator at least 4 hours. Make up as desired, let rise double, and bake. Can be refrigerated about 1 week.

Refrigerator Hot Rolls

Margaret Hartman's recipe for old-time flavor with time-saving convenience

2 c. warm water
2 pkg. dry yeast
6 c. flour
1/2 c. sugar
2 tsp. salt
1/2 c. shortening
1 egg

Put yeast in warm water and set aside for 5 minutes. Mix 3 cups flour, sugar, and salt with yeast mixture. Beat ingredients until smooth with spoon. Add shortening and egg and beat until smooth. Add 3 cups flour and knead until completely blended. Put in greased bowl and cover. Place in refrigerator until ready to cook. Take out what you need and let rise, work down and make into rolls. Let rise and bake at 350° about 20 minutes.

Sour Dough Starter and Rolls

STARTER:
2 c. unsifted flour
2 Tbsp. sugar
1 Tbsp. salt
1-1/2 c. water
1 Tbsp. vinegar

Combine flour, sugar, and salt in a stone crock. Mix well, add water, and beat to a smooth batter. Add vinegar. Cover with cheese cloth and set in a warm place until thoroughly sour. You determine this by the yeasty smell. Usually takes approximately 12 hours.

ROLLS:
1-1/2 c. sifted flour
1/4 tsp. baking soda
1/4 tsp. butter
2 Tbsp. baking powder
1/2 tsp. salt
1 c. sour dough starter

Mix all ingredients, roll out, cut, and let rise about one hour. Bake at 425° for 20 minutes, or until lightly browned. Makes about 12 large rolls.

Yeast Biscuits

Arbie Brumit was really excited about our cookbook and this is one of the recipes that she sent to us.

4-1/2 c. flour
1 tsp. salt
4 tsp. baking powder
1/2 tsp. soda
1/4 c. sugar
2 pkg. dry yeast
1/2 c. warm water
2 c. buttermilk
1/2 c. melted shortening

Sift together flour, salt, baking powder, soda, and sugar. In a separate dish, dissolve yeast in the warm water. Add buttermilk and shortening. Gradually add liquid mixture to dry ingredients. Place in covered dish in refrigerator overnight. May be used as needed. Keeps well for a week in refrigerator. No rising, no kneading. Just pat out on floured board, cut as biscuits, bake in greased pan at 425° for 12 minutes, or until browned.

Honey Bunches

Wayne thinks Rachel is a real "Honey" when she makes these.

3 c. oatmeal
2 c. coconut
1 c. flour
1-1/2 c. brown sugar
1 c. margarine
1/3 c. honey

In mixing bowl, mix oatmeal, coconut, and flour. In a saucepan, heat brown sugar, margarine, and honey and bring to a boil. Pour over first mixture. Bake in small greased muffin tins at 350° for 10 minutes. Let cool briefly and remove.

Apple Cranberry Muffins

1 c. flour
1/2 c. quick oats
1 tsp. baking powder
1 tsp. ground cinnamon
1/4 tsp. salt
1 large egg
3/4 c. packed dark brown
   sugar
1/4 c. margarine
1 tsp. vanilla
3/4 c. diced unpeeled tart
   apples
3/4 c. fresh or frozen
   cranberries
1/4 c. raisins

Preheat oven to 350°. Grease muffin cups or use foil liners. Mix flour, oats, baking powder, cinnamon, and salt in large bowl. Break egg into another bowl. Add sugar and whisk until smooth. Whisk in margarine and vanilla. Stir in apples, cranberries, and raisins. Pour over dry ingredients. Fold in just until dry ingredients are moistened.

Spoon batter into muffin cups. Bake 20 to 25 minutes or until browned and firm to the touch. Turn out onto a rack. Let cool. Store 1 to 2 days in a plastic bag or airtight container before reheating and serving. Do not freeze. Makes 12 muffins.

Pineapple Muffins

1/2 c. oleo
1-1/2 c. sugar
2 eggs, beaten
1 tsp. vanilla
1 large can crushed
   pineapple
2-1/2 c. flour
2-1/2 tsp. baking powder
1/2 tsp. salt

Cream oleo and sugar. Add eggs, vanilla, and pineapple. Add dry ingredients and mix well. Bake in greased muffin tins at 350° for 18 minutes. Makes 2 dozen.

Bran Muffins

Terry Scott, a great cook from Crawford, enjoys making these.

1-1/2 c. sugar
2-1/2 c. flour
2-1/2 tsp. soda
1 tsp. salt
2 beaten eggs
1/2 c. oil
1 pint buttermilk
1/4 tsp. vanilla
3 heaping c. Raisin Bran

Mix dry ingredients. Add eggs, oil, buttermilk, vanilla, and Raisin Bran. Beat well. Keep in refrigerator and use as needed. Spray muffin pans. Bake at 375° until brown, approximately 20 minutes.

Plum Muffins

Christine made these for her girls when they were little and they loved them.

1-3/4 c. sugar
1 c. cooking oil
1 c. buttermilk
2 eggs
2 c. flour
1 tsp. salt
1 tsp. baking powder
1/2 tsp. soda
1 tsp. cinnamon
1 tsp. nutmeg
1 tsp. allspice
1 c. pecans, chopped
1 (16 oz.) can purple
  plums, drained and
  chopped

Spray mini muffin pans with Baker's Joy. Mix sugar, oil, buttermilk, and eggs. Add flour, salt, baking powder, soda, cinnamon, nutmeg, allspice, and pecans. Then add plums. Place in muffin pans. Bake at 350° about 20 minutes.

Blueberry Muffins — Wonderful!

We guarantee you'll love these!

1 can blueberries
3/4 c. oleo, softened
3/4 c. cooking oil
2-1/2 c. + 2 Tbsp. sugar
3 eggs
4-1/2 c. flour
1-1/2 Tbsp. Best O' Butter
  (a butter substitute)
1-1/2 Tbsp. baking powder
1-1/2 tsp. soda
1-1/2 c. buttermilk

Drain blueberries and reserve juice. Mix oleo and oil together. Add sugar, eggs, flour, Best O' Butter, baking powder, and soda. Add buttermilk and some juice. Use enough juice so that the mixture is like cake batter. Mix well. Gently mix in blueberries with a spoon. Grease muffin pans well. Bake at 400° for 13 to 15 minutes. Makes about 55 medium size muffins.

Salads

Carrot Slaw

2 lb. sliced cooked carrots,
   drained
1/2 c. Wesson oil
1 c. sugar
1/2 c. vinegar
1/2 tsp. salt
Pepper to taste
1 tsp. Worcestershire sauce
1 tsp. dry mustard
1 onion, sliced in rings
1 bell pepper, sliced in
   rings
1 c. chopped celery

Mix oil, sugar, vinegar, salt, pepper, Worcestershire sauce, and mustard. Cook until sugar is dissolved. Mix cooked carrots, onion, bell pepper, and celery. Pour liquid over vegetables.

Cabbage Slaw by Margaret Carter

We have taken this on many fishing trips to eat with all the fish we catch.

1 head cabbage
1 onion
1 green pepper
1/2 c. Wesson oil
1/2 c. vinegar
1 tsp. celery seed
1 tsp. salt
3/4 c. sugar

Shred cabbage, onion, and green pepper. Refrigerate in water for 2 hours. Drain. Combine remaining ingredients and pour over cabbage mixture.

Cole Slaw

Beth served this at Beta Sigma Phi parties in Lamesa.

1 med. head cabbage
8 slices bacon, cooked and
   crumbled
6 green onions, chopped

DRESSING:
1 (8 oz.) carton sour cream
1 c. Miracle Whip
2 Tbsp. brown sugar
2 Tbsp. vinegar
1/2 tsp. seasoned salt

Shred cabbage. Add bacon and onions.

Mix well. Pour over cabbage mixture and toss well.

Shoe Peg Corn Salad

One of Bertha Morgan's delicious recipes

1 c. chopped carrots
1 bell pepper, chopped
1 c. chopped celery
1/2 c. diced onion
1 can Shoe Peg corn
1 can French green beans
  with pimiento
1 can tiny English peas (Le
  Sueur)
1 tsp. celery seed
1 c. sugar
3/4 c. vinegar
1/2 c. Wesson oil
Salt and pepper to taste

Chop carrots, bell pepper, celery, and onion very fine. Mix with corn, green beans, and peas. In a small pan, mix celery seed, sugar, vinegar, oil, salt, and pepper and bring to a boil. Pour over vegetables and refrigerate overnight.

Patio Corn Salad

Terry Scott from Crawford serves this.

2 (12 oz.) cans corn,
  drained
3/4 c. diced unpared
  cucumber
1/4 c. diced onion
2 small tomatoes, coarsely
  chopped and drained
1/4 c. sour cream
2 Tbsp. mayonnaise
1 Tbsp. vinegar
1/4 tsp. dry mustard
1/2 tsp. salt
1/4 tsp. celery seed

Mix all ingredients and chill. Serves 8 to 10.

Cornbread Salad

2 pkg. cornbread mix
8 slices bacon, cooked
   crisp and crumbled
1 onion, chopped
1 bell pepper, chopped
2 tomatoes, chopped
1 pt. Miracle Whip
2 Tbsp. mustard
Salt and pepper to taste
1 tsp. sugar

Cook and crumble cornbread. Mix remaining ingredients and pour over cornbread. Stir and chill. Will keep 1 week in refrigerator.

Macaroni Salad

One of our favorite recipes from Oleta Smith, our former teacher and forever friend.

12 oz. shell macaroni
1 Tbsp. seasoned salt
1 tsp. salt
2 large onions, chopped
8 hard-boiled eggs, sliced
2 c. celery, chopped
1 c. green pepper, chopped
1/2 c. pimiento, diced
2 cans English peas
1-1/2 c. mayonnaise

Boil macaroni in salted water until tender. Drain. Blanch with cold water and drain again. Add seasoned salt, salt, onions, eggs, celery, green peppers, and pimientos. Toss lightly. Add English peas, toss lightly. Gently mix in mayonnaise. Chill several hours before serving. Garnish with cucumber slices, radishes, chives, etc. (This makes a very large salad.)

Lena's Relish

Shirley Draper's recipe

1 can black olives,
   chopped
1 can green chilies,
   drained
3 green onions, chopped
2 tomatoes, chopped
1 tsp. garlic salt
1-1/2 tsp. white wine
   vinegar

Make several hours ahead or let set overnight. (This is good with any meat).

Raw Broccoli Salad
From Betsy Pridmore of Tahoka, Texas

1 bunch raw broccoli,
    chopped
1 raw head cauliflower,
    chopped
1 green pepper, chopped
1 red onion, chopped
1 small jar pimientos

Mix well.

DRESSING:
1 c. mayonnaise
1/2 c. apple cider vinegar
1/2 c. sugar
1 tsp. dry mustard
Salt and pepper to taste

Mix, pour over vegetables, and refrigerate overnight.

Broccoli Salad
Oh-la-la! Mama Mia!

1 bunch fresh broccoli
4 medium avocados
1 carton cherry tomatoes
1 carton fresh mushrooms
1 bottle Vivé Italian
    dressing

Parboil broccoli until tender, then cool. Mix vegetables 1 hour before serving and marinate in dressing.

Cauliflower Salad

1 head of cauliflower
1 c. shredded cheese
1 bell pepper, chopped
1 c. Buttermilk Dressing
1/2 c. fresh mushrooms,
    diced
1 large tomato, diced
1 stalk celery, chopped
1/2 c. stuffed olives, sliced

Break cauliflower into wedges. Mix ingredients in large bowl and refrigerate before serving.

Broccoli Salad

Kathy Martin of Monahans came up with another champion recipe.

1 bunch broccoli
1/2 c. purple onion,
    chopped
8 to 10 slices bacon, fried
    and crumbled
1 c. sunflower seeds or
    almonds

Cut broccoli into small pieces and mix with remaining ingredients.

DRESSING:
1 c. mayonnaise
3 Tbsp. vinegar
2 or 3 Tbsp. sugar

Mix ingredients together and pour over broccoli mixture just before serving.

Green Bean and Broccoli Salad

The ultimate salad by Carolyn Askew from New Home

1 pkg. frozen green beans,
    cooked and drained
1 pkg. chopped broccoli,
    cooked and drained
1 can water chestnuts,
    chopped
1 can artichoke hearts
1 jar Ranch dressing
1 c. shredded cheese

Combine beans, broccoli, water chestnuts, and artichoke hearts and chill several hours. Before serving, add dressing and shredded cheese and toss together.

Broccoli-Cauliflower Salad

1 bunch broccoli
1 head cauliflower
Tomatoes to taste
1 bunch green onions,
    chopped

Use only florets from broccoli and cauliflower. Place them in a large covered bowl.

DRESSING:
1 c. mayonnaise
1/2 c. sour cream
1 Tbsp. vinegar
2 Tbsp. sugar
Salt and pepper

Mix ingredients, pour over florets, and let marinate overnight. Before serving, add tomatoes and onions.

Bean Salad

Molly Shofner says this is really good to take to church for a dinner.

1 can green beans
1 can yellow beans
1 can dark red kidney
   beans
1 onion, cut into rings
1 green pepper, cut into
   rings

Mix ingredients and cover with dressing.

DRESSING:
1/3 c. oil
2/3 c. vinegar
3/4 c. sugar
1 tsp. salt
1 tsp. pepper

Mix ingredients and pour over salad. Refrigerate overnight.

7 Layer Salad

This makes a large salad.

1 head lettuce, torn into
   small pieces
1 or 2 heads cauliflower
   diced thin
1 or 2 pkgs. frozen green
   peas, cooked, drained
   and cooled
1 purple onion, diced
1 large jar bacon bits
4 - 6 oz. mild Cheddar
   cheese, grated
1 pt. Hellman's real
   mayonnaise

Use a large, pretty glass bowl and layer ingredients in order listed. Spread mayonnaise completely over top to seal all ingredients. Refrigerate overnight or up to 24 hours before serving.

German Cole Slaw by Clarene Chambers

1 large head of cabbage,
   cut fine
3/4 c. sugar
1 onion, finely chopped

Sprinkle sugar over cabbage and onion and let stand while making dressing.

DRESSING:
2 Tbsp. sugar
1 tsp. celery seed
1 c. white vinegar
1 tsp. dry mustard
1 Tbsp. salt
3/4 c. oil

Bring ingredients to a boil. While boiling, pour over cabbage mixture. Stir. Let stand until cold, uncovered. Stir well and store covered. (This keeps for several days in refrigerator). For holidays, mix red and green cabbage.

Tossed Vegetable Salad
One of Faye Leverett's great recipes

1 (16 oz.) can green peas,
   drained
1 (16 oz.) can diced
   carrots, drained
1 (16 oz.) can whole kernel
   corn, drained
1/4 c. finely chopped
   onion
1/2 green pepper, sliced
1 (2 oz.) jar chopped
   pimientos

Mix well and set aside.

DRESSING:
1/2 c. cider vinegar
1 tsp. wine vinegar
1/2 c. oil
1/4 c. sugar
1/2 tsp. celery seeds
1 tsp. salad seasoning

Mix dressing until sugar is dissolved. Pour over salad and refrigerate overnight or several days.

Layered Potato Salad

3-1/2 lb. new potatoes
3 c. shredded green
   cabbage
3 c. shredded red cabbage
2 c. diced green pepper
2 small onions, sliced and
   separated into rings
4 hard-cooked eggs, sliced
1/2 tsp. salt
1/2 tsp. pepper
1/2 tsp. dried whole celery
   seed
3 c. mayonnaise, divided
Paprika

Cover potatoes with water and boil for 30 minutes or until tender; drain and cool slightly. Peel and cut potatoes into 1/4" slices. Layer half each of green cabbage, red cabbage, green pepper, onion, eggs, and potatoes in a large bowl. Sprinkle with half of each: salt, pepper, and celery seed. Spread with enough mayonnaise to cover, sealing at edge of bowl. Repeat layers. Cover and chill 24 hours. Sprinkle with paprika.

Carrots

Sam appreciates these when Betsy makes them.

1 pkg. carrots
2 Tbsp. chopped onion
1 bell pepper, chopped
1 can tomato soup
1/4 c. vinegar
1/4 c. sugar

Pack unpeeled, sliced carrots, which have been washed and rinsed, but not dried, in a saucepan and cover in water. Cook covered on low for 30 minutes. Sauté onion and bell pepper, add tomato soup, vinegar and sugar and simmer for 5 minutes. Pour over cooked carrots. Cool. Refrigerate overnight. Serve hot or cold.

Carrot Salad

2 lb. fresh carrots
2 green peppers, chopped
2 onions, chopped
1 can tomato soup
1/4 c. Wesson oil
1 tsp. dry mustard
1 tsp. salt
1 tsp. pepper
1 c. sugar
3/4 c. vinegar
1 tsp. Worcestershire sauce

Wash, peel, and slice carrots crosswise. Parboil carrots until just tender and drain. Mix remaining ingredients and then add carrots. Cover and let marinate for 12 hours.

Artichoke Salad

Virginia Leonard's salad became the hit of a teacher's luncheon at Lamesa High School.

1 box chicken flavored
 Rice-A-Roni
2 jars marinated artichoke
 hearts
1/3 c. sour cream
1/3 c. mayonnaise
1/4 tsp. curry powder
1/4 tsp. ginger
1/3 c. chopped green
 pepper
1/3 c. chopped green
 olives
1/2 c. diced green onions

Cook rice according to directions. Cool. Drain artichoke hearts (save liquid). Artichokes may need to be cut up. Make sauce of liquid from artichokes, sour cream, mayonnaise, and spices. Mix sauce and other ingredients and chill overnight.

Spinach Supreme Salad

Linda Givens of Lubbock serves this for parties of 10 to 12.

1 pkg. fresh raw spinach,
 washed and torn
3/4 head iceberg lettuce,
 shredded
1 box frozen peas, thawed
 and uncooked
8 sliced green onions
8 hard-boiled eggs,
 chopped
8 slices crisply fried bacon,
 crumbled
1 c. Parmesan cheese
2 c. sour cream
1 pt. mayonnaise
Salt to taste

Layer ingredients. Sprinkle layers with 1/2 cup of the Parmesan cheese. Mix mayonnaise and sour cream. Spread on top, sealing edges. Refrigerate 24 hours. Before serving, sprinkle remaining Parmesan on top.

Cucumber Salad

4 medium cucumbers,
  sliced
2 onions, sliced
1/2 c. buttermilk
2 Tbsp. vinegar
1/2 c. mayonnaise
Salt and pepper to taste

Mix all ingredients and sprinkle paprika on top. Chill and serve. This will keep for several days.

Cinnamon Apples by Inez Stone

Yummy! Yummy! Yummy!

4 Rome Beauty apples
1/2 c. sugar
1 c. water
1/2 c. cinnamon candy
  (red hots)

Peel and core apples. Boil sugar, water, and candy. When red hots are dissolved, add apples to liquid. Cook uncovered over gentle heat until tender. Turn apples frequently to let them absorb as much liquid as possible. Remove apples from pan. Boil the liquid until it forms a thick syrup (jelly-like). Pour over apples and chill. If you like, the apple center may be filled with chopped almonds, pecans, or raisins.

Cherry Pie Filling Salad

1 can Eagle Brand milk
1 can cherry pie filling
2 cartons Cool Whip
1 can Mandarin oranges,
  drained
1 can pineapple chunks,
  drained
1 can green grapes,
  drained
1 c. chopped pecans
1/2 can coconut

Mix Eagle Brand, pie filling, and all but 1 cup Cool Whip. Reserve 1 cup Cool Whip for top. Add oranges, pineapple, grapes, pecans, and coconut. Pour into dish and cover top with the reserved Cool Whip.

Cherry Salad

1 can Cherry pie filling
4 Tbsp. sugar
1 small pkg. cherry Jello
4 large bananas, diced
1 large can crushed
  pineapple, drained
1 small pkg. miniature
  marshmallows
1 c. chopped pecans

Mix cherry pie filling, sugar, and Jello. Fold in other ingredients. Put in pretty dish and chill.

Heavenly Hash

1 small pkg. miniature
  marshmallows
1 small can crushed
  pineapple, drained
1 pkg. whipping cream,
  whipped
3 bananas, sliced
1/4 c. pecans, chopped
  (opt.)

Combine all ingredients, making sure all marshmallows are coated with whipped cream. Chill and serve.

Apricot Fruit Salad

1 pkg. frozen strawberries,
  thawed
1/2 c. sugar
1 can apricot pie filling
2 bananas, sliced
1 small can crushed
  pineapple, drained

Mix strawberries and sugar until sugar is completely dissolved. Gently blend in remaining ingredients. Pour into pretty dish and chill until ready to serve.

Ambrosia
The way Little Mother made it

5 to 6 fresh oranges
1 (3-1/2 oz.) can coconut
1 large can pineapple rings,
   reserve juice

Peel oranges and cut into 1/4″ slices, cutting across the sections. In large serving bowl, layer 1/2 of the oranges, then 1/3 of the coconut. Layer the pineapple rings and then another 1/3 of the coconut. Add another layer using the remaining oranges. Top with remaining coconut. Pour reserved juice over top.

Watermelon Sparkle
A delicious summertime treat

1/2 c. sugar
1/3 c. light rum
3 Tbsp. lime juice
6 c. cubed watermelon

Combine first three ingredients and stir well. Pour over cubed watermelon. Cover and chill for 2 to 3 hours.

Melon Salad

1/2 average size
   watermelon
2 cantaloupes
2 honeydew melons
5 bananas
1 qt. fresh strawberries
2 large cans pineapple
   chunks, drained
1 small can frozen orange
   juice, undiluted
3/4 c. sugar

Use melon baller for all melons. Slice bananas and strawberries. Combine all fruit. Add sugar to orange juice and add to fruit. Chill until ready to serve. Makes approximately 25 servings.

Salad Fruit

3 Tbsp. brown sugar
3/4 tsp. ginger
3/4 tsp. lemon rind, grated
2 (16 oz.) cans peach
   halves, drained

Mix first 3 ingredients. Sprinkle evenly over top of each peach half. Bake at 375° for 8 to 10 minutes.

Country Club Fruit Salad
This fantastic recipe is from Linda Givens of Lubbock.

1 (13-1/2 oz.) can
  pineapple tidbits,
  drained
1 (16 oz.) can dark, sweet
  cherries, drained
1 (16 oz.) can light sweet
  cherries, drained
1 c. sugar
4 Tbsp. cornstarch
1/4 tsp. salt
3/4 c. orange juice
1/3 c. fresh lemon juice
1-1/2 c. juice from fruits
3 egg yolks, slightly beaten
2 envelopes gelatin
1/4 c. cold water
3 egg whites, beaten
6 Tbsp. sugar
1 c. cream, whipped
2 c. miniature
  marshmallows
1 c. pecans, chopped
2 (11 oz.) cans Mandarin
  oranges, drained
1 c. strawberries, sliced
  (optional)

Reserve juice from fruits. Combine 1 cup sugar, cornstarch, salt, orange juice, lemon juice, and juice from fruits. Cook over low heat, stirring constantly, until it begins to thicken. Stir a small amount of hot liquid into beaten egg yolks. Stir well. Add yolks to hot mixture. Continue cooking and stirring until thick. Dissolve gelatin in cold water, add to cooked mixture, and stir until gelatin is dissolved. Remove from heat and chill about 30 minutes. Beat egg whites until stiff, adding 6 tablespoons sugar, and fold into cooled mixture. Chill. Fold in whipped cream, fruit, marshmallows, pecans, oranges, and strawberries. Chill until firm.

Ben's Fruit Salad

1 cantaloupe
1 pt. fresh strawberries

Cut cantaloupe into bite-size pieces. Wash strawberries, remove tops, and quarter. Mix together and chill.

Cranberry Salad

2 c. raw ground
  cranberries
2 c. sugar
2 pkg. lemon flavored Jello
1 c. boiling water
1 apple, ground with peel
1 orange, ground with
  rind
1 c. chopped pecans

Combine cranberries and sugar and let stand. Dissolve Jello in water and let partially set. Add apple, orange, pecans, and cranberries and let set firm.

Coke Salad
One of Little Mother's best

1 (1 lb. 1 oz.) can black
  cherries, chopped
1 (15-1/4 oz.) can crushed
  pineapple
2 c. liquid (from cherries
  and pineapple)
2 pkg. cherry Jello
1-1/2 cups Coke (1 can)
1 c. chopped pecans

Drain juice from cherries and pineapple, then add water to measure 2 cups liquid. Heat liquid to boiling and add Jello. Stir until dissolved then add Coke. Chill until slightly thickened, then add pineapple, cherries, and pecans. Chill until firm.

Blueberry Salad

1 large pkg. black cherry,
  black raspberry or grape
  Jello
2 c. boiling water
1 (20 oz.) can crushed
  pineapple, undrained
1 can blueberry pie filling

Combine Jello and hot water. Mix well and add pineapple and pie filling. Put in pretty glass bowl and chill until firm.

TOPPING:
1 (8 oz.) pkg. cream
  cheese, softened
1 small carton sour cream
1/2 c. sugar
1/2 c. chopped pecans

Beat cream cheese, sour cream, and sugar together until creamy. Spread on top and sprinkle with pecans.

Avocado Mold Salad

1 (3 oz.) pkg. lime Jello
1 c. boiling water
2 (3 oz.) pkg. cream cheese
2 medium avocados (or 1
   large)
1/2 c. mayonnaise
1/2 c. crushed pineapple,
   drained

Dissolve Jello in water and cool until it starts to set. Blend cream cheese and avocado together, then add mayonnaise and crushed pineapple. Fold into Jello. Pour into mold and refrigerate until firm.

Raspberry Jello Salad

Thanks to Sue Elrod for this goody!

1 c. hot water
1 large pkg. raspberry Jello
2 c. cold water
1/2 c. chopped pecans
1 can blueberry pie filling
1 (8 oz.) carton Cool Whip

Mix hot water and Jello, boil for 3 minutes, and remove skim. Add cold water, pecans, and blueberry pie filling to Jello mixture. Pour into an 8″ × 8″ dish. Chill and top with Cool Whip.

Strawberry Salad

A terrific recipe from Rachel Huffaker

2 pkg. strawberry Jello
1-1/2 c. water
2 (10 oz.) pkg. frozen
   strawberries
1 c. mashed bananas
1 (9 oz.) can crushed
   pineapple
1 c. sour cream
1/2 c. chopped pecans
1/4 c. chopped celery

Dissolve Jello in boiling water and stir in strawberries, bananas, and pineapple. Pour 1/2 of mixture in bowl and chill until firm. Mix sour cream, pecans, and celery. Pour on top of chilled mixture. Then add the other 1/2 of Jello mixture and refrigerate until set. Cut in squares to serve.

Apricot Salad

1 large pkg. orange Jello
2 c. hot water
1 (20 oz.) can apricots,
   drained
1 (20 oz.) can crushed
   pineapple
1 c. juice from apricots
   and pineapple
3/4 c. marshmallows

Mix all ingredients together and congeal.

TOPPING:
2 Tbsp. butter
3 Tbsp. flour
1/2 c. sugar
1 egg
1 c. whipping cream,
   whipped
Cheese

Cook butter, flour, sugar, and egg until thick. Then cool. Blend in whipped cream. Spread over congealed apricot mixture. Sprinkle grated cheese over the dressing.

Cherry Salad

Carol Miller of Tahoka makes this quick and easy dish for her family.

1 can cherry pie filling
1 small can crushed
   pineapple
1 small pkg. red cherry
   Jello
4 bananas, sliced
1 c. pecans, chopped
1 c. miniature
   marshmallows

Mix all ingredients together and chill before serving.

Cream Cheese and Lime Jello

1 (15 oz.) can crushed
   pineapple
1 small pkg. lime Jello
2 (3 oz.) pkg. cream cheese
1/2 pt. whipping cream
1 c. chopped pecans
1 c. chopped celery

Boil pineapple, add Jello, mix, and cool. Add cream cheese and whipping cream. Beat with beater for 5 minutes. Add pecans and celery and mix with a spoon. Pour into a small pretty dish. Chill.

Apricot Salad by Aunt Virginia

1 (15-1/2 oz.) crushed
   pineapple
3/4 c. sugar
1 pkg. apricot Jello
1 (8 oz.) pkg. cream cheese
1 jar junior strained
   apricots (baby food)
1 (8 oz.) carton Cool Whip
1 c. pecans, chopped

Cook pineapple, sugar, and Jello on low heat until sugar dissolves. Blend cream cheese and apricots. Mix the two mixtures together. Chill in refrigerator. Fold in Cool Whip and pecans.

Orange Apricot Ring

1 (1 lb.) can apricot halves
2 (3 oz.) pkg. orange Jello
Dash of salt
1 (6 oz.) can frozen orange
   juice concentrate
1 c. cold water
1 can Mandarin
   oranges, drained (opt.)
1 small bunch seedless
   grapes (opt.)

Drain apricots, reserving syrup. Puree apricots in electric blender. Add enough water to reserved syrup to make 1-1/2 cup. Combine reserved syrup, Jello, and dash salt. Heat to boiling, stirring to dissolve Jello. Remove from heat. Add orange juice and stir until melted. Stir in apricot puree and water. Pour into a 5-cup ring mold and chill until firm. Unmold on lettuce. If desired, fill center with orange sections and frosted grapes around mold. Makes 8 to 10 servings.

Orange Jello Salad

1 pkg. orange Jello
3/4 c. pecans, chopped
1 (8 oz.) can crushed
   pineapple, drained
1 c. cottage cheese
1/4 c. celery, chopped fine

Mix Jello according to directions on package. When Jello is partially set, mix in pecans, pineapple, cottage cheese, and celery. Mix well and place in refrigerator until firm.

Zing Salad

2 pkg. raspberry Jello
2 c. boiling water
1 c. port wine
1 large can crushed
 pineapple
1 c. chopped celery
1 c. chopped walnuts
1 can cranberry sauce
1/2 pt. sour cream
1 (3 oz.) pkg. cream
 cheese, softened

Dissolve Jello in boiling water. Add wine, pineapple, celery, walnuts, and cranberry sauce. Pour into a 9″ × 13″ glass dish. Chill until firm.

Blend sour cream and cream cheese until smooth. Spread over Jello mixture and garnish with chopped pecans.

Lime Jello Salad

Bea Russell's favorite Jello salad

1 (3 oz.) pkg. lime Jello
1-1/2 c. hot water
2 (3 oz.) pkg. Philadelphia
 cream cheese
1 small can crushed
 pineapple
1 c. pecans, chopped

Dissolve Jello in hot water. Blend Jello mixture and cream cheese in blender for smooth mixture. Put in serving dish and add pineapple and pecans last. Refrigerate. Serves 6.

Banana Frozen Dessert

This was great at Spur's Golf Play Day.

3 ripe bananas, mashed
1 c. buttermilk
3/4 c. sugar
1 tsp. vanilla
1/2 c. chopped nuts
1 (8 oz.) carton Cool Whip

Mix and pour into a 9″ × 13″ dish. Freeze and cut into small squares to serve.

Apricot Frozen Salad

Nancy Simoneau has become famous for her recipe and her generosity in sharing apricots.

1 (12 oz.) can frozen
   orange juice
1 can water
3 c. mashed apricots (or
   shredded)
2 c. crushed pineapple
1/4 c. lemon juice
6 bananas, mashed
2 c. sugar

Combine all ingredients in blender and blend well. Pour into paper-lined muffin tins or plastic molds and freeze. After completely frozen, remove from muffin tins and store in Ziploc bags. Makes about 40.

Strawberry-Banana Frozen Salad

Nancy Norris serves this at church socials.

1 (8 oz.) pkg. cream cheese
3/4 c. sugar
1 (16 oz.) Cool Whip
1 large can crushed
   pineapple
3 bananas, sliced
2 small pkg. frozen
   strawberries (thawed,
   undrained)
1 c. chopped pecans

Blend cream cheese and sugar. Stir in Cool Whip. Add pineapple, bananas, strawberries, and pecans. Stir gently and pour into a large Pyrex dish and freeze. Set out 30 minutes before serving.

Cherry Frozen Salad

Beverly Womack's whopper of a salad!

2 - 3 bananas, mashed
2 Tbsp. lemon juice
1 small can crushed
   pineapple
1 small jar cherries
1 c. chopped pecans
1/2 c. sugar
1 (8 oz.) carton sour cream
1 tsp. vanilla

Add lemon juice to mashed bananas and blend. Add other ingredients and stir. Pour into buttered dish or muffin tins and freeze.

Tuna Salad I

A treat at lunch period birthday parties at Lamesa High School

1-1/2 c. macaroni
2 (6-1/2 oz.) cans albacore
 tuna
4 boiled eggs
2 Tbsp. minced onion
4 - 6 Kosher dills, chopped

Cook macaroni according to package directions. Drain and cool. Mash the boiled eggs with a fork to completely crumble them. Add tuna, mashed eggs, minced onion, and Kosher dills to macaroni. Mix thoroughly.

Tuna Salad II

Christine's version

1 can white tuna, drained
6 hard-boiled eggs, mashed
1/3 c. onion, chopped
3 Tbsp. sweet pickle relish
1/2 c. Miracle Whip
1/3 c. apple, chopped
2 Tbsp. pecans, chopped

Mix all ingredients with a hand mixer. Remove center from tomatoes and fill with tuna salad. Place on lettuce leaf. You can also spread on bread for sandwiches or serve as a dip.

Chicken Salad

Christine serves this for everyday sandwiches and also for parties.

1 c. chopped onion
4 boiled eggs (mashed with
 a fork)
1 c. celery, diced
4 c. cooked chicken, diced
 (Don't use canned
 chicken.)
1/3 c. sweet pickle relish
1-1/2 c. Miracle Whip
1/2 c. chopped pecans
1/2 apple, diced

Mix and serve. Makes 2 dozen sandwiches. For a luncheon use large tomatoes, take center out and fill with salad. Place on lettuce leaf. Serve with crackers.

Curried Rice Salad

1/3 c. sour cream
2 Tbsp. cold water
3/4 tsp. curry powder
1/2 tsp. oregano, crumbled
1/2 tsp. garlic powder
3/4 tsp. salt
1/8 tsp. pepper
1 tsp. vinegar
2 Tbsp. finely chopped
   parsley
1-1/2 c. boiling water
1-1/2 c. instant rice
1 small onion, sliced or
   diced (1/2 cup)
1-1/2 c. cubed cooked
   chicken or turkey
1 (10 oz.) pkg. broccoli
   florets, thawed
1/2 c. sliced celery
8 cherry tomatoes, halved
Lettuce leaves

Combine sour cream, water, spices, vinegar, and parsley in bowl and blend well. Set aside. Pour boiling water over rice and onion in 2-quart bowl. Cover with Saran Wrap and let stand 5 minutes. Stir in sour cream dressing. Add chicken, broccoli, celery, and tomatoes, mixing lightly. Spoon into lettuce-lined bowl or platter. Serve at once or cover and chill.

Chicken Salad

1 chicken, cooked and
   boned
1 c. chopped celery
3 boiled eggs, chopped
1 or 2 sour pickles,
   chopped
1 large jar diced pimientos
1/2 c. salad dressing
2 Tbsp. lemon juice
Lettuce leaves

Chop chicken into small pieces and mix with celery, eggs, pickles, pimientos, dressing, and lemon juice. Serve on lettuce leaves.

Crab Dip Mold

A gourmet dish from Linda McCutcheon of Brownfield

3 Tbsp. water
1 pkg. Knox gelatin
1 can cream of mushroom
  soup
1 (8 oz.) pkg. cream cheese
1 c. mayonnaise
1 c. chopped celery
2 whole green onions,
  chopped
1 can crab meat

Dissolve gelatin in water. Heat soup until it bubbles. Add gelatin and set aside. Combine other ingredients. Add soup mixture, pour into mold. Refrigerate at least 24 hours. Can be made 1 or 2 days ahead of time.

Shrimp Salad

2 pkg. lemon Jello
3-1/2 c. hot tomato juice
2 Tbsp. diced onion
3/4 tsp. salt
6 Tbsp. vinegar
4 Tbsp. sugar
1/2. tsp. cloves
1 Tbsp. horseradish
1 c. diced celery
1/2 c. pecans, chopped
1 pkg. frozen cocktail
  shrimp

Dissolve Jello in tomato juice. Then add onion, salt, vinegar, sugar, cloves, and horseradish. Chill until partially set (about 3 hours). Add celery, nuts, and shrimp. Chill overnight.

Shrimp-Rice Salad

2 c. cooked rice
1 (4 oz.) can sliced black
  olives
2 (6 oz.) jars artichoke
  hearts, chopped
1/2 c. green onions,
  chopped
1 (12 oz.) pkg. frozen baby
  shrimp, thawed
1/2 (12 oz.) jar creamy
  Italian dressing

Toss all ingredients and chill.

Oriental Seafood Salad

1/3 c. sour cream
2 Tbsp. cold water
1 Tbsp. soy sauce
1/2 tsp. garlic powder
1/2 tsp. salt
1/8 tsp. pepper
1/2 tsp. ground ginger
2 Tbsp. finely chopped
   parsley
1-1/2 c. boiling water
1-1/2 c. instant rice
1 small onion, sliced or
   diced
1-1/2 c. cleaned, cooked
   shrimp
1 (9 oz.) pkg. frozen cut
   green beans, thawed
1 c. bean sprouts, trimmed
1/2 red or green pepper,
   diced

Combine sour cream, water, soy sauce, spices, and parsley in bowl and blend well. Set aside. Pour boiling water over rice and onion in 2-quart bowl. Cover with Saran Wrap and let stand for 5 minutes. Stir in sour cream dressing. Add remaining ingredients, mixing lightly.

Lime Salad Dressing

From Faye Kennedy of Lubbock

1/3 c. frozen lime
   concentrate
1/3 c. honey
1/3 c. salad oil
Poppy seed

Mix limeade, honey, and salad oil in blender until thick. Add small amount of poppy seed.

Poppy Seed Dressing

A great dressing for fruit

1-1/2 c. sugar
2/3 c. vinegar
3 Tbsp. lemon juice
2 tsp. dry mustard
1 tsp. salt
2 c. vegetable oil
2 Tbsp. poppy seeds

Combine sugar, vinegar, lemon juice, mustard, and salt in blender. Blend well. Add oil slowly while blender is running. Continue blending until mixture is thick. Stir in poppy seeds. Cover and refrigerate until thick.

Entrées

Three Day Brisket
Joan Gardner delights her family by serving this.

Brisket
2 Tbsp. Liquid Smoke
1 tsp. salt
1 tsp. onion salt
1 tsp. garlic salt

FIRST DAY:
Baste the brisket well with Liquid Smoke and salt. Wrap in foil and refrigerate overnight.

SECOND DAY:
Sprinkle onion salt and garlic salt on brisket. Wrap in foil again and bake at 300° for about 5 hours. Let cool and refrigerate overnight.

THIRD DAY:
Slice thin and pour sauce over brisket. Wrap in foil and bake at 300° to 325° for about 2 hours.

SAUCE:
3 Tbsp. brown sugar
1 c. catsup
1/2 c. water
6 Tbsp. oleo
4 Tbsp. Worcestershire
   sauce
2 tsp. celery seed
3 tsp. ground mustard
1 tsp. black pepper
2 tsp. salt

Mix together and bring to a boil. Pour over meat.

Fabulous Brisket
Many thanks to Margaret Hartman of Brownfield for this fabulous entrée

1 (6 - 8 lb.) brisket
2 tsp. garlic powder
2 tsp. celery salt
2 tsp. onion salt
1/4 of small bottle of
   Worcestershire sauce
1/2 bottle of liquid smoke
1 bottle barbeque sauce

Prick brisket with a fork on both sides. Sprinkle both sides with remaining ingredients, except barbeque sauce. Using heavy duty foil, put fat side up and wrap tightly. Place on a cookie sheet and allow to set overnight in refrigerator. Place in roasting pan and bake 5 hours at 250°. Mix drippings with bottled barbeque sauce.

Mexican Dish in a Hat

These little hat bowls are easy to make and fun to serve.

Flour tortillas
Cooking oil

Fill Fry Daddy 1/2 full with oil. (You can use a deep, narrow pan rather than a Fry Daddy.) Drop one flour tortilla into hot oil. Press down in center with a long-handled ladle. Cook 1 minute or until browned. Drain on paper towels. This makes a small bowl in the shape of a hat. Fill with the following ingredients.

2 lb. ground beef, browned and drained
1 bowl shredded Cheddar cheese
1 bowl shredded Mozzarella cheese
1 bowl raisins
1 bowl chopped onions
1 bowl shredded coconut
1 bowl chopped pecans
1 bowl sour cream
1 bowl picante
1 bowl avocado dip
1 bowl sliced jalapenos
1 bowl chopped tomatoes
1 bowl shredded lettuce
1 bowl chopped black olives

Set this up buffet style and let each person make their own. Serve with chips.

Beef Kabobs

This makes a fun summertime meal.

1 Tbsp. lemon juice
3 Tbsp. salad oil
1 clove garlic, crushed
1/4 tsp. salt
1 tsp. water
Dash pepper
Dash Accent
2 lb. stew meat
Fresh mushrooms
Apples
Pineapple chunks
Carrot chunks
Celery
Green pepper
1/4 c. honey
1/4 c. pineapple juice
1/4 tsp. ground ginger
Rice

Mix lemon juice, salad oil, garlic, salt, water, pepper, and Accent. Add meat and marinate at least two hours. Drain off marinade and reserve. String meat alternately on skewers with some or all of the vegetables.

To the drained marinade, add honey, pineapple juice, and ginger. Brush this mixture over the skewers as they cook on the grill. Cook for 15 to 20 minutes. Serve on rice.

Beef Burgundy

A melt-in-your-mouth dish from Lee Moore.

2 Tbsp. soy sauce
2-1/2 Tbsp. flour
2 lb. Pikes Peak roast,
   trimmed and cut into
   1″ cubes
1 c. dry red wine
4 carrots
2 onions
1 clove garlic, diced
1/4 tsp. marjoram
1/4 tsp. thyme
1/4 tsp. black pepper
1 (6 oz.) can mushroom
   buttons, drained
Cooked rice

Mix soy sauce and flour in dish, then add cubed meat. Toss to coat. Add wine and let marinate. Cut carrots in 1/2″ chunks and slice onions. Put all ingredients except rice in a browning bag. Toss one time to coat. Punch holes as directed on browning bag package. Bake at 325° for 2 to 2-1/2 hours. Serve on rice.

Texas Red Chili
Christine's recipe for Bobby and Joel

1/8 lb. suet, finely
  chopped
3 lb. round steak, cubed
  (OR hamburger meat)
6 Tbsp. chili powder
1 Tbsp. ground oregano
1 Tbsp. crushed cumin
  seed
1 Tbsp. salt
1/2 to 1 Tbsp. cayenne
  pepper
2 large garlic cloves,
  minced (about 2-1/2
  Tbsp.)
1 Tbsp. Tabasco "if you
  dare"
1-1/2 qt. water
1/4 c. white cornmeal

Fry suet until crisp. Add cubed steak or hamburger to suet and brown lightly. Add seasonings and water. Cover and simmer 1-1/2 hours. Skim off fat. Stir in cornmeal and simmer, uncovered for 30 minutes.

Mexican Beef Hash
A great prepare-ahead-and-freeze dish

1 lb. ground beef
1 c. chopped onion
1 c. chopped green pepper
1 Tbsp. chili powder
2 tsp. salt
1/4 tsp. pepper
1 c. uncooked rice
2 (1 lb.) cans tomatoes

Brown ground beef and drain. Add onion and green pepper and cook until onion is clear. Add chili powder, salt, pepper, and rice and mix well. Line 2 (1-1/2 qt.) casserole dishes with foil. Divide mixture evenly into each dish. Pour 1 can tomatoes over each casserole and mix lightly to blend. Cover and bake in 350° oven for 20 minutes.

Remove from oven, leave covered, and cool to room temperature. Place casseroles in freezer. When hash is frozen, lift foil from dish. Wrap in freezer paper, seal, label, date, and return to freezer. Recommended storage time is 3 to 6 months.

To serve, take package from freezer, remove wrappings and place in casserole dish. Cover and bake in 350° oven for 1-1/2 hours.

Hawaiian Meatballs

1 lb. ground chuck
1 egg
1/4 c. dry bread crumbs
2 Tbsp. milk
1 tsp. salt
1/8 tsp. nutmeg
2 Tbsp. cornstarch
1 beef bouillon cube,
　　dissolved
1 Tbsp. soy sauce
1 (13-1/2 oz.) can
　　pineapple chunks,
　　drained
3/4 c. pineapple liquid
1/4 c. cider vinegar
1 (11 oz.) can Mandarin
　　oranges, drained

Mix meat, egg, bread crumbs, milk, salt, and nutmeg. Shape into 3/4″ balls. Brown meatballs, about 5 minutes. Remove skillet from heat and remove meatballs. Add cornstarch, bouillon cube, and soy sauce to meat drippings. Heat until it thickens. Add reserved pineapple liquid and vinegar. Bring to a boil, then reduce heat to low. Add meatballs, pineapple, and oranges. Heat covered for 10 minutes on low. Serve with rice or use for appetizer with cocktail picks. Makes 6 main dish servings or 12 to 15 appetizer servings.

Mexican Beef and Chip

Beverly says this is the quickest dish in the South!

1 lb. ground beef
1 sm. onion, chopped
1 clove garlic, minced
1 can cream of mushroom
　　soup
1 (4 oz.) can chopped
　　green chilies
1 pkg. tortilla chips
1 (10 oz.) can enchilada
　　sauce
2 c. shredded Monterey
　　Jack cheese

Brown ground beef in skillet and drain. Add onion and garlic. Sauté until onions are soft. Add soup and chilies. Layer chips, meat mixture, enchilada sauce, and cheese. Cover and cook until bubbly and cheese is melted, about 6 to 8 minutes.

Spaghetti with Meatballs

A REAL spaghetti dish.

1 lb. lean ground beef
1/3 c. dry bread crumbs
1 egg
1 med. onion, grated
1 Tbsp. minced parsley
1-1/2 tsp. salt
1/8 tsp. pepper
2 Tbsp. olive oil
2 garlic cloves, crushed
1 (1 lb.4 oz.) can Italian
   peeled tomatoes
1 (6 oz.) can tomato paste
1 paste can of water
1 tsp. crushed dried basil
1 (8 oz.) pkg. thin
   spaghetti

Mix together beef, crumbs, egg, onion, parsley, 1 teaspoon salt, and pepper. Shape into 16 to 20 small balls. In a large skillet, heat oil. Add meatballs and slowly brown. Remove meatballs and set aside.

In a large saucepan, add garlic, tomatoes, tomato paste, the paste can full of water, basil, and remaining 1/2 teaspoon salt. Bring to a boil. Simmer, stirring often for 1/2 hour. Add meatballs and simmer another 1/2 hour.

Cook spaghetti according to package directions. Serve with meatballs and sauce.

Spaghetti Sauce by Nadine Rogers

1 lb. ground round
2 med. onions, chopped
2 cans tomato paste
1/2 small bottle Ketchup
1/4 c. various meat sauces
Chili powder to taste
1/2 tsp. salt
1/4 tsp. pepper
1/2 tsp. garlic powder
2 to 3 c. water
10 oz. spaghetti, cooked
Cheese, grated
Mushrooms (opt.)

Brown meat with onions. Add sauces, seasoning, and water. Add more water if needed. Cook over low heat for at least 2 hours. (4 or 5 hours are better.) Pour over prepared spaghetti and top with grated cheese and mushrooms.

Spaghetti Pie

Tahoka's very own Joey Rash serves this to her family.

6 oz. spaghetti
1 lb. lean ground beef
1/2 c. onion, chopped
1/4 c. green pepper,
    chopped
1 (8 oz.) can tomatoes, cut
    up
1 (6-oz.) can tomato paste
1 tsp. sugar
1 tsp. oregano
1/2 tsp. garlic salt
2 Tbsp. margarine
1/3 c. grated Parmesan
    cheese
2 well-beaten eggs
1/2 c. Mozzarella cheese,
    grated (2 ounces)

Cook spaghetti according to package directions, drain. Cook meat, onion, and green pepper in large skillet until meat is brown. Drain. Stir in tomatoes, tomato paste, sugar, oregano and garlic salt; heat through. Combine spaghetti, margarine, Parmesan cheese, and eggs. Press into a buttered 10" pie plate, forming a "crust." Fill crust with meat mixture. Bake uncovered in a 350° oven for 20 to 25 minutes. Sprinkle with cheese. Bake 5 minutes more or until cheese melts. Let stand 5 minutes.

Christine's Hash

Christine's girls love this with hot cornbread.

1 diced onion
3 or 4 peeled and diced
    potatoes
1/4 c. bacon drippings
1-1/2 c. chopped, cooked
    roast
Salt and pepper to taste

Cook onion and potatoes in bacon drippings, until tender. Add salt and pepper. Add roast and cook until meat is hot.

Pepper Steak Deluxe

1-1/2 lb. sirloin or round
   steak, about 1" thick
1/4 c. vegetable oil
1 c. water
1 med. onion, sliced
1/2 tsp. garlic salt
1/4 tsp. ginger
2 green peppers, sliced
4 servings instant rice
1 Tbsp. cornstarch
2 - 3 tsp. sugar (opt.)
2 Tbsp. soy sauce
2 tomatoes

Trim fat from steak and cut into strips. Heat oil in large skillet. Add steak and cook, turning frequently, until brown, about 5 minutes. Stir in water, onion, garlic salt, and ginger. Heat to boiling; reduce heat. Cover and simmer 15 minutes. Add green pepper during last 5 minutes of simmering. While steak is simmering, cook instant rice according to package directions.

Blend cornstarch, sugar, and soy sauce; stir into steak mixture. Cook, stirring constantly, until mixture thickens and boils. Boil and stir for 1 minute. Slice tomatoes and place on steak mixture. Cover and cook over low heat just until tomatoes are heated through. Serve with rice.

Swiss Steak

Nadine Rogers of Lubbock enjoys serving this to her family and friends.

2 lb. sirloin steak, cut into
   serving pieces
Flour
Salt
Pepper
1 pkg. dried onion soup
2 green peppers, sliced
1 large can whole tomatoes
1 can cooked carrots
1 can mushrooms
1 can mushroom soup
2 to 4 Tbsp. picante sauce

Flour, salt. and pepper meat, and tenderize with mallet on both sides. Put into 9" × 13" pan and sprinkle with dry onion soup. Place sliced peppers over soup. Add tomatoes, carrots, mushrooms, mushroom soup, and picante sauce. Seal with foil and bake 325° for 2 hours.

Swiss Steak Deluxe

2 lb. round steak, cut into
   small slices
2 cans diced tomatoes
1 med. sliced onion
1 Tbsp. Worcestershire
   sauce
1/4 tsp. pepper
1 tsp. vinegar
1 clove garlic, minced
2 Tbsp. catsup
2 Tbsp. brown sugar
1 tsp. salt

Brown steak on both sides. Mix remaining ingredients, and pour over meat, and cook at 300° for 1-1/2 to 2 hours.

Snazzy Individual Meatcups

These are delicious and children love them.

1 lb. ground beef
1/2 c. barbeque sauce
1 Tbsp. minced onion
2 Tbsp. brown sugar
1 (8 oz.) can large size
   biscuits
1 c. grated Cheddar cheese

Brown beef and drain. Add barbeque sauce, onion, and brown sugar. Set aside. Spray muffin tins with Pam and then place 1 biscuit in each muffin tin, pressing dough up the sides and forming a rim around the top. Spoon meat mixture into cups and sprinkle with grated cheese. Bake at 400° for 10 to 12 minutes.

Terrific Pizza

Chloie Jan Wells can compete with Pizza Inn with this recipe.

2 c. warm water
2 pkg. yeast
1/2 c. oil
1/2 c. sugar
1-1/2 tsp. salt
5 c. flour
1 jar Ragu spaghetti sauce
Mozzarella cheese
Pepperoni, hamburger,
   mushrooms, etc.

Mix water, yeast, oil, sugar, salt, and flour. Let rise 1 to 1-1/2 hours. Grease pizza pans. Use flour and pinch off dough needed. This makes crusts for 4 pizzas. Use extra flour to coat the dough to keep it from sticking. Press in pan and place in 400° oven. Cook crust a little to prevent soggy crust. Turn dough over and cook 5 more minutes. Spread Ragu on crust, then cheese, then toppings, then more cheese. Place in oven until cheese melts. For a quick crust, use boxed Hot Roll Mix.

Lasagna

Aunt Ruth has a winner with this one.

1 lb. Italian sausage, or
  ground beef
1 clove garlic, minced
1 Tbsp. chopped parsley
1 Tbsp. basil
1-1/2 tsp. salt
1 (1 lb.) can tomatoes (2
  cups)
2 (6 oz.) cans tomato paste
  (1-1/2 cups)
1 (10 oz.) pkg. lasagna
  noodles
2 (12 oz.) cartons large
  curd cream style cottage
  cheese
2 eggs, beaten
2 tsp. salt
1/2 tsp. pepper
2 Tbsp. chopped parsley
  (opt.)
1/2 c. grated Parmesan
  cheese
1 lb. Mozzarella cheese,
  thinly sliced

Brown meat slowly, then drain. Add next 6 ingredients to meat and simmer, uncovered, until thick, (about 45 minutes). Stir occasionally. Cook noodles in boiling salted water until tender. Drain and rinse in cold water. Combine cottage cheese with next 5 ingredients.

Place 1/2 noodles in 9″ × 13″ pan. Cover with 1/2 cottage cheese mixture. Layer 1/2 Mozzarella cheese slices and then 1/2 meat mixture. Repeat layers. Bake at 375° for 30 minutes. Cool 10 to 15 minutes before cutting. This freezes nicely.

Rump Roast

Christine makes this for special guests.

1 (4 to 5 lb.) roast
Salt and pepper
1 pkg. carrots, peeled and
  cut into 3″ chunks
4 med. size potatoes,
  peeled and quartered
1 onion cut into rings
1 pkg. dry onion soup
1 can cream of mushroom
  soup
2-1/2 c. water
1 small can diced
  mushrooms (opt.)

Place roast in roasting pan and salt and pepper to taste. Place carrots, potatoes, and onion rings around meat. Mix soups and water, pour over vegetables, and cover pan. Bake at 325° for 3-1/2 to 4 hours.

Stuffed Peppers

1 lb. ground beef
1/4 c. chopped onion
1 (12 oz.) can whole kernel
   corn, drained
1 (8 oz.) can tomato sauce
1 c. cooked rice
1/4 c. A-1 steak sauce
1/4 tsp. pepper
6 large green peppers

Brown ground beef and drain. Add onion and cook until done. Stir in corn, tomato sauce, rice, steak sauce, and pepper. Set aside.

Cut tops off peppers and remove seeds. Spoon meat mixture into peppers. Arrange in 9″ square baking dish. Bake at 350° for 30 to 35 minutes, or until peppers are done.

Fried Steak And Gravy
We could eat this twice a day.

2 lb. tenderized round
   steak, cut into serving
   portions
1 tsp. salt
1 tsp. pepper
1 c. flour
3/4 c. Crisco

Salt and pepper meat. Place flour in paper bag and drop steak in bag and shake well. Heat oil in a skillet to 375°. Fry steak in hot oil until browned, turning steak once. Reserve 1/4 c. drippings for gravy.

GRAVY:
1/4 c. flour
1/4 c. meat drippings
2 to 3 c. milk
1/4 tsp. salt
1/4 tsp. pepper

Add flour to oil, mix, and cook until bubbly, stirring constantly. Add 2-1/2 cups milk. If it is too thick, add more milk stirring constantly. Stir in salt and pepper.

Mexicali Boat

This makes an unusual dish and an attractive table setting.

1-1/2 lb. ground beef
1 (8 oz.) jar taco sauce
1 (8-3/4 oz.) can whole
   kernel corn, drained
1 pkg. dry onion soup mix
1-1/2 tsp. chili powder
2 pkg. RapidRise yeast
2/3 c. lukewarm water
   (125° to 130°)
1 Tbsp. sugar
1 tsp. salt
2 Tbsp. margarine,
   softened
2 eggs, room temperature
3 c. flour
1/2 c. chopped tomato
Sesame seed (opt.)
Sour cream (opt.)

In large skillet, over medium heat, brown beef and then drain. Stir in taco sauce, corn, soup mix, and chili powder. Simmer 2 minutes and set aside.

Mix yeast in warm water and set aside for about 5 minutes. Then add sugar, salt, and margarine and blend. Add one egg and mix completely. Reserve 1 cup of the flour and blend in the remaining flour. Add enough of the reserved flour to make a soft dough. On lightly floured surface, knead about 4 minutes.

Roll dough into 16″ × 9″ rectangle. Spoon beef mixture down center third of dough length. Top with tomato. Bring long edges of dough together over filling, pinching firmly at 2″ intervals and seal ends. Gently place on a greased baking sheet. Cover with a damp cloth. Place a large shallow pan on counter and half-fill with boiling water. Place baking sheet over pan. Let dough rise 15 minutes.

Beat remaining egg and brush on loaf. Sprinkle with sesame seed. Bake at 400° for 20 minutes or until done. Cool slightly on wire rack. Serve warm with sour cream.

Rolled Roast

1 (5 - 6 lb.) rolled cross
   ribs of beef
Salt and pepper to taste
Garlic salt to taste

Sprinkle meat with salt, pepper, and garlic salt. Place on rack in a shallow baking pan. Bake at 325° for 2-1/2 hours or until tender.

Spanish Noodles

Inez Bessire has enjoyed making this for her boys.

1 large onion, chopped
   fine
2 Tbsp. shortening
1-1/4 lb. ground beef
1 (5 oz.) pkg. egg noodles
1/2 tsp. black pepper
1/2 tsp. red pepper
1 tsp. celery seed
2 tsp. chili powder
1 tsp. salt
1 can English peas, drained
2 cans tomato soup

Brown onion in shortening. Add beef and brown. Cook noodles as directed on package and drain. Put half of noodles in deep casserole. Put in one half of beef and onions, then a layer of seasoning. Add 1/2 can peas and 1 can tomato soup. Repeat for second layer. Cover. May be put in refrigerator or freezer. Bake 1 hour at 350°or until mixture is bubbly. Serves 6

Chinese Beef & Peppers

3/4 lb. boneless chuck, cut
   into thin strips
1 large onion, sliced (about
   1 cup)
1 garlic clove, minced
1 Tbsp. oil
3/4 tsp. ginger
1 cup green and/or red
   pepper strips
1-1/2 c. beef bouillon (Or
   use 2 beef bouillon
   cubes dissolved in 1-1/2
   cups boiling water)
3 Tbsp. soy sauce
2 Tbsp. sherry wine
   (optional)
1-1/2 c. instant rice

Sauté beef, onion, and garlic in oil in large skillet until meat is browned. Add ginger, green pepper, bouillon, soy sauce, and wine. Bring to a boil. Stir in rice. Cover, remove from heat, and let stand for 5 minutes.

Beef Enchilada Rice

1/2 lb. lean ground beef
1 Tbsp. oil
1/3 c. diced onion
1 clove garlic, finely
   minced
1 (3 oz.) can green chilies,
   diced
1-1/2 to 2 tsp. chili
   powder
1/2 tsp. oregano
1 (8 oz.) can whole
   tomatoes in juice
1/2 tsp. salt
3/4 c. water
1-1/2 c. instant rice
2 tsp. chopped fresh
   parsley
2 slices (1 oz. each)
   American cheese, cut in
   strips

Brown beef in oil in skillet. Add onion and sauté with beef until tender. Add garlic; sauté 15 seconds. Add chilies, chili powder, oregano, tomatoes with juice, salt, and water. Break up tomatoes and bring to boil. Add rice. Stir, cover, and remove from heat. Let stand 5 minutes. Sprinkle dish with chopped parsley. Place cheese on top. Replace cover. Let stand 3 to 5 minutes until cheese has melted.

Swedish Meat Balls in Curry Sauce

1 lb. ground beef
1/2 c. dry bread crumbs
1 egg
1/2 small onion, grated
2/3 c. milk
1/4 tsp. black pepper
1/4 tsp. nutmeg
1 tsp. salt
1 bouillon cube (dissolved
   in 1/4 c. water)

Mix all ingredients except bouillon and form into 1-1/2" balls for a main dish, or 3/4" balls for serving as hors d'oeuvres. Brown well in bacon drippings. Add bouillon to skillet, cover tightly and simmer 20 to 25 minutes. Serve with hot curry sauce.

CURRY SAUCE:
1/4 c. butter, melted
1/4 c. flour
2 c. milk
2 Tbsp. catsup
2-3 tsp. curry powder
2 tsp. lemon juice
1/2 tsp. salt
Dash pepper

Blend butter and flour, then blend in milk a little at a time. Add remaining ingredients and cook, stirring, until thickened.

Beef and Bean Burritos

1 lb. ground beef
1 medium onion, chopped
1 clove garlic, minced
2 tsp. chili powder
1 tsp. dried whole oregano
1/2 tsp. ground cumin
1/2 tsp. salt
1/4 tsp. pepper
1 (16 oz.) can refried beans
1 (10 oz.) can enchilada
   sauce, divided
6 (8") flour tortillas
Shredded lettuce

Cook beef, onion, and garlic in a large skillet until meat is browned, stirring to crumble meat. Drain. Add chili powder and next 4 ingredients. Simmer 5 to 10 minutes. Add beans and 1/2 cup enchilada sauce. Heat thoroughly. Wrap tortillas securely in aluminum foil and bake at 350° for 10 minutes or until heated. Remove tortillas from foil and spoon about 1/2 cup ground beef mixture on each tortilla. Roll tightly and place seam side down on serving platter lined with shredded lettuce. Spoon remaining enchilada sauce over tortillas. Garnish and serve with choice of toppings: shredded lettuce, shredded cheese, sliced ripe olives, chopped tomatoes, sour cream, or taco sauce.

Chilies Rellenos

4 (4 oz.) cans whole green
   chilies, drained
1-1/2 c. shredded Swiss
   cheese (6 oz.)
1-1/2 c. shredded Cheddar
   cheese (6 oz.)
6 eggs, beaten
3/4 c. milk
1/4 tsp. salt
1/4 tsp. pepper

Rinse chilies and remove seeds. Set chilies aside. Combine cheeses. Stuff each chili with 3 tablespoons cheese. Arrange chilies in a lightly greased 12" × 8" × 2" baking dish. Sprinkle remaining cheese on top. Combine eggs and remaining ingredients, mixing well. Pour over chilies. Bake at 350° for 30 minutes or until set.

Swiss Meat Loaf
Kathy Martin's delicious entrée

2 lbs. hamburger meat
3/4 c. diced Cheddar
   cheese
3/4 c. diced Swiss cheese
2 beaten eggs
1/2 c. chopped onion
1/2 c. chopped green
   pepper
1-1/2 tsp. salt
1/2 tsp. pepper
1 tsp. celery salt
1/2 tsp. paprika
2 c. milk
1 c. dried bread crumbs

Mix together in order as given. Press into one big or two small loaf pans. Bake at 350° for 1-1/2 hours.

Ring Meat Loaf

2 eggs, beaten
3/4 c. milk
2/3 c. bread crumbs
2 Tbsp. chopped onion
1 tsp. salt
1/2 tsp. chili powder
1/2 tsp. pepper
1-1/2 lb. ground beef

Combine eggs, milk, bread crumbs, onion, salt, chili powder, and pepper. Add beef and mix well. Shape meat into a ring in an 8″ round baking dish. Bake at 375° for 45 to 50 minutes. Drain excess fat.

SAUCE:
1/4 c. hot-style catsup
1 tsp. brown sugar
1/2 tsp. dry mustard

Combine catsup, brown sugar, and mustard and spread on top of meat. Cook uncovered for 5 minutes.

Runzas (Yeast dough filled with hamburger & cabbage)

Karen Slife of Hewitt serves this to Brent, Conor, Nathan, and Jacob.

DOUGH:
2 c. warm water
2 pkg. active dry yeast
1/2 c. sugar
1-1/2 tsp. salt
1 egg
1/4 c. margarine, melted
  and cooled
6-1/2 c. flour

HAMBURGER FILLING:
1-1/2 lb. hamburger meat
1/2 c. chopped onion
3 c. shredded cabbage
1-1/2 tsp. salt
1/2 tsp. pepper
Dash Tabasco
Sliced mushrooms to taste
1/2 c. water
16 slices American cheese

Mix first 4 ingredients until dissolved. Add egg and melted margarine. Stir in flour. Put in refrigerator for 4 hours. Roll dough into rectangular shape and cut into 16 squares. Divide hamburger mixture between squares. Lay one slice of cheese on top. Pull sides up and seal by pressing edges together. Place on greased cookie sheet. Bake 20 minutes at 350°.

Brown hamburger and onion and drain. Add cabbage, seasonings, mushrooms, and water. Simmer 15 to 20 minutes. Cool completely before putting into dough.

HINT:
To save time, use a French roll and scoop out the middle. Fill with meat mixture. You can also use pita bread. You can substitute ground turkey for the ground hamburger.

Meatloaf

Virginia Goggan's specialty

3 lb. hamburger meat
Salt and pepper to taste
1 Tbsp. chili powder
1 tsp. celery salt
2 - 3 eggs, slightly beaten
2 c. instant oats
2 cans cream of mushroom
  soup
1 can tomato juice
1 beef bouillon cube
1 onion, finely chopped
1-1/2 c. water

Mix meat, salt, pepper, chili powder, and celery salt. Then add eggs and oats. Mix thoroughly and divide in half. Form into two loaves. Place loaves in a hot, greased iron skillet and brown on both sides. Drain.

Dissolve bouillon cube in a small amount of hot water. Make sauce by blending mushroom soup, tomato juice, bouillon cube, onion, and water. Pour over loaves. Bake at 325° for 2 hours.

HINT:
The iron skillet must be very large and at least 3″ deep. Otherwise, after browning, place loaves in a large casserole dish to bake.

Chili for a Year

Virginia Goggans makes this up and freezes it in small containers.

8 onions, diced
4 Tbsp. bacon grease
8 lb. hamburger meat
8 lb. chili meat
32 pods garlic, diced
2 tsp. cumin
1 tsp. red pepper
24 Tbsp. Morton Chili
    Blend (1 pkg. and 11
    Tbsp.)
Salt and pepper to taste
Water

Sauté onion in bacon grease. Cook chili in electric dutch oven or very large pan. Brown meat. Add garlic, onion, cumin, red pepper, chili blend, salt, and pepper. Fill oven pan with water and bring to a boil. Cover and turn to low. Cook between 6 and 7 hours.

SMALL AMOUNT:
1 onion, diced
2 lb. meat
4 garlic pods
1/2 tsp. cumin
3 Tbsp. Morton Chili
    Blend
Salt and pepper to taste
Red pepper to taste
Water

Mix same as above and cook 2 to 3 hours.

Mexican Good Stuff

1 lb. hamburger meat
1 small onion, chopped
1/2 bell pepper, chopped
1/2 tsp. minced garlic
1 Tbsp. chili powder
1 tsp. salt
1 (6 oz.) can tomato sauce
1/2 c. milk
2 c. cooked rice
1 c. grated Cheddar cheese
1 pkg. flour tortillas

Cook first six ingredients together until done. Stir in tomato sauce, milk, and rice. Heat well. Remove from heat and add cheese. Place mixture in middle of warmed tortillas. Roll and serve with hot sauce. Serve with chips.

Salmon Croquettes

Christine serves this with hot biscuits and gravy.

1 small can salmon 1 egg, slightly beaten 8 soda crackers, crushed	Mix salmon and egg. Add cracker crumbs and mix. Make 4 to 6 patties. Brown both sides in hot skillet with small amount Crisco.

Spicy Grilled Catfish

One of our all-time favorites

2 Tbsp. lemon-pepper 2 Tbsp. blackened redfish seasoning 6 (6 oz.) catfish fillets 1/2 c. margarine, melted 1/4 c. lemon juice	Combine seasonings and set aside. Place fish in a single layer in a lightly greased fish basket. Combine butter and lemon juice; brush on each side of fish. Grill fish over hot coals for 5 minutes on each side, basting with butter mixture when turning. Sprinkle each side with seasoning mixture. Baste and grill 3 additional minutes on each side or until fish flakes easily when tested with a fork.

Shrimp and Rice a la Bobby

Bobby's special treat for Ben and Clay

1-1/2 c. instant rice 1 box frozen green peas 1 (10 oz.) pkg. frozen cooked shrimp Soy sauce to taste (opt.)	Cook rice according to package directions and set aside. In separate dish, cook peas according to package directions. Rinse shrimp in cold water. Toss all together in a large serving bowl. Serve with crackers or hot bread.

Tuna Delight

1 (6 oz.) pkg. macaroni,
  cooked
1 can cream of mushroom
  soup
1 (7 oz.) can white tuna,
  drained
1 large can cut green
  asparagus or 1 small can
  green peas
Green pepper, cut into
  rings
1/2 tsp. salt
1/4 tsp. pepper
1 cup grated cheese

Rinse macaroni and place in buttered baking dish. Reserving a small amount of cheese for the top, mix remaining ingredients and pour on top of macaroni. Sprinkle with reserved cheese. Bake at 325° for 30 minutes.

Fish Batter

Bea Russell of Lamesa gave this to Bobby.

1 c. flour
1 c. water
2 tsp. baking powder
Dash salt

Mix all ingredients with a wire whip. Dip fish and fry in hot grease. This is also good for onion rings.

Baked Fish by Rachel Huffaker

1-1/2 lb. fillets
1/2 tsp. seasoned salt
1 Tbsp. margarine
1-1/2 c. light mayonnaise
1/2 c. Mozzerella cheese,
  grated
2 Tbsp. green onions,
  chopped
1/2 tsp. paprika

Sprinkle fish with seasoned salt and dot with margarine. Bake fish at 350° for 10 minutes. Mix mayonnaise, cheese, and onion and pour over fish. Bake about 15 minutes, or until flaky and cheese is bubbly. Garnish with paprika.

Tuna Fish Rolls a la Virginia

1 can refrigerator biscuits
1 can tuna
1/2 c. celery, chopped fine
1 egg
1/2 c. milk
1 can cream of chicken
   soup

Mash each biscuit flat. Mix tuna, celery, and egg. Place tuna mixture on biscuit and roll up and seal. Place roll in baking dish. Mix milk and soup and pour over rolls. Bake at 350° for 30 to 40 minutes.

Tuna Casserole

Bobby's dream and Clay's nightmare

1 can cream of mushroom
   soup (or cream of
   celery)
1/2 c. milk
1 sm. can tuna, drained
1 c. cooked green peas
2 c. cooked shell macaroni
1 c. grated Cheddar cheese
1/4 c. potato chips,
   crushed

Blend soup and milk. Add tuna, peas, and macaroni and mix completely. Pour into a greased casserole dish. Top with cheese and potato chips. Bake at 350° until bubbly.

Tuna and Rice Supreme

1-1/2 c. water
1 can cream of mushroom
   soup
1/2 c. chopped onion
1 tsp. lemon juice
1/4 tsp. salt
Dash pepper
1-1/2 c. instant rice
1 (10 oz.) pkg. frozen green
   peas
1 (7 oz.) can tuna, drained
1/2 c. grated cheese

In a saucepan, combine water, soup, onion, lemon juice, salt, and pepper. Bring to a boil, stir occasionally. Pour half of mixture into a greased 1-1/2 quart casserole. Add rice, peas, and tuna. Add remaining soup mixture. Sprinkle with cheese. Cover and bake at 375° for 20 to 25 minutes, stirring once after 10 minutes.

Indonesian Fried Rice

Dennis, Marina, and Carrie get this treat from Kathy Martin of Monahans.

2 medium chopped onions
1/8 c. salad oil
10 large shrimp, cooked
   and chopped
2 Tbsp. butter
4 cloves garlic, minced
6 chopped scallions
4 sprigs parsley
2 tomatoes, 1 sliced for
   garnish, 1 chopped
Salt and pepper to taste
1 (8 oz.) can whole string
   beans
Soy sauce to taste
3 c. cooked rice
1 hard scrambled egg

Cook 2/3 onions in oil until crisp. Remove onions and add shrimp to oil. Fry until water is out of shrimp and has evaporated from oil and shrimp are slightly browned. Remove from oil. Remove 3 to 4 tablespoons of the oil. Add butter. When butter is bubbly (but not browned) add garlic and rest of onion. Fry until soft. Add 2/3 scallions and 1/2 parsley. Stirring constantly, fry until slightly soft. Add chopped tomatoes, salt, and pepper. Fry about 10 minutes while continuing to stir. Add beans, shrimp, and a big dash of soy sauce. Cook until brown. Add rice to frying mixture. Mix well and stir constantly. Add rest of scallions and parsley to frying pan. Cook for 10 to 15 minutes. Put in bowl and put fried onions and scrambled egg in strips on the top. Garnish with sliced tomatoes.

Marinated Salmon Steaks

A taste of Alaskan cuisine by Nadine Rogers

4 (1″) salmon steaks
1/3 c. orange juice
1/3 c. soy sauce
2 Tbsp. parsley
2 Tbsp. cooking oil
1 clove garlic, crushed

Mix orange juice, soy sauce, parsley, cooking oil, and garlic and pour over steaks. Let chill 4 to 6 hours, turning occasionally. Drain and reserve marinade. Place fish in greased wire grill basket. Cook over medium coals 8 minutes. Baste, turn, and cook until fish flakes easily. Heat remaining sauce and serve with steaks. Can be baked in 350° oven uncovered for 35 minutes in marinade. Do not turn steaks if you cook in oven.

Shrimp Scampi

1/4 c. vegetable oil
1 red pepper, diced
1-1/4 lb. raw shrimp,
    shelled and deveined
1 clove garlic, chopped
1/4 tsp. salt
1/4 c. fresh parsley
2 Tbsp. butter
2 Tbsp. lemon juice
1-1/2 c. rice

Heat oil in large skillet. Add pepper and cook for 3 to 4 minutes, stirring constantly. Add shrimp, garlic, and salt; cook for 5 minutes, turning shrimp once. Remove from heat, stir in parsley, butter, and lemon juice. Cook rice according to package directions, and serve shrimp mixture over rice.

Cajun Shrimp
Hot, Spicy, and G-r-r-reat!

1 c. margarine
1 onion, chopped
3 cloves garlic, minced
1 tsp. red pepper
1 tsp. black pepper
1/2 tsp. white pepper
1/2 tsp. crushed red
    pepper
1/2 tsp. thyme
1/2 tsp. rosemary, crushed
1/8 tsp. oregano
1 tsp. Worcestershire sauce
1 lb. frozen cocktail
    shrimp
1/2 c. water
1/4 c. beer (opt.)
2 c. hot cooked rice

Melt 1/2 cup margarine in a large skillet. Add onion and next 9 ingredients. Cook for 1 minute, stirring constantly. Add shrimp and cook for 2 minutes, stirring constantly. Add remaining 1/2 cup margarine and water. Cook 2 minutes, stirring occasionally. Stir in beer and cook 1 minute. Remove from heat. Serve over hot rice.

Seafood Cacciatore

3/4 lb. cleaned shell fish
1/2 c. chopped onion
1 garlic clove, minced
1 Tbsp. oil
1 (28 oz.) can whole
  tomatoes
1 (8 oz.) can tomato sauce
1/2 tsp. salt
1/2 tsp. oregano
1/2 tsp. basil
1/8 tsp. cayenne pepper
1 medium green pepper,
  cut into strips
1-1/2 c. instant rice

In a large skillet, lightly sauté fish, onion, and garlic in oil. Add tomatoes, tomato sauce, salt, seasonings, and green pepper. Bring to a full boil. Stir in rice. Cover, remove from heat, and let stand for 5 minutes.

Onion-Baked Catfish

1 (8 oz.) carton sour cream
1 c. Miracle Whip salad
  dressing
1 pkg. Ranch salad
  dressing mix
1 (6 oz.) can French fried
  onion rings
6 catfish fillets (about 2
  pounds)

Combine sour cream, Miracle Whip, and Ranch dressing mix in a small bowl. Measure 3/4 cup mixture into a shallow dish. Reserve remaining dressing mixture to serve with fish.

Crush onion rings and place in a flat dish. Dip fillets into dressing mixture, then roll in crushed onion rings. Arrange fillets in an ungreased 10″ × 15″ baking pan. Bake at 350° for 20 to 25 minutes or until fish is flaky.

Cowabunga Catfish

2 eggs, beaten
1/4 c. water
1 Tbsp. taco seasoning mix
6 (6 oz.) catfish fillets
3/4 c. flour
1 (10 oz.) pkg. tortilla
  chips, crushed
6 slices Monterey Jack
  cheese
1/2 c. sour cream
1/2 c. picante sauce

Combine eggs, water, and taco seasoning mix and set aside. Dredge fillets in flour and dip in egg mixture. Then dredge in crushed tortilla chips. Arrange fillets in a lightly greased 14″ × 11-1/2 ″ × 3″ baking dish. Bake at 375° for 30 minutes. Top with cheese slices and bake an additional 5 minutes. Serve with sour cream and picante sauce.

Pork Chops

6 pork chops
1/2 c. orange juice
1 tsp. salt
1/2 tsp. dry mustard
4 Tbsp. brown sugar

Preheat oven to 350°. Put pork chops in baking dish. Mix orange juice, salt, mustard, and brown sugar. Mix well and pour over pork chops. Cover with foil. Bake at 350° for 50 to 60 minutes

Pork Chops, Potato, and Onion Casserole

4 to 6 pork chops
3 - 5 large potatoes
2 onions
Salt and pepper to taste
1 can cream of mushroom
 soup
1/3 can of water
1 Tbsp. butter

Brown pork chops and set aside. Cut potatoes and onions in slices and layer in casserole dish. Salt and pepper to taste. Mix soup with water and pour over top of potatoes and onions. Dot with butter. Put pork chops on top. Cook at 350° for 1 hour.

Grilled Brown-Sugar Pork Chops
Laura Ives' treat for Terry and Dustin

1/4 c. brown sugar
1/4 c. apple juice
2 Tbsp. oil
1 Tbsp. soy sauce
1/2 tsp. ground ginger
Salt and pepper to taste
1/4 c. water
1 tsp. cornstarch
6 boneless loin pork chops,
 about 1/2" thick

Start fire in grill and place rack about 6 inches above coals. In 2-quart saucepan combine brown sugar, apple juice, oil, soy sauce, ginger, salt, and pepper. Bring to boil over medium heat, stirring until sugar dissolves. In small bowl stir 1/4 cup water into cornstarch to dissolve, then add to mixture in saucepan. Return to boil, stirring. When mixture is slightly thickened, remove from heat. Grill pork chops over hot coals 10 to 12 minutes, turning once. Brush with sauce; grill 5 minutes longer until pork is well glazed and cooked through, turning once more and brushing with sauce.

Easy Pork Chops

Christine's treat for Arlys. She has several.

6 to 8 pork chops (3/4 to
   1″ thick)
1 Tbsp. mustard
Salt and pepper to taste
1/4 to 1/2 tsp. celery salt
1/4 tsp. garlic salt
2 Tbsp. flour
2 large onions, cut unto
   rings
1 green pepper, cut into
   rings
1-1/2 c. water

Brush each chop with mustard. Sprinkle with seasonings and flour. Brown both sides in small amount of oil. Lay onions and green pepper on top of pork chops and add water. Cover and cook on medium heat until tender.

Bean's Ole

1 lb. Pinto beans
1 can chopped green
   chilies
1/2 to 1 c. diced, onion
2 Tbsp. chili powder
2 garlic cloves (crushed)
1 tsp. salt
1 tsp. cumin
1 tsp. oregano
1 small pork roast
1 c. diced tomato
1 c. shredded cheese
1 c. diced lettuce
1 small pkg. Fritos
1/2 c. diced onion (opt.)
Picante sauce (opt.)

Soak beans in 7 to 8 cups water overnight and drain. Mix first 8 ingredients and cover with water. After mixing, add pork roast, cover and simmer all day. Remove roast and bone, then return meat to mixture in small pieces. Cook an additional 30 minutes. Crush Fritos and line large bowl, put in meat and bean mixture, top with tomato, cheese, and lettuce. Add additional diced onion and picante sauce if desired. Can also serve in individual portions.

Bacon-stuffed Cabbage
Mayme Martin's 1950 Classic

1 medium head of cabbage
1/2 lb. bacon
2 Tbsp. bacon fat
1 small onion, chopped
1/2 green pepper, diced
1 can chopped tomatoes
  (2 c.)
1 c. cooked rice
1 tsp. salt
1/4 tsp. pepper
1 can onion soup,
  undiluted

Cook or steam cabbage gently for 5 minutes or until leaves are limp and easily separated. Cool to handle. Cook bacon until crisp; drain, and crumble. Sauté onion and green pepper in 2 tablespoons bacon fat until soft. Drain tomatoes, reserve juice. Combine bacon, onion, pepper, tomatoes, rice, salt and pepper in bowl and mix well. Break or cut out rib of each cabbage leaf so it will roll easily. Spoon about 1/4 cup of the filling onto each cabbage leaf. Fold over ends of leaf; roll up tightly to enclose filling. Fasten with wooden pick. Place filled leaves in large skillet. Combine onion soup and reserved tomato juice, pour over and around cabbage. Cover and bake at 300° for 20 to 30 minutes.

Ham and Potato Casserole
We have really enjoyed this recipe from Nancy Simoneau.

1/4 c. chopped onion
1/4 c. oleo
1/4 c. flour
1/2 tsp. salt
1/4 tsp. pepper
1/4 tsp. dry mustard
1-1/2 c. milk
1 (8 oz.) pkg. shredded
  Cheddar cheese (2 c.)
1/2 lb. ham, cut in slices
6 c. potato slices,
  precooked

Sauté onion in oleo. Blend in flour and seasonings. Gradually add milk while stirring constantly. Cook until thickened. Add 1-1/2 cups cheese. Stir until cheese is completely melted. Reserve 1 cup potato slices and add remaining potato slices to cheese sauce. Pour into a 2-quart casserole dish. Arrange ham and reserved potato slices on top of casserole. Bake at 350° for 30 minutes. Top with remaining cheese. (We also like this when substituting American cheese for the Cheddar cheese.)

Broiled Ham with Sweet and Sour Sauce

1-1/2 to 2" thick center
  slice cut of precooked
  ham
1/2 c. grape jelly
1/2 c. prepared mustard

Heat jelly and mustard in pan, stirring until well blended. Let cool. Baste ham on both sides using all the sauce. Cook until hot and sauce has thickened on ham.

Elegant Ham and Asparagus

This makes a very attractive luncheon dish.

1 can Crescent Dinner
   Rolls
4 slices cooked ham
1 (15 oz.) can Extra Long
   Asparagus Spears,
   drained

Heat oven to 375°. Lightly grease cookie sheet. Separate dough into triangles. Cut each slice of ham diagonally. Place one triangle of ham on each roll. Place asparagus spears on wide end of each triangle. Roll up, starting at shortest side of triangle and rolling to opposite point. Place crescents point side down on prepared cookie sheet. Bake at 375° for 16 to 20 minutes, or until golden brown.

CHEESE SAUCE:
2 Tbsp. margarine or
   butter
2 Tbsp. flour
1 c. milk
1/2 c. shredded natural
   Swiss cheese (2 oz.)
1/4 tsp. pepper

In small saucepan, melt margarine, stir in flour until smooth. Cook over medium heat for 1 minute, stirring constantly. Gradually stir in milk. Cook until thick and bubbly, stirring constantly. Add cheese and pepper, and stir until cheese melts. Pour over warm roll-ups.

Hot Ham and Cheese Sandwiches

Try it — you'll like it!

1 loaf frozen Bridgford
   white bread, thawed
1 pkg. ham lunch meat
1 pkg. Swiss cheese slices

Roll out bread dough into a rectangle. Put a layer of cheese and a layer of meat centered in rectangle, then repeat. Fold edges of bread over and seal. (Seal the edges at the side also.) Turn over and place on a greased cookie sheet. Brush the top with butter. Let rise until doubled in bulk. Bake at 375° until browned. Cut into 1″ slices. These slices can then be cut into smaller pieces to be served as hors d'oeuvres.

Creamy Ham Roll-Ups

Sirita smiles a big smile when Brandie cooks this.

1 c. instant rice
1 (9 oz.) pkg. frozen
   onions in cream sauce
3/4 c. water
1 Tbsp. butter
1 (1-1/4 oz.) envelope
   cheese sauce mix
1 c. milk
1 (3 oz.) can chopped
   mushrooms, drained
1/2 tsp. curry powder
8 thin ham slices

Cook rice according to package directions and set aside. In 1-1/2 quart casserole, combine onions, 3/4 cup water, and butter. Cook covered in microwave on high for 3 minutes. Stir in cheese sauce and milk. Cook covered on high power for 6 minutes or until thickened and bubbly. Stir twice.

Add 1/2 cup onion sauce to cooked rice, along with mushrooms and curry powder. Spoon 1/4 cup rice mixture evenly on each ham slice. Roll up, jelly-roll fashion, starting on long side. Arrange ham rolls, seam side down, in 9″ × 13″ baking dish. Spoon onion sauce over filled ham rolls. Cook in microwave, covered 8 to 9 minutes, giving dish a half turn during cooking.

Company Pork Roast

5 lb. pork roast
Salt and pepper to taste
12 orange slices
12 whole cloves
1 c. orange juice
1/2 c. honey
2 sticks cinnamon
1 t. grated orange peel

Trim fat from roast and score. Sprinkle with salt and pepper. Attach orange slices to roast with cloves. Place on rack, fat side up, in roasting pan. Bake at 325°for 3 to 4 hours. Combine orange juice, honey, and cinnamon in a saucepan. Bring to a boil and simmer uncovered 15 minutes. Add orange peel. Baste roast with mixture every 15 minutes during last hour of roasting.

Spareribs With Apples And Squash
Little Mother's meal for company

4 lb. spareribs
1 Tbsp. salt
1/4 tsp. pepper
2 Tbsp. butter
1/2 c. minced onion
3 c. apple juice
1/2 c. cider vinegar
3 Tbsp. brown sugar
3 tsp. cinnamon
1-1/2 tsp. cornstarch
2 acorn squash
4 apples

Preheat oven to 350°. In 12″ × 14″ shallow roasting pan; place ribs meaty side up. Sprinkle with salt and pepper. Bake 45 minutes until well browned. Cook onion in butter until tender. Stir in 2-3/4 cup apple juice, vinegar, brown sugar, and cinnamon and heat to boiling. Mix remaining apple juice (1/4 cup) with cornstarch, gradually add to hot liquid, stirring constantly, and cook until thickened. When ribs are brown, reduce heat to 300°. Remove all liquid from pan. Pour apple juice mixture evenly over ribs. Cover pan with foil and bake 1 hour. Cut each squash into 8 wedges and each apple in half, discarding seeds and cores. Add to ribs, spooning some of the liquid over them, and bake covered, 45 minutes, or until ribs, squash and apples are tender.

Pizza Rye
A Tennessee recipe given to us by Arbie Brumit

2 loaves party rye bread
1 lb. sausage
1 lb. Velveeta cheese, grated
1 tsp. soy sauce
1 tsp. Worcestershire sauce
1/2 tsp. garlic powder

Cook sausage, drain, and chop fine. Add cheese, soy sauce, Worcestershire sauce, and garlic powder. Spread on bread slices. Freeze on cookie sheets. Then store in plastic bags in freezer. Take out as needed and cook in 350° oven only until hot and cheese bubbles. (Do not Microwave.)

Ham Loaf by Wanda Henson

1 lb. cured ham, ground
1 lb. fresh pork, ground
2 eggs
2/3 c. cracker crumbs
1-1/4 c. milk

Have ham and pork ground together. Mix other ingredients well and add to meat mixture. Will make 1 large or 2 small loaves. Bake at 350° for 45 minutes.

  HAM LOAF GLAZE:
1 Tbsp. prepared mustard
1/2 c. brown sugar
1/2 c. water
1/4 c. vinegar

Mix mustard and sugar with small amount of water. Add remaining water and vinegar. Mix well and pour over ham loaf while cooking.

Easy Pineapple Baked Ham

1 (2-1/2-inch thick) center-
  cut fully cooked ham
  slice (4 to 5 pounds)
1 (8 oz.) can crushed
  pineapple, undrained
1/2 c. firmly packed dark
  brown sugar
1/2 tsp. ground cloves

Place ham in heavy-duty aluminum foil; seal tightly, and place in a $9'' \times 13'' \times 2''$ pan. Bake at 350° for 1 hour. Combine pineapple, brown sugar, and cloves; spread over ham. Bake, uncovered, 1 hour or until meat thermometer registers 140°. Let stand 15 minutes before slicing.

Pork and Noodles

1 lb. boneless pork, cubed
1 Tbsp. flour
1 Tbsp. oil
1 apple, sliced
1 small onion, sliced
1 clove garlic, minced
1/2 c. sliced celery
1 c. water
1/4 tsp. salt
Dash pepper
5 oz. uncooked egg
  noodles
1/2 c. sour cream (opt.)

Coat pork with flour and brown in oil. Place in a glass baking dish. Add apple, onion, garlic, celery, water, salt, and pepper. Cover and bake at 350° for 1 hour. Cook noodles according to package directions, drain, and set aside. Serve with sour cream over noodles.

Pork Tenderloin With Orange Sauce

4 to 5 lb. pork tenderloin
Salt
Pepper
1 small onion, sliced
1/4 c. celery, chopped
1/8 tsp. oregano
1/8 tsp. cloves
1 c. orange juice
2 Tbsp. Marsala cooking
   wine
1 tsp. cornstarch
Cooked rice

Sprinkle pork with salt and pepper and place in roasting pan, fat side up. Mix onion, celery, oregano, cloves, orange juice, and wine and pour over roast. Cook at 350° for 25 to 30 minutes per pound, basting frequently with the pan juices. When meat is done, drain juice from pan and use cornstarch to thickened. Serve over rice.

Holiday Ham

Bobby, Ben, and Clay look forward to this special-occasion meal.

1 ham, with bone
1 (15-1/4 oz.) can
   pineapple slices, reserve
   liquid
1 c. brown sugar
1/4 c. honey

Choose ham according to size needed for occasion. Score ham by making 1/4" cuts about 1" apart over surface of ham. Make cuts diagonally, then make cuts perpendicular to those. This will give a diamond-shape surface. Put ham in large roasting pan. Attach pineapple slices to surface of ham with toothpicks. Blend brown sugar, pineapple juice, and honey to make a basting sauce. Bake ham, covered, at 325° for 15 minutes per pound, basting ham with basting sauce every 30 minutes. If you run out of sauce before you finish baking, use the juices in the pan and continue basting.

After removing ham from pan, pour juices into a bowl. Refrigerate juices several hours. Remove hardened grease. Heat remaining juices and serve as a meat sauce.

Country Style Stuffed Peppers

4 green, red, or yellow
   peppers
8 oz. pork sausage
1/4 c. chopped onion
1-1/2 c. cooked rice
2 c. shredded mild
   Cheddar cheese (8 oz.)
1 tomato, chopped

Preheat oven to 375°. Remove tops and seeds from peppers. Crumble sausage into skillet and cook with onion. Drain. Stir in rice, 1-1/2 cups cheese, and tomato. Fill peppers with sausage mixture and top with remaining cheese. Arrange in 9″ square baking pan. Add 1/4 cup water. Bake for 30 minutes or until peppers are tender. Makes 4 servings.

Chicken And Rice

Carol Miller's version of a good Sunday dinner

1 can onion soup
1 can water
2 chicken bouillon cubes
1 c. rice
1 chicken, cut up
3/4 stick oleo, melted
Paprika

Simmer soup, water, and bouillon cubes until cubes are dissolved. Pour rice in baking dish and cover with soup. Dip seasoned chicken in melted oleo and place on top of rice. Sprinkle with paprika. Cover and bake at 250° for 2-1/2 to 3 hours.

Chicken And Spaghetti

1 large hen
2 (10 oz.) pkg. spaghetti,
   cooked
2 c. chicken broth
1 large onion, chopped
1 green pepper, chopped
1 c. chopped celery
1 tsp. oleo or butter
1 c. chopped pimientos
1 c. sliced stuffed olives
2 cans cream of mushroom
   soup

Cook hen until tender. Remove meat from bones and chop coarsely. Boil spaghetti in chicken broth, drain, and reserve broth. Cook onion, pepper, and celery in butter until tender. Combine all ingredients, add salt and pepper to taste. Simmer about 10 minutes. Serves 12 to 15. This is such a large recipe you may want to cut it in half.

Chicken and Rice

Christine often makes this for Arlys.

1 1/4 c. uncooked rice
1 can cream of mushroom
  soup
1 can cream of chicken
  soup
1 can cream of celery soup
1 small can green chilies
4 green onions (tops too),
  chopped
1 chicken, skinned and cut
  in regular pieces
Salt and pepper

Place rice in 9″ × 13″ dish, sprayed with Pam. Add next 5 ingredients to rice and mix well. Salt and pepper chicken and place on top of rice mixture. Cover with foil. Bake at 300° for 2 hours. You can use same recipe with pork chops. (Put casserole in oven just before you leave for Sunday School. When you get home from church, lunch will be ready.)

Italian Chicken and Rice

1-1/2 c. water
1 c. uncooked rice
1 (14-1/2 oz.) can chopped
  tomatoes, undrained
1 (8 oz.) jar Cheez Whiz
1/4 c. finely chopped
  onion
1-1/2 tsp. Italian
  seasoning, divided
1 (2-1/2 to 3 lb.) chicken,
  cut up and skinned
2/3 c. grated Parmesan
  cheese

Preheat oven to 375°. Stir together water, rice, tomatoes, Cheez Whiz, onions, and 1 teaspoon Italian seasoning. Pour into a greased 9″ × 13″ baking dish. Top with chicken. Sprinkle with Parmesan cheese and remaining Italian seasoning. Bake for 45 to 50 minutes, or until chicken is tender. Let stand for 5 minutes. Makes 4 to 6 servings.

Chicken Enchiladas

Nancy McCord and Amy enjoy making this together.

1 (3 - 4 lb.) chicken
1/2 c. margarine
1-1/2 c. chopped onion
2 (10 oz.) cans Rotel
1 (28 oz.) can tomatoes
1 (2 lb.) box Velveeta
   cheese
30 corn tortillas
Cooking oil
2 c. sour cream

Boil or microwave chicken, until tender. Cool, bone, and cut into bite size pieces. Set aside. Sauté onions in margarine until tender. Add tomatoes and Rotel. Simmer until it cooks down. Cut up cheese and add. Stir until melted. Add chicken. Fry tortillas in oil until soft. Add 1 heaping tablespoon of mixture to each tortilla and roll up. Place in 9″ × 13″ baking dish. Pour remaining mixture on top. Top with sour cream. Bake at 350° for 30 minutes.

Baked Chicken with Honey

1 chicken, skinned and cut
   for frying
Salt and pepper to taste
1/2 c. honey
1/4 c. water

Salt and pepper each side of chicken. Mix honey with 1/4 cup water. Brush each side of chicken with this mixture. Place pieces of chicken in greased baking dish and cover with foil. Bake at 375° for 30 to 40 minutes. Remove foil and return chicken to oven until it is slightly browned.

Mom's Chicken Enchiladas

A favorite from Paige Pridmore Harston of Tahoka, Texas

2 cans cream of chicken
   soup
2 cans boned chicken
1 c. milk
1 onion, chopped
1 small can jalapeno
   peppers or chopped
   green chilies
1 large pkg. Doritos
1-1/2 c. grated Cheddar
   cheese (Longhorn)

Heat all ingredients except cheese and Doritos. When warm, place in casserole dish over crushed Doritos. Cover with cheese. Place in 325° oven until it bubbles. Serve hot.

Mexican Chicken
A Brownfield delight from Bertha Morgan

1 stick oleo
1 small onion, chopped
2 cans boned chicken
2/3 small can green chilies
1/2 lb. Velveeta, chunked
1 small can taco sauce
2/3 small can Pet milk
1 pkg. Doritos

Melt oleo and add onion, chicken, and green chilies. In a separate pan, combine Velveeta, taco sauce, and milk. Heat until Velveeta is melted and ingredients are blended.

In a long Pyrex dish, layer Doritos, chicken mixture, and cheese mixture. Then repeat layers. Bake at 350° for 20 minutes or until bubbly.

Polynesian Chicken
Clarene has come up with a complete harmonic blend of flavors with this one.

1 lb. skinless, boneless
  chicken breasts
2 Tbsp. butter or
  margarine
1 green pepper, cut into 1"
  pieces
1/8 tsp. pepper
1/4 tsp. salt
1 (15 oz.) can pineapple
  chunks, undrained
1/2 c. plus 2-1/2 Tbsp.
  water, divided
1/3 c. apple cider vinegar
  or distilled white
  vinegar
1 tsp. ginger
2 Tbsp. brown sugar
2 Tbsp. soy sauce
2-1/2 Tbsp. cornstarch
4 servings hot buttered rice
Toasted slivered almonds
  (opt.)

Cut chicken into 2" strips. In large skillet, melt butter, then sauté chicken and green pepper just until chicken changes color. Season with salt and pepper. Stir in pineapple, 1/2 cup of the water and the next 4 ingredients. Cover, simmer 10 to 12 minutes, or until chicken is cooked. Combine cornstarch and the remaining 2-1/2 tablespoons of water, then stir into chicken mixture. Cook until sauce is thickened, stirring constantly. Serve over rice and garnish with almonds. Serves 4.

Sweet and Sour Chicken

Lottie Jo is like Ford, she has a better idea!

2 chickens, cut-up (or
  chicken breasts)
1 bottle creamy Russian
  Dressing
1 pkg. dry onion soup mix
1 (10 oz.) jar apricot
  preserves

Place chicken pieces in a baking dish. In a separate dish mix dressing, soup mix, and preserves. Pour over chicken. Bake covered at 325° for about one hour. Remove cover and bake 20 to 30 minutes longer.

Christine's Chicken And Broccoli

4 chicken breasts
1 box frozen broccoli
  spears
1/3 c. mayonnaise
1 can cream of chicken
  soup
1 can cream of mushroom
  soup
1 tsp. lemon juice
Salt and pepper to taste
6 oz. sliced Swiss cheese
Parmesan cheese

Boil chicken until tender, strip from bone, and cut into small pieces. Cook frozen broccoli according to package directions. Blend mayonnaise, soups, lemon juice, salt, and pepper for sauce. Grease 10″ × 10″ dish. Layer broccoli, cheese, and chicken. Pour sauce over all ingredients. Sprinkle Parmesan cheese on top of dish. Bake at 350° for 30 minutes.

Chicken With Ranch Dressing And Bacon

Wallace Combest from Waco loves to make this.

6 deboned chicken thighs
6 slices of bacon
1 pkg. dry Ranch dressing
  mix

Lay out bacon strips. Place chicken on bacon. Sprinkle dressing on chicken (about 1 teaspoon for each piece of chicken). Wrap bacon around the chicken. Place chicken in pan with rack and bake for about 1 hour at 250°. You can also substitute shrimp for the chicken.

Jambalaya
A fantastic entrée from Nadine Rogers

4 chicken breasts (boned
   and cut into chunks)
1/2 c. bacon drippings
1 Smoked Sausage link cut
   into bite-size pieces
1 green pepper, chopped
3 bunches green onions,
   chopped
1 med onion, chopped
3 ribs of celery, chopped
1 clove garlic, minced
3 c. chicken stock or 2
   cans chicken broth
1 large can tomatoes (put
   through blender)
Salt
Pepper
Red pepper
Tabasco
1 lb. raw shelled shrimp
2 c. raw rice, cooked
   separately

Brown chicken, in hot bacon grease. Remove chicken and heat sausage. Remove sausage and sauté vegetables in remaining grease. Add chicken stock and tomatoes. Simmer 5 minutes. Add seasonings, chicken, and sausage. Cook 10 minutes. Last 3 minutes add shrimp and cooked rice and adjust seasoning. Serves 10 to 12.

Baked Parmesan Chicken by Clarene Chambers

1 egg, beaten
1 Tbsp. milk
1/2 c. grated Parmesan
   cheese
1/4 c. flour
1 tsp. paprika
1/2 tsp. salt
1/8 tsp. pepper
1 (2-1/2 to 3 lb.) fryer, cut
   up and skinned (or use
   chicken breasts)
1/4 c. margarine, melted

Combine egg and milk, stir well, and set aside. Combine cheese, flour, paprika, salt and pepper; mix well. Rinse chicken and pat dry. Dip in egg mixture, then dredge in flour mixture. Place chicken in a baking dish, pour margarine over chicken. Bake at 350° for 1 hour or until tender.

Old-Fashion Chicken Pie
One of Bertha Morgan's favorites

**Biscuit dough prepared
   ahead of time**
**1 chicken, cooked and
   boned (reserve fat and
   broth)**
2 - 3 small potatoes
6 slender carrots
**1 c. onion, cut into tiny
   chunks**
4 Tbsp. flour
1/4 tsp. chives (opt.)
1/8 tsp. ginger (opt.)
1/8 tsp. thyme (opt.)

Cook vegetables until nearly tender. Roll a top crust to fit casserole allowing an extra inch all around. Make slits in the crust for steam vents. In a casserole dish, place fairly large pieces of chicken and vegetables.

Good chicken gravy demands care and accuracy. Melt 4 tablespoons chicken fat and add 4 tablespoons flour and stir over low heat until lightly brown. Add 2 cups chicken broth, stirring constantly until thick. Reduce heat. Season to taste, adding any of the optional ingredients. Pour hot gravy over vegetables and chicken.

Adjust pastry centered over pie. Fold dough under to make a double layer, at the same time fitting just inside the rim. Press fork around rim. Having vegetables hot keeps pastry flaky. Glaze pastry with slightly beaten egg white. Bake pie promptly at 425° about 30 minutes.

Lum's Turkey
Lum Holder fixed this and Ben and Clay "tasted" three platefuls!

Turkey
Poultry seasoning

Wash turkey thoroughly. Season with poultry seasoning inside and out. Cook on grill with fire on each side of turkey. No fire directly under the turkey. Cook until thermometer in turkey pops out.

Chicken Continental

3/4 lb. slivered raw
  chicken
1 (4 oz.) can sliced
  mushrooms, drained
1 garlic clove, crushed
2 Tbsp. oil
1 (13-3/4 oz.) can chicken
  broth
1 (9 oz.) pkg. frozen cut
  green beans
1 tsp. salt
1/2 tsp. tarragon
Pepper to taste
1-1/2 c. instant rice

Sauté chicken, mushrooms, and garlic in oil in large skillet until chicken is lightly browned. Add broth, beans, salt, tarragon, and pepper. Bring to a full boil. Stir in rice. Remove from heat; cover and let stand for 5 minutes. Makes 4 servings.

Sweet and Sour Chicken with Pineapple

This is a favorite of Laura Ives.

4 tsp. cornstarch
1/4 c. sugar
1/4 c. wine vinegar
2 Tbsp. catsup
1 Tbsp. soy sauce
1 Tbsp. dry sherry
1/2 tsp. ground ginger
1/4 tsp. salt
1/4 c. chicken broth
3 Tbsp. salad oil
1-3/4 lb. chicken breasts
  cut in 1/2" × 2" strips
1 clove garlic, minced or
  pressed
1 med. onion, thinly sliced
1 med. green pepper,
  seeded and cut in thin
  strips
1 can pineapple chunks,
  drained
Sweet and sour sauce
  (directions given)
About 4 c. cooked rice

Stir together cornstarch, sugar, wine vinegar, catsup, soy sauce, sherry, ginger, salt and broth. Blend completely and set aside. Place wok over high heat. When wok is hot, add 2 tablespoons oil. When oil is hot, add chicken and garlic, stir fry until chicken is opaque (about 4 minutes), then remove from wok and set aside. Add remaining 1 tablespoon oil to wok. When oil is hot, add onion and green pepper. Stir fry for about 1 minute or until tender-crisp. Return chicken to wok, add sweet and sour sauce and pineapple. Stir until liquid boils and thickens. Serve over cooked rice.

Chicken Chili Pie

Virginia Goggans makes this for Joe.

1 chicken, cooked and
 boned, and cut into
 small pieces
1 c. broth
1 small onion, chopped
1 bell pepper, chopped
1 can cream of mushroom
 soup
1/4 tsp. garlic salt
2 tsp. chili powder
8 oz. Cheddar cheese,
 grated
1 can Rotel tomatoes with
 hot diced chilies
8 to 10 corn tortillas

Spray dish with Pam. Mix ingredients together except tortillas. Break tortillas in small pieces and line a 9″ × 13″ dish with tortillas. Pour mixture over tortillas. Bake at 350° until brown and onions are tender.

Chicken Divan

3/4 lb. boned skinned
 chicken, slivered
2 tsp. oil
1 c. water
1 Tbsp. dry sherry wine
1 (10 oz.) pkg. frozen
 broccoli spears
1 can cream of chicken
 soup
1-1/2 c. instant rice
1 Tbsp. grated Parmesan
 cheese

In skillet, brown chicken lightly in oil, stirring occasionally. Add water, wine, broccoli, and soup. Bring to a full boil. Stir in rice. Cover, remove from heat, and let stand 5 minutes. Arrange chicken, broccoli and rice mixture on serving platter. Sprinkle with cheese and serve.

Zesty Chicken

1 can cream of mushroom
  soup
1 (8 oz.) jar Cheez Whiz
1/2 c. milk
2 c. diced cooked chicken
3 Tbsp. chopped jalapeno
  peppers
2 Tbsp. instant minced
  onion
4 c. corn chips, crushed

Heat together soup and Cheez Whiz until blended. Gradually stir in milk. Add chicken, peppers, and onion. Cook until bubbly. Layer half of the corn chips in a casserole dish and pour cheese mixture over. Add remaining corn chips on top. Bake at 350° until bubbly.

Turkey And Dressing
Virginia And Christine's recipe for Christmas dinner

1 (18 to 20 lb.) turkey or 2
  large hens
8 c. cornbread crumbs
6 c. biscuits, torn in pieces
8 eggs slightly beaten
3 cans cream of mushroom
  soup
2 c. onions, chopped
2 c. celery, chopped
Salt and pepper to taste
1 tsp. poultry seasoning
13 to 15 c. chicken broth

Cook meat until tender, set aside to cool. Crumble cornbread and biscuits in very small pieces. Add eggs and mix. Add soup, onion, celery, salt, pepper, and poultry seasoning. Mix well. Add 3 or 4 cups hot broth and mix well. Repeat until you use enough broth that your dressing looks soupy. Mix well. Cook dressing in roasting pan or a large 16-1/2″ × 12″ × 4″ foil pan. If you use a foil pan, put it on a cookie sheet. Bake 2 hours at 350°, covered with foil. Remove foil, lower temperature to 250°, and cook 1 more hour. Serves 35 to 40. (Hint: You can do a lot of the preparation the day before you need the dressing.)

GRAVY:
8 c. broth
3/4 c. flour
1 c. water
Salt and pepper to taste
2 boiled eggs, diced
Turkey giblets

If you need more broth, use hot water. Boil broth. Mix flour and 1 cup water in a jar, shaking until flour is dissolved. Add to hot broth. Cook about 10 minutes. If you want thicker gravy, mix a little more flour and water and add to gravy. Salt and pepper to taste. Add eggs and turkey giblets.

Turkey or Chicken and Dressing
One of Oleta Smith's wonderful recipes

1 turkey or chicken, size
   by number of servings
   needed
6 c. cold biscuit crumbs
4 c. cold cornbread crumbs
1 large chopped onion
   (cooked in 1 c. water
   until tender)
1 tsp. salt
3 c. broth
2 tsp. sage
1/2 tsp. black pepper
2 c. water or more
6 raw eggs

Cook turkey or chicken until done by your favorite method. (Braising or stewing will give more broth.) Mix all ingredients together except eggs. Blend until smooth then add raw eggs. Blend thoroughly. Place in greased flat pan and cook at 350° until firm about 1 hour.

GIBLET GRAVY:
Turkey or chicken giblets
1 c. water
2 c. broth
1/2 c. flour
1/2 c. sweet milk
1 tsp. salt
3 boiled eggs

Cook giblets in 1 cup water until tender. Chop giblets. Take 2 cups broth, add 1/2 cup flour. Mix well. Add 1/2 cup sweet milk and 1 teaspoon salt. Stir while cooking over medium heat until mixture coats the spoon. Add chopped giblets and 3 chopped hard cooked eggs. Stir and serve hot with chicken and dressing.

Chicken in Lemon Sauce

1 chicken, cut into serving
   pieces
2-1/2 c. water
2 bay leaves
1 tsp. Accent
2 tsp. salt
2 small onions, peeled
1 (9 oz.) pkg. frozen
   artichoke hearts
2 Tbsp. flour
2 egg yolks
2 Tbsp. lemon juice

Put chicken in a large saucepan. Add 2 cups of water, bay leaves, Accent, and salt. Bring to boil. Cover and simmer for 35 minutes. Add onions and continue boiling for 15 minutes. Then add artichoke hearts and continue boiling for another 10 minutes. In a small bowl, blend together remaining water, flour, egg yolks, and lemon juice until smooth. Gradually add to chicken mixture, stirring constantly, until thickened.

French Chicken

An international classic from Kathy Martin

1 small jar dried beef
6 boned chicken breasts
6 slices bacon
1 can cream of mushroom
  soup
1 (8 oz.) container of sour
  cream

Line a 9″ × 13″ baking dish with dried beef. Wrap each chicken breast with a slice of bacon and place on dried beef. Bake for 30 minutes at 350°. Drain grease. Mix mushroom soup and sour cream together and pour over chicken. Bake for additional 30 minutes.

Chicken Stuffed Potatoes

A pretty and very tasty recipe from Veta Ford

3 large potatoes
1/2 c. sour cream
1/2 c. milk
4 oz. cream cheese with
  chives
1 c. cooked, boned,
  chopped chicken
1 c. onion, chopped
1 Tbsp. oleo
Salt and pepper to taste
1-1/2 c. grated Cheddar
  cheese
Parsley flakes (optional)

Bake potatoes. Split in half and scoop out insides. Put into a large bowl. Save skins. Add sour cream, milk, and cream cheese. Mix well. Then add chicken. Sauté onion in oleo, then add to potato mixture. Add salt and pepper and mix well. Stuff potato shells and sprinkle with Cheddar cheese. Bake at 375° for 15 minutes. Garnish with parsley.

Chicken Enchiladas

Terri Bessire makes this for Harold, Leah, and Andy.

1 chicken (OR 4-6 chicken
  breasts)
1 can cream of mushroom
  soup
1 can cream of chicken
  soup
1 can Rotel tomatoes,
  diced
1/2 c. chicken broth
Corn tortillas
1 c. Cheddar cheese, grated

Boil chicken and save broth. Bone and cube chicken. Mix soups, tomatoes, and broth and heat thoroughly. Layer 1/2 of torn corn tortillas in bottom of 9″ × 13″ baking dish. Sprinkle 1/2 of cheese on tortillas. Add 1/2 of cubed chicken. Then add 1/2 of sauce mixture. Repeat layers. Cook 30 minutes uncovered at 350°. Use as much chicken and cheese as you like.

Hot Chicken Salad Sandwiches

Clois Crawford of Lubbock says these make a "fun" bridge or luncheon dish.

2 c. cooked chicken (or
   turkey)
2 c. finely chopped celery
1/2 c. chopped toasted
   almonds
1/2 tsp. salt
2 tsp. grated onion
2 Tbsp. lemon juice
1 c. mayonnaise
Pepperidge sandwich bread
Butter to taste
1 can cream of chicken
   soup
1 carton sour cream

Combine chicken, celery, almonds, salt, onion, lemon juice, and mayonnaise. Make sandwiches and butter the outside of each sandwich. Place in casserole. Mix soup and sour cream and cover sandwiches with mixture. Bake at 325° for 1 hour.

Bar-B-Q Sauce by Arlys

The hit of the initiation of Yellow Dogs

1 gallon Kraft Hickory
   Smoke sauce
1 c. brown sugar
1/2 can beer
2 oz. Worcestershire sauce

1 c. Kraft sauce
1 tsp. brown sugar
2 Tbsp. beer
Dash of Worcestershire

Melt brown sugar in beer and add to Kraft sauce. Warm to completely mix and dissolve sugar. Add Worcestershire sauce. Let set overnight. Use the following amounts for 1 cup of sauce.

Barbeque Sauce a la Debbie

1 (2 lb.) bottle catsup
2 Tbsp. brown sugar
1/4 c. Worcestershire
   sauce
1/4 c. honey
2 Tbsp. A-1 steak sauce
2 Tbsp. liquid smoke
2 tsp. chili powder
2 tsp. salt
2 tsp. lemon juice
1 tsp. garlic salt
1 tsp. dry mustard
1/2 tsp. Tabasco
1 large onion, finely
   chopped

Mix all ingredients. Store in refrigerator. This is especially good over pork ribs.

Marinade For Chicken Or Pork

1/3 c. orange juice
1/3 c. soy sauce
2 Tbsp. parsley
2 Tbsp. cooking oil
1 clove garlic, crushed

Mix all ingredients and pour over meat. Let set 4 to 6 hours in refrigerator, turning meat occasionally.

Roast Gravy

Christine has made this for years for her family.

5 Tbsp. bacon drippings
1/3 c. flour
5 c. liquid from roast
1 Tbsp. Kitchen Bouquet
Salt and pepper to taste

Add flour to hot bacon drippings, mix well and add liquid from roast. If you need more liquid, add water to make 5 cups or more. Add Kitchen Bouquet and salt and pepper. Mix well and cook about 3 to 5 minutes.

Gravy

1/4 c. shortening (This
    can be Crisco or fat
    from frying meat.)
1/3 c. flour
3 c. milk
Salt and pepper to taste

Heat shortening and add flour. Stir well, using a fork. Add milk and stir constantly. Cook 3 to 5 minutes.

Taco Soup

This recipe from Mary Taylor is sure to become a Texas tradition.

1 lb. hamburger meat
1 med. onion
1 pkg. taco seasoning mix
1 pkg. Ranch dressing mix
1 (15 oz.) can pinto beans,
    with juice
1 can kidney or black
    beans, with juice
1 can hominy, drained
3 (14-1/2 oz.) cans diced
    tomatoes
1 (6 oz.) can chopped
    green chilies
Salt and pepper to taste
1-1/2 c. water
1 c. grated Cheddar cheese
    (opt.)

Brown meat and onion and drain. Add the taco seasoning mix and the Ranch dressing mix to the meat and onion and dissolve completely. In a separate large saucepan, mix the remaining ingredients, except cheese. Then add the meat mixture. Sprinkle each bowl of soup with cheese to serve. This is also good with cheese chunks.

Broccoli-Cheese Soup

5 c. fresh broccoli stalks,
    about 1 large bunch
3 c. chicken stock (canned
    or homemade)
1 small onion, minced
3 - 4 Tbsp. butter
1 tsp. ground coriander
1/2 tsp. salt
1/8 tsp. white pepper
1 c. shredded sharp
    Cheddar cheese

In large saucepan, place broccoli stalks in chicken stock and bring to a boil. Reduce heat and simmer about 20 minutes or until very tender. Meanwhile, in small pan, sauté onion in butter until soft, about 4 minutes. When broccoli has cooked, transfer to food processor fitted with a steel blade and process with stock and sautéed onions until coarsely pureed. Return to large saucepan and add coriander, salt, and pepper. Heat through and stir in cheese to melt. Ladle into bowls. Serves 4.

7 Bean Soup

A pint jar filled with this mix makes a nice gift.

MIX:
1 lb. red (kidney) beans
1 lb. pintos
1 lb. navy beans
1 lb. great northern beans
1 lb. lentils
1 lb. split peas
1 lb. black-eyed peas

Blend thoroughly. This will make 8 to 9 two-cup portions.

SOUP:
2 c. bean mix
2 qt. water
1 lb. ham, diced
1 large onion, diced
1 clove garlic, minced
1/2 to 3/4 tsp. salt
1 (16 oz.) can chopped
   tomatoes, undrained
1 (10 oz.) can tomatoes
   and green chilies,
   undrained

Sort and wash 2 cups bean mix. Place in water and soak overnight. Drain beans. Add 2 quarts water and next 4 ingredients. Cover and bring to a boil, reduce heat and simmer 1-1/2 hours or until beans are tender. Add remaining ingredients. Simmer 30 minutes stirring occasionally.

Spinach Florentine Soup

From Luanne Klaras of Nick's Restaurant in Waco

3 Tbsp. butter
2 tsp. chopped onion
1 pkg. frozen chopped
   spinach
1 tsp. lemon juice
1 c. chicken broth
1 c. milk
1 c. cream
Pepper
Salt to taste
1/4 tsp. nutmeg
Parmesan cheese (opt.)

Sauté onion in butter. Cook spinach in lightly salted water, drain thoroughly. Process spinach, butter, onion, lemon juice, and chicken broth. Add milk, cream, pepper, salt, and nutmeg. Sprinkle with Parmesan cheese, if desired. Serve hot.

Clam Chowder

2 cans clam pieces, drain
   and reserve juice
1 c. diced onion
1 c. diced celery
4 c. diced potatoes

  WHITE SAUCE:
3/4 c. margarine
Scant 1/2 c. flour
1 qt. half and half
1/2 tsp. sugar
1/2 tsp. salt
Pepper

Prepare vegetables and put in pan. Add clam pieces and just enough water to cover vegetables. Simmer until tender. Add white sauce and clam juice. Simmer slowly.

Melt margarine; add flour to make a paste. Cool. Add half and half, sugar, salt, and pepper. Cook over low heat until thick and smooth.

Bill's Tortilla Soup
Given to us by Jim and Sue Hooks of Woodway, Texas

1 small onion, chopped
2 garlic cloves, mashed
1 (4 oz.) can diced green
   chilies
2 Tbsp. oil
1 (8 oz.) can stewed
   tomatoes
2 c. chicken broth
1 c. beef bouillon
1 tsp. ground cumin
1 tsp. chili powder
1 tsp. salt
1/4 tsp. pepper
4 corn tortillas
Oil for frying tortillas
1 c. Monterrey Jack or
   Cheddar cheese, grated

Using a medium saucepan, sauté onion, garlic, and green chilies in oil until soft. Add tomatoes, chicken broth, and beef bouillon. Mix in spices and simmer for 1 hour. Cut tortillas into quarters, then into 1/2″ strips. Fry strips in hot oil until crisp. Drain. Add fried tortilla strips to soup and simmer 10 minutes. Ladle into bowls and top with cheese. Additional spices may be added to suit taste.

Cowboy Stew

Roy Rogers and the Lone Ranger would have jumped off their horses for a bowl of this stew from Faye Nordyke Kennedy.

1-1/2 lb. ground beef
1/2 c. chopped onion
1 bell pepper, chopped
Salt and pepper to taste
1 Tbsp. hot sauce (picante)
1/2 tsp. chili powder
1 can Ranch Style beans
1 can whole kernel corn,
    drained
1/2 to 3/4 lb. Cheddar
    cheese, grated
Cornbread, cooked

Brown meat, onion, and pepper; stir well. Add seasonings. Then add beans and corn. Simmer on low heat for 1-1/2 to 2 hours. Serve over hot cornbread and sprinkle with grated cheese.

Potato Soup

4 medium potatoes, cubed
1 medium onion, chopped
    fine
4 slices bacon, fried and
    crumbled
1/4 stick oleo
1-1/2 c. water
1/2 tsp. salt
1/8 tsp. celery salt
1 tsp. Lea & Perrins sauce
2 c. milk
3/4 c. Cheez Whiz

Cook potatoes, onion, bacon, oleo, and water until done. Add remaining ingredients and cook until cheese melts. Serve with cornbread.

Corn Chowder

A delicious after-golf dish from Frances Austin of Lubbock

2 c. water
2 c. diced potatoes
1/2 c. chopped onion
1/2 c. diced celery
2 Tbsp. margarine (opt.)
1/2 tsp. dried whole basil
1 large bay leaf
1 can cream-style corn
2 c. milk
1 c. canned tomatoes
2 tsp. salt
1/8 tsp. pepper
1/2 c. shredded cheese
   (opt.)
1 Tbsp. minced fresh
   parsley (opt.)

Combine water, potatoes, onion, celery, margarine, basil, and bay leaf in large kettle or saucepan. Bring to a boil, reduce heat, and simmer for 10 minutes or until potatoes are tender. Discard bay leaf. Stir in corn, milk, tomatoes, salt, and pepper. Heat thoroughly. Add cheese and stir until cheese is melted. Garnish with parsley. Serves 8 to 10.

Casseroles

Beef Jalapeno Cornbread by Mary Brandon

1 c. + 2 Tbsp. yellow
   cornmeal
2 eggs
3/4 tsp. salt
1 tsp. soda
1/2 c. bacon drippings
1 c. milk
1 can cream style corn
1-1/2 lb. ground beef,
   browned and drained
1 large onion, chopped
2 to 4 jalapeno peppers
3/4 lb. Cheddar cheese,
   grated

Mix cornmeal, eggs, salt, soda, bacon drippings, milk, and corn. Grease a long baking dish and pour in half of the cornbread mixture. Layer meat, onion, pepper, and cheese. Then cover with the remaining cornbread mixture. Bake at 350° for 50 minutes.

Beefy Baked Beans

1 pound ground beef
1 medium onion, chopped
1 (32 oz.) can pork and
   beans
1 (8 oz.) can tomato sauce
1/2 c. catsup
3 Tbsp. brown sugar
1 Tbsp. Worcestershire
   sauce
1/2 tsp. salt
1/4 tsp. pepper

Cook ground beef and onion in a large skillet until meat is browned, stirring to crumble meat, drain. Stir in remaining ingredients. Pour mixture into a lightly greased 2-quart casserole. Bake, uncovered, at 350°for 1 hour.

Chinese Tuna Casserole X

1/2 c. chopped onion
1 can tuna
1 can cream of mushroom
   soup
2/3 c. milk
1/2 c. chopped celery
1 (5 oz.) can Chow Mein
   noodles
1 small can cashew nuts

Sauté onions and add other ingredients, reserving half of the noodles and nuts. Pour into casserole dish, cover top with reserved noodles and nuts. Bake at 350°until bubbly.

Border Patrol Special

Christine's family has enjoyed this casserole for years.

2 lb. ground hamburger
  meat
1 chopped onion
1 can cream of mushroom
  soup or cream of
  asparagus soup
1 can cream of chicken
  soup
1 can Cheddar cheese soup
1 can chopped pimientos
1 (8 oz.) can green chilies
1 large pkg. flour tortillas
1/2 lb. grated Velveeta
  cheese
1/4 lb. grated Mozzarella
  cheese

Brown meat and onion. Mix soups together and add pimientos and green chilies. Form layers of the meat mixture, tortillas (torn into pieces), soup mixture, and cheese. Begin layering again, starting with meat. Bake in a 9" × 13" baking dish at 350° until bubbly and brown.

Cheeseburger Pie

1 lb. hamburger meat
1-1/2 c. chopped onion
1/2 tsp. salt
1/4 tsp. pepper
1/2 tsp. picante sauce
  (opt.)
1-1/2 c. milk
3 eggs, beaten
3/4 c. Bisquick
2 tomatoes, sliced
1 c. shredded Cheddar
  cheese

Preheat oven to 400°. Grease pie plate. Cook and stir meat and onion in skillet over medium heat until meat is done. Stir in salt, pepper, and picante sauce; spread in pie plate. Beat milk, eggs, and Bisquick until smooth, 15 seconds in blender on high or 1 minute with hand mixer. Pour over meat. Bake 25 minutes. Top with tomatoes and sprinkle with cheese. Bake 8 to 10 minutes longer. Serves 6 to 8.

Lum's Casserole

Lum Holder's mother served this in the 1930s.

1 lb. sausage, browned and
  crumbled
1 onion, chopped
1 bell pepper, chopped
2 c. macaroni, cooked
Red pepper to taste
2 cans tomatoes

Cook onion and pepper in sausage grease until wilted. In large casserole dish, layer macaroni, sausage, and vegetables, then repeat layers. Sprinkle generously with red pepper. Pour tomatoes over all. Bake at 350°until completely heated.

Cheese-Sausage Cornbread

2 Tbsp. butter
1/3 c. chopped onion
1/4 c. chopped green
  pepper
1 (8 oz.) pkg. brown and
  serve sausage links,
  thawed
1 (8-1/2 oz.) pkg. corn
  muffin mix
1 (8-3/4 oz.) can whole
  kernel corn, drained
1 egg
1/4 c. milk
1 c. shredded Monterey
  Jack cheese (4 oz.)

Preheat oven to 400°. Sauté onion and pepper in butter until tender, about 5 minutes. Brown sausage according to package directions; drain. Combine muffin mix, sautéed vegetables, corn, egg, and milk. Stir only until all ingredients are combined. Pour mixture into well-buttered 9″ round cake pan or skillet. Arrange sausage in spoke fashion on top of dough. Bake until golden and wooden pick inserted near center comes out clean, or about 30 minutes. Remove from oven and sprinkle cheese over top. Let stand 10 minutes. Cut into wedges and serve.

Tuna-Noodle Casserole

We love this casserole from Sammye Middleton of O'Donnell.

1 pkg. egg noodles
1 small can of tuna
1 large bay leaf
1 medium onion, sliced
Salt and pepper to taste
2 c. grated Velveeta cheese
1 can cream of mushroom
  soup
1 soup can of water

Grease 9″ × 13″ dish with butter. Spread half of noodles (uncooked) in bottom of dish. Crumble tuna and bay leaf evenly over noodles. Add sliced onion, salt, and pepper as desired. Spread remaining noodles and cheese evenly. Add soup and water thoroughly mixed. Bake in covered dish for 1 hour at 300°.

Cherokee Casserole

The color contrast of the olives on the cheese makes this a very attractive dish.

1 lb. ground beef
1 Tbsp. cooking oil
3/4 c. chopped onion
1-1/2 tsp. salt
1/4 tsp. pepper
1/8 tsp. oregano
1/8 tsp. garlic powder
1 can chopped tomatoes
1 can cream of mushroom
   soup
1 c. instant rice
2 or 3 slices cheese, cut in
   1/2″ slices
6 stuffed olives, sliced

Brown meat in oil. Add onion and cook until tender. Stir in all ingredients except cheese and olives. Bring to a boil, reduce heat and simmer for 5 minutes. Stir occasionally. Put in baking dish and add cheese. Broil until cheese melts. Garnish with olive slices.

Chicken Casserole

8 chicken breast halves,
   skinned and boned
1/2 c. water
1/4 tsp. salt
1/2 tsp. pepper
2 Tbsp. minced onion
1 can cream of mushroom
   soup, undiluted
1 can cream of chicken
   soup, undiluted
1-1/3 c. milk
1 c. herb-seasoned stuffing
   mix
1 c. cornbread stuffing mix
1/2 c. butter or margarine,
   melted

Place chicken in a baking dish. Add water; sprinkle with salt, pepper, and onion. Cover and bake at 350° for 30 minutes or until tender. Remove chicken from baking dish, reserving 1 cup broth. Cut chicken into bite-sized pieces, and place in a lightly greased 9″ × 13″ baking dish. Combine soups and milk in a medium saucepan. Cook until thoroughly heated; pour over chicken. Combine stuffing mixes; sprinkle over soup mixture. Combine butter and reserved chicken broth; pour over stuffing mixture. Bake, uncovered, at 350° for 30 minutes or until thoroughly heated.

Gad-About's Casserole

This is a sure-fire hit from Patsy Sanders.

3 medium onions
2 lb. hamburger meat
Salt and pepper to taste
1-1/2 tsp. Lawry's seasoned
 salt
1/4 tsp. garlic powder
 (opt.)
1/4 tsp. red pepper (opt.)
2 cans mushroom soup
1 soup can water
1/2 lb. American cheese
2 Tbsp. jalapeno Cheez
 Whiz (opt.)
1 (12 oz.) pkg. egg noodles
 (8 c. uncooked noodles)
Parmesan cheese
Paprika

Sauté onions in small amount cooking oil. When clear, add hamburger and cook until browned. Drain grease and add seasonings. In a large pan, heat soup, water, cheese, and Cheez Whiz until cheese is melted and well-blended. Cook egg noodles according to package directions. Grease 2 large baking dishes with cooking oil. Place the noodles, meat mixture and soup mixture in alternate layers in baking dishes. Top with Parmesan cheese and paprika. Bake at 350° for 10 minutes, or until heated thoroughly. This dish can be frozen and is good to double ingredients to serve a large crowd.

Spanish Rice

This is also good with ground turkey or veal.

2 Tbsp. oil
1 lb. ground beef
1 c. chopped onion
1 c. green pepper, chopped
1 c. uncooked rice
2 tsp. chili powder
1-1/2 c. water
1 tsp. seasoned salt
1/2 tsp. cumin
1/2 tsp. pepper
1 (8 oz.) can tomato sauce
1 (14-1/2 oz.) can
 tomatoes, drained and
 chopped

Heat oil in a large skillet over medium heat. Add beef, onion, and green pepper. Cook until meat is lightly browned. Drain liquid. Stir in remaining ingredients. Reduce heat, cover, and simmer for 20 minutes or until rice is tender. Serves 6.

Enchiladas

1 lb. ground beef
1/2 jalapeno pepper, diced
1-1/3 c. chopped onion,
   divided
1 Tbsp. oil
1 (8 oz.) can tomato sauce
1 (16 oz.) can whole
   tomatoes, undrained
   and chopped
1 (10 oz.) can tomatoes
   with green chilies,
   undrained and chopped
1/2 tsp. sugar
1/8 tsp. salt
1/8 tsp. pepper
1-1/2 tsp. flour
1 Tbsp. water
2 c. shredded Cheddar
   cheese (8 oz.)
2 c. shredded Monterey
   Jack cheese (8 oz.)
12 (6") corn tortillas

Cook beef in a large skillet until meat is browned, stirring to crumble meat. Drain and set aside. Sauté jalapeno pepper and 1/3 cup onion in hot oil until tender. Add tomato sauce and next 5 ingredients, stir well. Bring to a boil, reduce heat, and simmer for 15 minutes, stirring occasionally.

Combine flour and water, stir into tomato mixture. Cook over medium heat, stirring constantly, for 1 minute or until it thickens. Combine cheeses and remaining onion. Set aside 1 cup of cheese mixture for top of casserole.

Using tongs, dip a tortilla into hot tomato mixture, sprinkle about 2 tablespoons ground beef and about 1/4 cup cheese mixture down center of tortilla. Roll up jellyroll fashion and place, seam side down, in a lightly greased 9" × 13" × 2" baking dish. Repeat procedure with remaining tortillas. Spoon remaining sauce over tortillas. Cover and bake at 350° for 25 minutes. Sprinkle with reserved 1 cup of cheese mixture. Bake, uncovered, for 4 minutes or until cheese melts.

Green Enchiladas

The lady golfers of Tahoka always look forward to this dish from Novis Curry.

1 lb. ground beef
Salt and pepper to taste
1/4 tsp. chili powder
1 large onion, chopped
1/2 lb. grated Cheddar
   cheese
15 corn tortillas
1 stick oleo
4 Tbsp. flour
2 c. milk
1/2 lb. Velveeta cheese
1 (4 oz.) can green chilies

Cook ground beef, salt, pepper, chili powder, and onion until meat is brown, then drain. Add Cheddar cheese to cooked meat mixture. Soften corn tortillas in hot grease. Roll meat in tortillas and place in 9" × 13" Pyrex dish, that has been sprayed with Pam. In double boiler, melt oleo. Slowly add flour to make a paste. Add milk, stirring constantly. Add Velveeta and green chilies. Cook until thick. Pour on top of enchiladas. Bake at 350° about 20 minutes, or until bubbly. (Freezes well before baking.)

Green Enchiladas a la Bea Russell

2 lb. ground Beef
1 onion, chopped
Garlic to taste
3 tsp. chili powder
1 tsp. salt
1 large can evaporated
  milk
1 can cream mushroom
  soup
1 can chopped green
  chilies
1 can enchilada sauce
8 to 10 flour tortillas
1-1/2 c. cheese, grated
3 Tbsp. onion

Brown meat and onion with garlic, chili powder, and salt. Add evaporated milk, soup, green chilies, and enchilada sauce. Quarter tortillas. Line pan with foil and layer with tortillas, meat, cheese, and onion. Bake until hot and cheese melts.

Green Chili Enchiladas

1 can cream of chicken
  soup
1 sm. can evaporated milk
1/2 lb. Velveeta cheese
1 can chopped green
  chilies
1 sm. jar chopped
  pimientos
2 Tbsp. picante sauce
1 lb. hamburger meat
1 c. chopped onion
1 pkg. flour tortillas

Heat soup, evaporated milk, and Velveeta until heated through and smooth. Add green chilies, pimientos, and picante sauce.

In skillet, brown hamburger meat and drain. Add onion and heat until onion is clear.

Fill each tortilla with meat and cheese sauce, and arrange in a greased baking dish. Top with remainder of cheese sauce. (You can also layer tortillas, meat, and cheese sauce.) Bake at 350° for 15 minutes.

Lasagne Casserole

A great recipe from Terry Scott of Crawford

MEAT SAUCE:
1 lb. Italian sausage or
   ground meat
1 clove garlic, minced
1 Tbsp. whole basil
1-1/2 tsp. salt
1 lb. can stewed tomatoes
   (2 c.)
1 (12 oz.) can tomato paste
10 oz. noodles, cooked,
   drain, and rinsed

Brown meat slowly, spoon off fat. Add next 5 ingredients. Simmer, uncovered, for 1/2 hour stirring occasionally.

CHEESE FILLING:
3 c. cottage cheese
1/2 c. grated Parmesan
   cheese
2 Tbsp. parsley flakes
2 eggs, beaten
2 tsp. salt
1/2 tsp. pepper
1 lb. Mozzarella cheese,
   sliced

Mix first 6 ingredients. Place 1/2 noodles in a 9″ × 13″ baking dish. Spread with 1/2 cheese filling, 1/2 mozzarella cheese, and 1/2 meat sauce. Repeat layers. Bake at 375° for 30 minutes. Let stand for 10 minutes before cutting. Serves 12.

Mexican Casserole

This makes a great after-the-ball-game meal.

1 lb. hamburger meat
1 can cream of mushroom
   soup
1 c. water
1 small can chopped green
   chilies
1 small can condensed
   milk
1 large can mild enchilada
   sauce
1 pkg. Doritoes
1 c. grated cheese

Brown hamburger meat and drain. Add all ingredients except cheese and Doritoes and simmer about 30 minutes. Layer enough Doritoes to cover the bottom of a 9″ × 13″ baking dish. Pour mixture over Doritoes and cover with cheese. Place in 350° oven until cheese melts.

Mexican Cornbread Casserole

Debbie's absolute favorite! (Except for chocolate chip cookies, Red Velvet cake, and toffee.)

1 lb. ground beef
1/4 c. chopped onion
2 Tbsp. chopped jalapenos
    or 1 small can chopped
    green chilies
2 eggs, beaten
1 (1 lb.) can cream style
    corn
2/3 c. milk
1 (6-1/2 oz.) envelope
    cornbread mix.
4 slices American cheese

Preheat oven to 425°. Brown meat until crumbly, drain off excess fat, and add onions and peppers. Cook until onions are clear. Combine eggs, 1 cup corn, and milk, and add to cornbread mix. Stir until moistened. Pour half of cornbread batter into greased 9″ square pan. Top with beef mixture, cheese slices, and remaining corn. Pour other half of cornbread batter on top. Bake for 25 to 30 minutes. Makes 6 servings.

Seafood And Rice Casserole

2-1/2 c. water
1 c. rice
2 Tbsp. margarine
2 (4-1/2 oz.) cans shrimp,
    rinsed and drained
1 (8 oz.) jar cheese spread
1 (6 oz.) can crabmeat
1 green pepper, chopped
1/2 c. onion, chopped
1 (4 oz.) can green chilies,
    chopped and drained
1/4 c. green onions with
    tops, sliced
1/4 tsp. garlic powder
2 Tbsp. bread crumbs

Bring water to a boil in medium pan. Stir in rice and margarine. Cover and simmer 20 minutes. Remove from heat. Let stand covered until all liquid is absorbed. Add remaining ingredients, except bread crumbs; mix well. Pour into greased baking dish. Sprinkle with bread crumbs and bake at 350° for 30 minutes.

Vegetables & Side Dishes

Squash Supreme Casserole

A fantastic vegetable dish from Inez Stone of Stanton

2 c. cooked yellow squash,
    drained
1 c. commercial sour
    cream
1 (10-3/4 oz.) can cream of
    chicken soup, undiluted
1 carrot, grated
1 small onion, chopped
Salt and pepper to taste
1 box herb-seasoned
    crumbs (croutons)
1 Tbsp. margarine

Mash squash; add sour cream, soup, carrots, onion, salt, and pepper. Sprinkle a layer of crumbs in a shallow casserole dish, then spoon squash mixture over crumbs. Cover with additional crumbs and dot generously with margarine. Bake at 350° for 30 to 45 minutes.

Yellow Squash Casserole

A great recipe from that lady aviator from Tahoka

2 lb. yellow squash, sliced
    and cooked
2 eggs
1 small jar Cheez Whiz
1 small can chopped green
    chilies
1 small onion, chopped
1 can cream of chicken
    soup
1/2 c. cracker crumbs

Drain squash and place in a greased 1-1/2 quart casserole. Mix remaining ingredients, except cracker crumbs, and pour over squash in casserole. Add cracker crumbs to top. Bake at 350° for 30 to 40 minutes.

Baked Squash

4 c. squash
1 Tbsp. onion flakes
2 Tbsp. sugar
1 Tbsp. flour
1/2 tsp. salt
1 c. milk
2 Tbsp. butter
1 c. grated cheese
1 c. bread crumbs

Cook squash until tender. Drain and place in baking dish. Sprinkle with onion flakes. Mix sugar and flour, and then add salt, milk, and butter. Cook until thick and add cheese; mix well and pour over squash. Sprinkle with bread crumbs (or cracker crumbs). Bake at 350°until brown.

Squash Dressing

A wonderful recipe from Pasty Sanders, a great cook and a fantastic Sunday School teacher.

1 pkg. cornbread mix,
   cooked
2-1/2 c. milk
1/2 c. onion, chopped
1/2 c. celery, chopped
1 can cream of chicken
   soup
2/3 c. oleo
2 c. squash, cooked

Cook cornbread and mix with milk, onion, celery, soup, and oleo. Spread squash over bottom of oblong baking dish and pour other mixture over it. Bake at 350° for about 30 minutes or until brown.

Zucchini Casserole

A real "cheesy" recipe from Betsy Pridmore

2 zucchini squash, sliced
4 yellow squash, sliced
1 large onion, chopped
Salt and pepper to taste
1 (8-oz.) pkg. cream cheese
1 lb. American cheese,
   grated
1/4 lb. Cheddar cheese,
   grated
1 c. bread crumbs
1/2 stick butter, melted

Cook squash and onion in small amount of water for 25 minutes. Drain and add salt and pepper. Add cream cheese and let cool. Add American cheese and mix well. Place in casserole dish and top with Cheddar cheese. Sprinkle bread crumbs over cheese. Pour melted butter on top of crumbs. Bake at 350° for 25 to 30 minutes. Serves 10.

Vegetable Casserole

1 can English peas and
   onions
1 can asparagus
1 can long green beans
1 can water chestnuts,
   sliced
1 sm. jar Cheez Whiz

Put into casserole dish in layers and bake at 350° for 15 to 20 minutes.

Sauerkraut a la Wessie

Wessie Carroll makes this for Eldon and we get to enjoy.

1 large can sauerkraut
2 Tbsp. butter
2 Tbsp. brown sugar (may
   need a little more)

Mix sauerkraut, butter, and brown sugar; stir well. Cook until sugar is dissolved. Serve hot. Add more brown sugar to taste.

Chinese Cabbage

1/2 large head cabbage
1 Tbsp. vegetable oil
1 clove garlic, crushed
1 tsp. sugar
1/4 tsp. salt
1/4 tsp. pepper
1/4 tsp. paprika
4 Tbsp. water
1/4 c. chopped almonds

Shred cabbage. Heat oil in a large pan and fry garlic until golden color. Add cabbage, sugar, salt, pepper, paprika, and water. Cover mixture, remove lid and stir occasionally. Cook cabbage until browned. Cauliflower or spinach may be substituted for cabbage. Add almonds before serving. Serves 4.

Cabbage Casserole

We appreciate all the delicious recipes Betsy Pridmore shared with us, including this one.

1 head cabbage, cooked
   and drained
1 stick garlic cheese
1 small onion, chopped
1 can cream of mushroom
   soup
1 stick butter, melted
Salt and pepper to taste

Spread 1/2 of the cabbage in a baking dish. Top with 1/2 of the cheese and all of the onion. Add the remaining cabbage and cheese. In a small bowl, blend soup, butter, salt, and pepper. Pour this over the casserole. Bake at 350° for 20 minutes.

Spinach Madaline

2 pkg. frozen chopped
  spinach
4 Tbsp. butter
2 Tbsp. flour
2 Tbsp. chopped onion
1/2 c. evaporated milk
1/2 c. liquid from spinach
1 (6 oz.) roll Jalapeno
  cheese
1/2 tsp. black pepper
3/4 tsp. celery salt
3/4 tsp. garlic salt
1/2 tsp. salt
1 tsp. Worcestershire sauce
Red pepper to taste
1 c. buttered bread crumbs

Cook spinach according to directions. Drain and reserve liquid. Melt butter in pan and add flour, stirring until completely blended but not browned. Add onion and cook. Add milk and liquid from spinach slowly, stirring constantly to avoid lumps. Cook until smooth and thick. Add cheese and seasonings. Stir until melted. Combine with cooked spinach. Put in casserole dish. Top with buttered bread crumbs. Bake until warm. Freezes well. Serves 6.

Sour Cream Potatoes

Jan Hughes makes this often for Mickey, Haley, and Whitney.

1 (2 lb.) pkg. frozen hash
  brown potatoes
1 stick melted margarine
1 large carton sour cream
8 oz. grated Cheddar
  cheese
1 bunch chopped green
  onions, blades too
1 can cream of mushroom
  soup

Put potatoes in a 9″ × 13″ dish. Mix remaining ingredients, pour over potatoes. Bake at 350° 1 hour and 15 minutes.

Au Gratin Potatoes

3 - 4 large potatoes, diced
1 onion, finely chopped
Salt and pepper to taste
1 can cream of mushroom
  soup
1 soup can milk
1/2 c. grated American
  cheese

Mix potatoes and onion in casserole dish. Add salt and pepper. In a small microwave bowl, beat soup and milk until completely blended. Then add cheese and heat until cheese is melted and mixture is completely blended. Pour over potatoes. Bake at 300° until tender, about 45 minutes.

Potato Casserole
This prize recipe comes from Clarene Chambers.

8 medium sized potatoes
1/2 tsp. salt
1/2 tsp. pepper

 SAUCE:
1 stick oleo
1/2 c. flour
4 or 5 c. milk
1 small can chopped
  pimiento
1/2 lb. grated American
  cheese
Salt and pepper to taste

Boil potatoes with jackets on. Peel and dice. Place potatoes in baking dish and sprinkle with salt and pepper.

Melt oleo and mix with flour. Add milk, stir, and cook until thick. Add chopped pimiento and cheese. Stir until melted. Pour over potatoes and bake at 350° for 30 minutes.

Jalapeno and Potato Casserole

4 potatoes, peeled and
  sliced
1 small bell pepper, sliced
1 small jar pimientos
1/2 stick oleo
1 Tbsp. flour
1 c. milk
1/2 roll garlic cheese,
  cubed
1/2 roll jalapeno cheese,
  cubed
Salt and pepper to taste

Layer potatoes in buttered casserole dish with bell pepper and pimientos. Melt oleo in pan, add flour, and stir until well blended. Add milk and cheese and cook until melted. Pour over potatoes and bake at 350° for 45 minutes to one hour. (Easy to double.)

Potato Boats

6 medium potatoes
1 tsp. salt
1/4 tsp. pepper
1/4 c. butter
1/2 c. sour cream
2 Tbsp. chives, chopped
3 slices bacon, cooked and
  crumbled
1-1/4 c. shredded Cheddar
  cheese

Bake potatoes 1 hour at 400° or until tender. Cut in half lengthwise. Scoop potatoes out of shells. Mash, add remaining ingredients, except cheese, and beat until light and fluffy. Spoon back into shells. Sprinkle with cheese and bake, uncovered, at 350° for 15 to 20 minutes.

Grilled Fancy Potatoes

An elegant and easy way to serve the ever popular potato.

6 medium potatoes
3 medium onions, thinly
  sliced
1 Tbsp. Best O' Butter (a
  butter substitute)
1 tsp. lemon pepper
1/2 tsp. garlic salt

Wash potatoes well. Place each potato on heavy-duty foil and cut horizontally into 1/4" slices. Place an onion slice between each potato slice. Combine seasonings and sprinkle mixture between potato and onion slices. Wrap potatoes to seal. Grill over medium-hot coals for 40 minutes or until potatoes are done, turning after 20 minutes. These are also good baked at 350° for 1-1/2 hours if you are not using your grill.

Potato Casserole

1 c. sour cream
1/2 c. milk
1 Tbsp. instant dried
  onion
5 c. diced cooked potatoes
Salt and pepper to taste
2 Tbsp. dry fine bread
  crumbs
1 Tbsp. butter

Mix sour cream, milk, and onion. Pour half of mixture over potatoes in a large casserole dish. Sprinkle with salt and pepper, repeat. Mix crumbs and butter together and sprinkle over casserole. Bake at 350° for 20 to 25 minutes. Easy to make ahead and heat when needed.

Potato Patties

1-1/2 c. leftover mashed
  potatoes
1 egg
4 Tbsp. flour
1/2 tsp. salt
1/8 tsp. pepper
2 tsp. onion flakes
1-1/2 c. crushed Corn
  Flakes

Mash cold potatoes with fork until soft. Add egg and mix well. Add flour, salt, pepper, and onion flakes and stir until well blended. Crush Corn Flakes on wax paper. Drop potato mixture by tablespoonfuls onto Corn Flakes and pat into patties, covering both sides. Fry in small amount of hot grease, or in a non-stick skillet sprayed with Pam. Brown lightly on both sides.

Sweet Potato Surprise

A magical dish from Bitsy Wells — You serve it and it disappears.

3 medium sweet potatoes,
   boiled and peeled
1-1/4 c. brown sugar
1-1/2 Tbsp. cornstarch
1/4 tsp. salt
1/8 tsp. cinnamon
1 tsp. grated orange peel
1 (16 oz.) can apricot
   halves, reserve liquid
2 Tbsp. butter
1/2 c. chopped pecans

Slice sweet potatoes and arrange in the bottom of a buttered 10″ × 6″ × 1-1/2″ baking dish. In a saucepan, combine brown sugar, cornstarch, salt, cinnamon, and orange peel. Drain apricots and reserve liquid. Stir 1 cup of reserved apricot syrup into sugar mixture. Cook and stir over medium heat until boiling. Boil 2 minutes. Add apricots, butter, and pecans. Remove from heat and stir until butter melts. Pour mixture over sliced sweet potatoes. Bake uncovered at 375° for 25 minutes.

Sweet Potatoes

3 c. cooked and mashed
   sweet potatoes
1/2 c. milk
2 eggs, beaten
1-3/4 tsp. vanilla
1/2 c. sugar
1/2 tsp. salt
1/2 c. butter

Mix milk, beaten eggs, and vanilla and add to potatoes. Add sugar, salt, and butter and mix well.

TOPPING:
1/2 c. brown sugar
1/2 c. flour
1 c. pecans, chopped
1/3 stick butter, softened

Mix well and sprinkle on potato mixture and bake at 350° for 30 to 35 minutes.

Sweet Potato Casserole

Lola Caldwell says that even a vegetable-hater will love this.

5 c. mashed sweet potatoes
2 c. sugar
2 large cans Pet milk
4 eggs, beaten
1-1/2 sticks oleo, melted
1 Tbsp. nutmeg
1 Tbsp. cinnamon
1 Tbsp. vanilla

Mix ingredients well and pour into 1 large or 2 small casserole dishes sprayed with Pam. Bake at 350° for 15 minutes.

TOPPING:
4 c. Rice Krispies
1 c. brown sugar
1 c. pecans, chopped
1 stick oleo, melted

Mix ingredients and pour over filling. Bake until set, or about 10 to 12 minutes. Don't let topping brown. Serves 12 people.

Golden Crisp Onion Rings

A favorite at the Inklebarger house

1 c. flour
1 tsp. baking powder
1/4 tsp. salt
1 egg, beaten
1 c. milk
1 Tbsp. salad oil
3 large onions

Sift together flour, baking powder, and salt. Add egg, milk, and salad oil. Add dry ingredients and beat until smooth. Slice onions and separate into rings. Dip a few at a time into batter. Fry in shortening until golden brown.

Baked Onions

Jimmy Kendrick's fantastic side dish for cookouts

Onions
Butter
Garlic pepper
Lemon pepper

Remove outer layer of onion skin. Make several slashes in onions, but do not cut completely through. Set each onion on a piece of Saran Wrap large enough to cover and seal onion. Put butter between wedges of onion and sprinkle with peppers. Seal in Saran Wrap and place in microwave. Bake on high setting until tender, about 4 minutes.

Hot Sauce Olé

8 qt. chopped tomatoes
1-1/2 c. chopped jalapeno
   peppers
1 large onion, chopped
4 cloves garlic, diced
1/2 c. salt
1 tsp. pepper
1-1/2 tsp. cumin
1-1/2 tsp. oregano

Mix all ingredients and boil 20 to 25 minutes. Pour into sterilized jars. Process in cooker for 5 minutes at 5 pounds.

Brownfield Hot Sauce

Connie Hogue gave this recipe to Bobby when they were teaching at the Intermediate School.

1 gal. ground tomatoes
4 ground onions
1 carrot
1 c. hot peppers, diced
1/2 c. vinegar
1/4 c. oil
2 Tbsp. salt
1/2 c. sugar
1 Tbsp. mustard seed
1 Tbsp. celery seed
1 Tbsp. black pepper

Mix all ingredients and bring to a boil. Simmer for 45 minutes. Seal in sterilized jars. Makes 10 to 11 pints.

Hot Sauce

From a dear friend

8 c. ripe tomatoes
4 c. bell peppers
3 c. onions
2 c. celery
2 Tbsp. salt
1-1/2 c. sugar
3 c. vinegar
1 tsp. cinnamon
3/4 to 1 c. chopped hot
   peppers, use more if you
   dare

Boil tomatoes in hot water, until they crack. Put in cold water, let them set, then peel and core. Mash tomatoes with a potato masher before you mix with other ingredients. Chop peppers, onions, and celery, and mix with other ingredients. Cook in large pan about 1 hour; stir often. Pour into sterilized jars. Seal. (Hint: If you like chunky sauce don't use a food processor. You can use a small onion chopper.)

Pinto Beans
Dedicated to Rachael Huffaker

1 small pkg. dried pinto
  beans
1 tsp. salt
4 slices bacon, cut into 2"
  strips

First, go through beans and remove all rocks and broken beans. Put beans in a bowl and cover them with water, wait a minute, then take out any skins or whole beans that float to the top. Rinse beans thoroughly, cover with water, and soak for 8 hours or overnight. Before cooking, drain, rinse, and cover with fresh water, then add salt and bacon. Be sure to simmer beans slowly so they won't break and lose their shape. You can either cook these in a large saucepan or in a crockpot. Cook until tender, or about 3 to 4 hours.

Red Beans And Rice
A Family Favorite

1/2 lb. dried pinto beans
1 qt. water
1/2 lb. cooked ham, cubed
1 c. onion (chopped)
1 c. celery (chopped)
1 large clove of garlic,
  minced
3/4 tsp. salt or to taste
1/4 to 1/2 tsp. crushed red
  pepper
1 (4 oz.) can green chilies,
  drained
Hot cooked rice

Sort and wash beans. Place in a large Dutch oven. Cover with water 2" above beans. Cover and bring to a boil. Cook 5 minutes. Remove from heat and drain beans and rinse. Add water to completely cover beans and soak 8 hours. Drain and rinse. Add water to cover beans again, add next 7 ingredients, and bring to a boil. Cover, reduce heat,and simmer 2 hours, or until beans are tender, stirring occasionally. Serve over hot rice.

Artichokes Au Gratin

Nancy Askew Warren's recipe has great flavor plus the convenience of advance preparation.

2 pkg. frozen artichoke
  hearts
1/4 c. butter
3/4 tsp. salt
Pepper to taste
1 med. onion, chopped
1/2 tsp. dry mustard
1/3 c. flour
1-1/2 c. milk
2 cans mushroom buttons,
  drained
1 c. grated Swiss cheese
1/4 c. dry bread crumbs
Paprika

Cook artichoke hearts as directed on package. Drain. Put in baking dish. Combine remaining ingredients, except cheese, bread crumbs, and paprika, into a sauce. Pour over artichoke hearts. Sprinkle cheese, bread crumbs, and paprika on top. (May refrigerate now, bake later). Bake at 450° for 15 minutes.

Liz's Frozen Okra Dish

This is from Mary Margaret Stewart of Waco.

Frozen okra, slightly
  thawed
Salt and pepper to taste
Oleo
Corn Flakes, crushed
Parmesan cheese
Milk

Fill casserole dish with okra. Salt and pepper to taste. Dot generously with oleo. Sprinkle with Corn Flakes and Parmesan cheese. Cover with milk. Bake at 375° until slightly brown and bubbly.

Frank's Okra

Frank Richerson of Waco makes this all the time.

1 large onion, chopped
1 tsp. sugar
1 tsp. salt
1 tsp. pepper
1 tsp. Cavender's Greek
  seasoning (or to taste)
1 can stewed tomatoes
Fresh or frozen okra in
  quantity desired

Cover chopped onion with water and add seasonings. Boil for 10 minutes. Add tomatoes and bring to a boil. Add okra. Cook until tender, or approximately 15 minutes. This will not be "slimy."

Broccoli And Corn Casserole

1 (16 oz.) can cream style
   corn
1 (10 oz.) pkg. frozen
   chopped broccoli,
   cooked and drained
1 egg, beaten
3/4 c. cracker crumbs
1 Tbsp. instant minced
   onion
1 Tbsp. melted butter
1/4 tsp. salt
1/8 tsp. pepper
1/2 c. cracker crumbs
1 Tbsp. melted butter
1/4 tsp. onion salt (opt.)
1/4 tsp. cayenne pepper
   (opt.)
1/2 c. Cheddar cheese,
   grated

Mix corn, broccoli, egg, the 3/4 cup cracker crumbs, onion, 1 tablespoon melted butter, salt, and pepper. Put in 1-quart casserole dish. Mix 1/2 cup crumbs with 1 tablespoon butter; sprinkle over vegetables. Sprinkle onion salt and cayenne pepper over crumbs. Bake uncovered at 350° for 35 minutes. Top with cheese and bake an additional 5 minutes.

Broccoli Casserole Abilene Style

1/2 c. onion, chopped
1/2 c. celery, chopped
1/4 c. butter
1 can cream of mushroom
   soup
1 can cream of celery soup
1 jar jalapeno Cheez Whiz
1 c. rice, cooked
1 pkg. frozen chopped
   broccoli, cooked
1/2 c. chopped almonds
   (opt.)

Sauté onion and celery in butter. Add soups and Cheez Whiz to onion mixture and blend thoroughly. Fold in rice, broccoli, and almonds. Pour into 9" × 13" casserole dish and bake at 350° for about 20 minutes.

Corn Pudding

A great side dish from Beverly Womack and it has become a
Thanksgiving tradition.

2 cans cream-style corn
2 eggs
3/4 c. cornmeal
1/2 c. Wesson oil
1/2 tsp. baking powder
1 tsp. garlic salt
1 (4 oz.) can chopped
   green chilies
1-1/2 c. Longhorn cheese,
   grated

Mix all ingredients except cheese and pour into a greased 9" × 13" casserole dish. Bake at 350° for 40 minutes. Then sprinkle cheese on top and bake another 10 to 15 minutes.

Corn Casserole

A real gem of a vegetable dish from Benna Askew of Dallas

2 Tbsp. butter
1 (8 oz.) pkg. cream cheese
Pepper to taste
2 cans whole kernel corn,
   drained
1 (4 oz.) can green chilies,
   chopped
1/4 tsp. garlic salt
2 Tbsp. milk

Melt butter and cream cheese and stir together over low heat. Add pepper to taste. Add remaining ingredients. Put in casserole dish and bake at 350° for 20 to 25 minutes.

Grilled Corn-On-The-Cob

Linda Bartley says these are super good!!!

Roasting ears

Leave roasting ear in husk. Soak corn in water for about 15 minutes. With husk left on the corn, place corn on grill or in oven at 350°. Cook about 25 to 35 minutes.

Baked Corn

From Margaret Hartman of Brownfield

2 (16 oz.) cans whole
   kernel corn, drained
2 Tbsp. oleo
1/2 tsp. salt
8 oz. cream cheese
2 (4 oz.) cans chopped
   green chilies
1/4 c. milk
1/4 tsp. garlic salt

Mix all ingredients and bake 20 to 25 minutes at 350°.

Carrots with Pizzazz

Christine's family enjoys these.

3 lb. carrots
1/2 c. Wesson oil
1 c. sugar
1/2 c. vinegar
1/2 tsp. salt
Pepper to taste
1 tsp. Worcestershire sauce
1 tsp. dry mustard

Peel, slice, and cook carrots. Then drain and put into casserole dish. Mix remaining ingredients and cook until sugar is dissolved. Pour over carrots. Will keep for weeks. Good hot or cold.

Carrot Ring

A beautiful center piece and a delicious vegetable dish from Sylvia Lehman of Lubbock

1 c. Crisco
1/2 c. brown sugar
1 egg
1 Tbsp. water
1-1/4 c. sifted flour
1/2 tsp. baking powder
1/2 tsp. nutmeg
1/2 tsp. salt
1/2 tsp. cinnamon
1 c. grated carrots

Cream Crisco and sugar. Add egg, water, and dry ingredients which have been sifted together. Add carrots. Bake in ring mold 45 minutes to 1 hour in 350° oven. Turn over on platter. (Nice to fill center with English peas.)

Glazed Carrots

1 lb. carrots, cut into 2"
   strips
2 Tbsp. Wesson oil
1/4 c. water
2 Tbsp. brown sugar
1/4 tsp. salt

Cook carrots in Wesson oil over medium heat until lightly browned. Mix remaining ingredients and pour over carrots. Cover and cook on low heat, about 15 minutes.

Deluxe Cucumbers

4 medium cucumbers,
   peeled and sliced
1-1/2 c. milk
1 tsp. salt
1/2 tsp. pepper
1 c. dry bread crumbs
4 Tbsp. butter

Mix cucumbers, milk, salt, and pepper. Fold in bread crumbs. Pour in greased 1-quart casserole. Dot with butter, bake at 350° for 30 minutes.

Hominy a la Wessie Carroll

1 can cream mushroom
   soup
1/2 c. cream or half and
   half
1 tsp. celery seed
1/4 tsp. cayenne pepper
1 pkg. shredded almonds
1 can hominy

Mix soup, cream, celery seed, and pepper. Heat to boil then add almonds. Pour over hominy and bake 30 to 40 minutes at 350°.

Golden Hominy

2 cans hominy
1 tsp. minced onion
2 tsp. seasoned salt
2 tsp. melted butter
1 c. crushed Corn Flakes

Place hominy in baking dish. Sprinkle onion, seasoned salt, and dot with butter. Sprinkle Corn Flakes on top. Bake at 400° for 20 minutes.

Baked Beans

These are good with grilled steaks or hamburgers.

2 (1 lb.) cans pork and
   beans
1 small onion, minced
1/4 c. catsup
1/4 c. brown sugar
3 Tbsp. molasses
1 Tbsp. Worcestershire
   sauce
1/4 tsp. ground cloves
2 or 3 Tbsp. bacon
   drippings
3 strips of bacon

Mix all ingredients except bacon in a casserole dish. Place bacon across top of beans. Cover and bake at 350° for one hour. Remove cover and bake for 30 minutes more. These can be frozen very nicely. Easy to double.

Creole Beans

Shirley Draper of Tahoka makes this for what's-his-name.

1-1/2 c. onions, thinly
   sliced
1 c. chopped green pepper
1 c. diced celery
3 Tbsp. butter
2 tsp, salt
1 tsp. pepper
3 c. diced fresh tomatoes
   or 1 can tomatoes,
   drained
3 c. cooked green beans or
   2 cans whole green
   beans

Sauté onions, pepper, and celery in butter. Add remaining ingredients and cook until thoroughly heated.

Green Bean Casserole

1 (1 lb.) can green beans
1 can cream of mushroom
   soup
1/2 c. soy sauce
1 small can water
   chestnuts, chopped
1 can onion rings

Mix beans, soup, soy sauce and chestnuts in buttered casserole dish. Bake at 350° for 20 minutes. Then add onion rings on top of beans and bake 5 to 10 minutes longer.

Green Beans Deluxe

1 Tbsp. butter or
   margarine
2 small onions, sliced and
   separated into rings
2 (16 oz.) cans cut green
   beans, drained
1/4 c. picante sauce
1 Tbsp. plus 1 tsp. diced
   pimiento
1/8 tsp. lemon juice

Melt butter in a saucepan; add onion and sauté until tender. Add remaining ingredients. Cover and heat thoroughly.

Bean Casserole

2 boxes frozen peas
2 boxes frozen French
   green beans
1 box frozen baby lima
   beans
1 diced onion
1 carton cream, whipped
1/2 c. mayonnaise
1 tsp. garlic salt
1 can mushrooms
1 large can Parmesan
   cheese

Cook peas, beans, and limas by directions on package. Combine all ingredients except cheese. Place in casserole, alternating layers with cheese. Bake at 350° for 20 minutes.

Deviled Eggs

6 eggs
1/2 tsp. salt
1/2 tsp. mustard
1 tsp. vinegar
1/2 tsp. mayonnaise
Paprika

Boil eggs for 8 to 10 minutes and remove shells. Cut eggs in half. Remove yolk and mash with a fork. Add salt, mustard, vinegar, and mayonnaise and mix with yolk. Put into egg white halves and sprinkle with paprika.

Macaroni and Cheese

This is a favorite of Christine's grandchildren.

12 oz. macaroni
Salt
1 Tbsp. Wesson oil
1-1/2 lb. Velveeta Cheese
3 Tbsp. margarine
2 c. milk

Cook macaroni according to directions. (Hint: If you add 1 tablespoon Wesson oil to water, it will eliminate foam.) Drain well. Add other ingredients and heat over low setting. Stir occasionally to keep from sticking. Cook until all cheese is melted. Garnish with paprika if desired. (Add additional milk when reheating.)

Rice Casserole

This is a great side dish for any meat.

1 c. rice
6 Tbsp. oleo
1 small can mushrooms
  pieces
1 can water chestnuts,
  chopped
1 can onion soup
1 soup can water

Brown rice in oleo. Add mushrooms, water chestnuts, soup, and water. Place in casserole dish and cover. Bake at 350° for 30 minutes, or until all liquid is absorbed.

Sour Cream Rice

Nancy Askew Warren sent this from Ft. Stockton.

4-1/2 c. cooked rice
2 c. sour cream
2 (7 oz.) cans chopped
  green chilies
1 (4 oz.) jar pimientos
1 lb. grated cheese (mix
  Cheddar and Jack)

Combine rice and sour cream. Pour 1/2 in baking dish. Combine green chilies, pimientos, and 1/2 of the cheese, then spread on top of rice mixture. Put other 1/2 rice on top and sprinkle the remaining cheese on top. Bake, uncovered for 30 minutes at 350° or until lightly browned.

Baked Almond Rice

3 c. hot chicken broth or
   water
1-1/2 c. regular rice,
   uncooked
1-1/4 tsp. salt
3/4 c. slivered almonds
3 Tbsp. butter

Mix broth, rice, and salt in ungreased 9″ × 13″ baking dish. Cover tightly with aluminum foil. Bake at 350° for 25 to 30 minutes, until liquid is absorbed and rice is tender. Just before serving, brown almonds in butter and add to hot, cooked rice and mix. Serves 6 to 8.

Florentine Rice

1 c. rice
1 (10 oz.) pkg. frozen
   chopped spinach
3 Tbsp. chopped onion
2-1/2 c. water
1 tsp. salt
1/4 c. oleo
1/4 tsp. pepper
1 (8 oz.) pkg. Cheddar
   cheese, cubed

Add rice, spinach, and onion to boiling salted water. Cover, reduce heat, and simmer for 25 minutes. Add remaining ingredients and mix well. This makes 6 to 8 servings.

Rice Dressing
One of our longtime favorites from Sybil Jordan

2 eggs, well-beaten
2 c. cooked instant rice
1/2 c. salad oil
1 large can Carnation milk
1 onion, chopped
1/8 tsp. garlic salt
1 (.25 oz.) can parsley
   flakes
Salt and pepper to taste
1/2 lb. grated American
   cheese

Spray baking dish with Pam. Mix all ingredients together and mix well. Bake at 300° for 45 minutes to 1 hour.

Green Rice

From Savannah Walker of Washington, D.C.

2 c. boiled rice
1 c. chopped parsley
2 c. milk
1-1/2 c. sharp cheese, cut
   into chunks
2 eggs, beaten with 1/2 c.
   Wesson oil
1 medium onion, chopped
Touch of garlic
1 jar pimiento

Mix and bake in buttered dish at 350° until brown.

Cakes, Candies & Cookies

Amazin' Raisin Cake
From Nancy Askew Warren of Ft. Stockton

3 c. unsifted flour
2 c. sugar
1 c. mayonnaise
1/3 c. milk
2 eggs
2 tsp. baking soda
1-1/2 tsp. ground
   cinnamon
1/2 tsp. ground nutmeg
1/2 tsp. salt
1/4 tsp. ground cloves
3 c. chopped apples
1 c. seedless raisins
1/2 c. chopped pecans

Mix all ingredients except apples, raisins, and pecans. Beat for 2 minutes on low speed. Batter will be very thick. Stir in apples, raisins, and pecans. Spoon batter into greased and floured pans, whatever size or shape you prefer. Bake at 350° for 45 minutes. Cool in pans for 10 minutes, then remove and cool. If you want a layer cake, fill and frost with whipped cream or cream cheese icing.

Apple Pie Cake
This is from Bea Russell of Lamesa.

1 c. white sugar
1 c. brown sugar
2 c. flour
1 tsp. soda
1 tsp. cinnamon
1 c. pecans, chopped (opt.)
2 sticks melted oleo
1 tsp. vanilla
2 eggs, beaten
1 c. chopped apples

Mix sugars, flour, soda, cinnamon, and pecans. Add remaining ingredients and mix well. Bake in 9″ × 13″ pan at 350° until done, about 35 minutes.

Fudge Cup Cakes
This recipe from Clarene Chambers will delight children of all ages.

1 stick margarine
1 sq. bitter chocolate
2 eggs
1 c. sugar
3/4 c. flour
1 tsp. vanilla

Melt margarine and chocolate on low heat (or microwave). Beat eggs, add sugar, and mix well. Add flour and chocolate mixture. Add vanilla. Put in 12 baking cups. Bake at 350° for 25 to 30 minutes. (You may add pecans to batter or sprinkle on top, as desired)

Applesauce Cake

1 c. sugar
1/3 c. butter
1 egg
2 c. flour
1 tsp. baking powder
1 tsp. cinnamon
1/2 tsp. salt
1/4 tsp. cloves
1 c. applesauce
1 c. raisins (opt.)

Cream sugar and butter. Add egg. Sift flour with baking powder, cinnamon, salt, and cloves. Alternately add flour and applesauce to mixture. Fold in raisins. Bake in loaf pan at 350° for 45 minutes to 1 hour.

Apricot Brandy Pound Cake

Linda Givens says these make super gifts if baked in freezer loaf pans.

1 c. butter
2-1/2 c. sugar
6 eggs
1 tsp. vanilla, orange, lemon, AND rum extract
3 c. sifted flour
1/4 tsp. soda
1/2 tsp. salt
1 c. sour cream
1/2 c. apricot brandy

Cream butter and sugar. Add eggs, one at a time, beating well after each addition. Add extracts. Then add sifted dry ingredients alternately with sour cream and brandy. Blend well. Bake in a tube pan (not a bundt pan or batter will overflow) for 1 hour and 15 minutes at 325°. This can also be baked in 3 freezer loaf pans.

Banana Split Cake

Graham cracker crust
2 (8 oz.) pkg. cream cheese
2 c. powdered sugar
3 bananas
1 small can crushed pineapple, drained
1 large carton Cool Whip
1 c. chopped pecans
1 c. Maraschino cherries, chopped

Make a graham cracker crust in a 9″ × 13″ Pyrex dish. Blend cream cheese and sugar. Layer over crust. Slice bananas and place over cream cheese mixture. Layer pineapple over bananas. Cover with Cool Whip. Garnish with pecans and cherries.

Banana Nut Cake

Wayne Huffaker said this reminds him of his grandmother's gravy icing.

3/4 c. butter
2 c. sugar
6 Tbsp. buttermilk
1 tsp. soda
3 eggs
2-1/4 c. flour
1 c. pecans, chopped
1 tsp. vanilla
4 bananas, mashed

Combine all ingredients and bake in a 9″ × 13″ pan at 350° for 40 to 50 minutes. This cake will fall in the middle.

ICING:
6 Tbsp. cornstarch
1 c. sugar
1 c. water
2 egg yolks
1 banana, mashed
4 Tbsp. orange juice or
   lemon juice
2 Tbsp. butter

Mix cornstarch, sugar, and enough water to make a paste. Then add egg yolks and mix well. Add mashed bananas and remaining water. Cook until thick. Remove from heat and add juice and butter.

Buttermilk Cake

Margaret Hartman of Brownfield makes this for Royce.

1 c. buttermilk
1/2 tsp. soda
2 c. sugar
1 c. Crisco
4 eggs
1 tsp. salt
1 tsp. vanilla or lemon
   flavor
3 c. flour

Mix buttermilk and soda together and set aside. Cream sugar and Crisco, then add eggs. Beat well. Add remaining ingredients and buttermilk mixture. Bake in a greased tube pan about 1 hour at 350°.

Turtle Cake

A favorite of Wey McNeil of Waco

1 pkg. German chocolate
   cake mix
1 stick soft oleo
2/3 c. oil
3 eggs
1-1/2 c. water
1 can Eagle Brand milk
1 (14 oz.) bag caramels (15
   oz. caramel sauce will
   work.)
1 c. chopped pecans

Mix cake mix, oleo, oil, eggs, water, and 1/2 can Eagle Brand milk. Pour half batter into 9″ × 13″ pan. Bake 20 minutes at 325°. Melt caramels and mix in other half can Eagle Brand milk, add pecans, and mix well. Pour mixture over baked cake and add rest of batter. Bake 30 to 40 minutes at 325°

ICING:
(I usually double this
   recipe)
1/2 c. sugar
1/4 c. milk
2 Tbsp. Cocoa
1 Tbsp. white Karo syrup
1/2 stick butter
1 c. powdered sugar
1 tsp. vanilla

Mix sugar, milk, cocoa, Karo syrup, and butter. Bring to a boil, stirring constantly. Remove from heat. Add powdered sugar and vanilla. Pour on warm cake.

Chocolate Applesauce Cake

Monte Hughes of Brownfield gives this cake as a gift.

1 c. shortening or oil
3 c. sugar
4 Tbsp. cocoa
3 c. applesauce
4 c. flour
2 tsp. salt
2 tsp. cinnamon
1 tsp. cloves
4 tsp. soda
2 c. chopped raisins or
   dates
2 c. chopped pecans

Mix shortening, sugar, and cocoa. Stir well then add applesauce. Mix flour with spices and soda, then add to applesauce mixture. Add raisins and nuts and mix well. Bake in tube pan at 325° for 2 hours. (You can also bake this in 2 loaf pans at 350° for 1 hour and 15 minutes.)

Carrot Pecan Cake

Very moist and keeps well. Freezes well too!

1-1/4 c. oil
2 c. sugar
2 c. sifted flour
2 tsp. baking powder
1 tsp. soda
1 tsp. salt
2 tsp. cinnamon
4 eggs
3 c. finely grated raw
   carrots
1 c. finely chopped pecans

Combine oil and sugar and mix well. Sift together remaining dry ingredients. Add half to oil-sugar mixture and blend. Add remaining dry ingredients alternately with eggs, one at a time, mixing well after each addition. Add carrots and pecans and mix well. Pour into 3 greased and floured layer pans. Bake at 325°for 35 to 45 minutes. Cool in pans. Remove cakes from pans and spread with glaze.

ORANGE GLAZE:
1 c. sugar
1/4 c. cornstarch
1 c. fresh orange juice
1 tsp. lemon juice
2 Tbsp. butter
2 Tbsp. grated orange peel
   (opt.)
1/2 tsp. salt

Combine sugar and cornstarch in saucepan. Slowly add orange juice and lemon juice, stirring until smooth. Add butter, orange peel, and salt. Cook over low heat until thick and glossy. Cool. Spread glaze between layers and on top and sides of cake.

Chocolate Cake

Donna Whitley's treat for her family

1 c. water
1/2 c. Wesson oil
1/4 c. cocoa
1 stick butter
1/2 c. buttermilk
1 tsp. soda
2 c. sugar
2 c. flour
2 eggs, beaten

Place water, oil, cocoa, and butter in saucepan and bring to a boil. Mix buttermilk and soda and let set. In large mixing bowl, add sugar and flour. Add boiling mixture, mix well. Add buttermilk-soda mixture and eggs. Blend. Pour into 9″ × 13″ pan. Bake at 350° for 25 to 30 minutes.

ICING:
1 stick butter
1/4 c. cocoa
1 box powdered sugar
1/4 c. milk

Place butter and cocoa in saucepan and bring to a boil. Add mixture to sugar and mix well. Add milk gradually and blend. Spread over cake.

Chocolate Chip Cake

The teachers at Lamesa High School always liked this.

1 pkg. yellow cake mix
1 small box instant vanilla
   pudding
1 small box instant
   chocolate pudding
4 eggs
1-1/2 c. water
1/2 c. oil
1 small pkg. milk
   chocolate chips
1 c. chopped pecans

Mix first six ingredients and beat well. Then add the chocolate chips and pecans and stir with spoon until blended. Bake in a bundt pan for 1 hour at 325°.

Chocolate Eclair Cake

1st Place Howard County Fair 1985 submitted by Linda Womack

1 lb. graham crackers
2 small pkgs. vanilla
   instant pudding
3-1/2 c. milk
1 (8 oz.) carton Cool Whip

Butter 9" × 13" pan. Line bottom with crackers. Beat pudding and milk at medium speed until thick. Fold in Cool Whip by hand. Pour half of the pudding over the crackers. Place another layer of crackers over this. Then pour the rest of the pudding over them. Last layer is crackers. Frost.

FROSTING:
2 oz. melted unsweetened
   chocolate
2 Tbsp. white Karo syrup
2 tsp. vanilla
3 Tbsp. margarine
1-1/2 c. powdered sugar
3 Tbsp. milk

Beat with mixer until smooth. Spread over cake then chill several hours.

Chocolate Sheath Cake

Sybil serves this hot with homemade ice cream.

2 c. unsifted flour
2 c. sugar
1 tsp. soda
1 stick butter
3-1/2 Tbsp. cocoa
1 c. water
1/2 c. Crisco
1/3 c. buttermilk
2 eggs, beaten
1 tsp. vanilla

Mix first three ingredients in a large bowl and set aside. Combine butter, cocoa, water and Crisco in a pan and bring to a boil. Pour over dry ingredients and mix well. Add buttermilk, eggs, and vanilla. Grease and flour a 9" × 13" cake pan. Bake at 400° for 30 to 40 minutes.

ICING:
2 c. sugar
1 stick butter
1/2 c. milk
2 Tbsp. cocoa
1/4 c. white Karo
1 tsp. vanilla

In a saucepan, mix ingredients and boil for 3 minutes. Cool and spread over cake.

Date Nut Cake

2 c. hot water
2 c. dates
2 tsp. soda
2 c. sugar
1-1/2 c. butter or
    margarine
2 eggs
2 c. pecans, chopped
2-2/3 c. flour
2 tsp. vanilla

Pour hot water over dates, add soda and mash. Set aside. Cream sugar and butter. Add eggs and beat well. Use half of the flour to coat the pecans. Add the remaining half of the flour alternately with the date mixture. Stir in the flour-coated pecans. Add vanilla and blend completely. Pour into a greased and floured tube pan and bake at 300° for about 1-1/2 hours, or until toothpick inserted comes out clean.

Dump Cake
Super easy and tangy tasty!

1 (22 oz.) can cherry pie
   filling
1 small can crushed
   pineapple (with juice)
1 pkg. yellow cake mix
1 c. melted butter
1 (3-1/2 oz.) can coconut
1 c. chopped nuts

Layer ingredients in order. Do not stir. Bake at 350° for 1 hour.

Five Flavor Cake
Emma McNutt of Thorton makes this flavorful cake to take when they travel.

2 sticks oleo
3 c. sugar
1/2 c. vegetable oil
5 eggs, beaten well
1 tsp. coconut flavoring
1 tsp. butter flavoring
1 tsp. lemon flavoring
1 tsp. rum flavoring
1 tsp. vanilla flavoring
1 c. milk
3 c. flour
1/2 tsp. baking powder

In large bowl, cream oleo and sugar. Add oil, eggs, flavorings, and milk. Beat well. Gradually add flour and baking powder. Beat until smooth. Bake at 350° for 1-1/2 hours.

ICING:
1 c. powdered sugar
1 tsp. each of the 5
   flavorings
3 Tbsp. milk

Mix thoroughly and spread on warm cake.

Fresh Apple Cake
One of Willie Mae Caswell's recipes and Bobby's favorite

4 c. peeled, diced apples
1 c. chopped pecans
2 c. sugar
3 c. flour
1/2 tsp. nutmeg
1/2 tsp. cinnamon
1/2 tsp. salt
2 tsp. soda
1 c. oil
1 tsp. vanilla
2 eggs

Mix apples, pecans, and sugar and let stand 1 hour. Stir often. Add dry ingredients to apples. Then add oil, vanilla, and eggs. Do not use a mixer. Pour batter into greased, floured tube pan. Bake 1 hour and 15 minutes at 350°.

Fresh Coconut Cake
This recipe from Betsy Pridmore requires patience, but the wait is sure worthwhile.

2 c. fresh frozen coconut
2 c. sour cream
2 c. sugar
1 box yellow cake mix

Mix coconut, sour cream, and sugar and set aside. Bake yellow cake mix in a 9″ × 13″ pan following package directions. Let cool and cut into 4 equal portions. Ice cake with the set aside mixture. Seal in a Tupperware container and refrigerate for 4 days.

Lemon Fruit Cake by Bertha Gardenhire
A classic recipe by a classy cook

1 lb. butter
1 lb. brown sugar
6 eggs, separated
4 c. flour
1 tsp. baking powder
1-1/2 oz. lemon extract
1/2 lb. candied cherries, diced
1/2 lb. candied pineapple, diced
1 lb. pecans, chopped

Mix butter and sugar. Add egg yolks, 2 cups flour, baking powder, and lemon extract. Add remaining 2 cups flour to cherries, pineapple, and pecans and coat well. Pour second mixture over the first and mix with hands. Beat egg whites and pour over mixture. Mixture will be very thick so you will need to mix by kneading. Put mixture into a tube pan and let it stand overnight before baking. Bake at 300° for 3 to 3-1/2 hours.

Hershey Cake

A recipe of Terry Scott, who is well-known at Woodway First Baptist Church as a terrific cook.

2 sticks butter or
  margarine
2 c. sugar
4 eggs
8 plain Hershey bars,
  melted
1-1/2 tsp. soda
1 c. buttermilk
2-1/2 c. flour
1/4 tsp. salt
2 tsp. vanilla
1 c. pecans, chopped

Beat butter and sugar well. Add eggs, one at a time and beat well after each egg. Add melted Hersheys to mixture. Add soda to buttermilk. Mix salt with flour. Alternating buttermilk and flour, add to above mixture. Add vanilla and pecans and blend thoroughly. Bake in tube pan for 1-1/2 hours at 350°.

Fresh Pear Cake

Virginia Goggans likes to make this for Ronn and Alan.

2 c. sugar
1-1/2 c. Crisco oil
3 eggs, well beaten
3 c. pears, grated
1 Tbsp. soda
1 tsp. salt
3 c. flour
1 c. pecans, chopped

Mix all ingredients. Bake in a bundt pan at 350° for 1 hour and 15 minutes.

GLAZE:
1-1/2 c. powdered sugar
2 - 4 tsp. milk
1/2 c. pecans

Blend sugar and milk and add pecans. Pour over warm cake.

Hell Cake
Contrary to the title, this has a heavenly taste.

1 box Duncan Hines
   Butter Cake mix
4 eggs
1/2 c. oil
1 can Mandarian oranges,
   undrained

Mix and beat like hell. Bake in 3 layer pans at 350° for 30 minutes.

ICING:
2 boxes lemon instant
   pudding
1 large can crushed
   pineapple
1 large carton Cool Whip

Beat and spread over cake. Refrigerate cake.

Hot Milk Cake
Wanda Henson made this every Saturday for Sunday lunch when her children were small.

5 egg whites
2 c. flour
1/2 tsp. salt
2 c. sugar
5 tsp. baking powder
2 c. milk, scalded

Beat egg whites separately. Sift dry ingredients 6 times. Pour milk over dry ingredients and beat. Fold in egg whites. Bake in greased and floured 9″ × 13″ dish for 30 minutes at 350°.

ICING:
1-1/2 c. sugar
1/2 stick oleo
1 c. milk
1 tsp. vanilla

Cook until mixture forms soft string and pour over cooled cake.

Hummingbird Cake from Hereford
From a friend of Aunt Mary Helen

1-1/2 c. Wesson oil
2 c. sugar
2 eggs
1 tsp. vanilla
3 c. flour
1 tsp. soda
1 tsp. cinnamon
1/2 tsp. salt
1 (8 oz.) can crushed
  pineapple
1/2 c. coconut
2 bananas, diced
1 c. chopped pecans

Do not use a mixer for this cake. Mix oil, sugar, eggs, and vanilla. Then add sifted dry ingredients. Mix well. Then add fruit and pecans and mix. Bake in greased and floured tube or bundt pan at 350° for 1-1/2 hours. Cool completely before removing from pan.

Italian Cream Cake
Virginia Goggans makes this by request from her family.

1/2 c. Crisco
1 stick oleo or butter
2 c. sugar
5 eggs, separated
1 c. buttermilk
1 tsp. soda
2 c. flour
1/2 tsp. salt
1 tsp. vanilla
1 can coconut

Cream Crisco and oleo, add sugar slowly and beat well. Add egg yolks. Alternately add buttermilk and dry ingredients, then add vanilla. Beat egg whites until stiff; fold into other mixture. Add coconut and blend well. Bake at 350° for 25 minutes. Will make 3 layers. Cake will freeze well.

ICING:
1 (8 oz.) pkg. cream cheese
1 stick butter
1/4 tsp. salt
1 box powdered sugar
1 c. pecans, chopped

Beat cream cheese and butter together. Add salt and powdered sugar and mix well. Blend in pecans.

Lemon Cake

Christine uses this for Jesus' birthday cake every Christmas.

1 Duncan Hines Yellow
  Cake Mix
1/2 c. liquid shortening
4 eggs
1 c. hot water
1 pkg. Lemon or Vanilla
  Instant Pudding

Blend all ingredients for 4 minutes and bake at 350°for 45 minutes to 1 hour in greased and floured tube pan.

 ICING:
2/3 c. sugar
2-2/3 Tbsp. water
1/3 c. white Karo
2 egg whites
1 tsp. vanilla
1 can coconut (opt.)

Mix sugar, water, Karo, and cook until it makes a thread. Beat egg whites until they make a peak. Add mixture to beaten eggs slowly. When you have used about half the mixture, cook the other half a little longer then add. Let icing cool some before putting on cake. (I use one can of coconut on icing.)

Marble Chocolate Chip Cupcakes

Charles sure likes Tracy's cupcakes!

1 (8 oz.) pkg. cream cheese
1-1/2 c. sugar
1 egg, slightly beaten
1/8 tsp. salt
1 (6 oz.) pkg. semi-sweet
  chocolate chips
1-1/2 c. flour
1 tsp. soda
1/2 tsp. salt
1/4 tsp. cocoa
1 c. water
1/2 c. vegetable oil
1 Tbsp. vinegar
1 tsp. vanilla

Combine cream cheese and 1/2 cup sugar and beat until smooth. Add egg, 1/8 teaspoon salt, and chocolate chips. Stir well and set aside.

Combine flour, remaining 1 cup sugar, soda, 1/2 teaspoon salt, and cocoa. Add water, oil, vinegar, and vanilla. Stir until well blended. Spoon batter into paper-lined muffin pans, filling half full. Spoon a heaping tablespoon of cream cheese mixture into center of each cupcake. Bake at 350° for 25 to 30 minutes or until cupcakes test done. Makes about 18 cupcakes.

Mayonnaise Cake

Fern says that this is one of Noel's favorites.

1 c. mayonnaise
1 c. sugar
3 Tbsp. cocoa
1 tsp. soda
2 c. flour
1 c. warm water
1 c. pecans, chopped
1 tsp. vanilla

Mix ingredients in order listed. Bake in bundt pan at 350° for 40 to 50 minutes. May also be baked in layers.

Milk Chocolate Cake

A special treat from Fern for Brenda, Janie, and Regina.

1/2 c. oleo
1-1/2 c. sugar
2 eggs
1 c. buttermilk
2 c. flour
2 squares baking chocolate
1 Tbsp. vinegar
1 tsp. soda
1/4 tsp. salt
1 tsp. vanilla

Cream oleo and sugar, add unbeaten eggs, beating after each. Add buttermilk alternating with flour. Then add chocolate which has been melted in top of double boiler along with a bit of Crisco. Dissolve soda in vinegar, add salt and vanilla. Add to cake mixture and blend well. Pour into 2 greased 9" cake pans and bake at 350°.

FILLING FOR BETWEEN LAYERS:
3/4 c. buttermilk
3/4 c. sugar
3 Tbsp. flour
1/8 tsp. salt
2 egg yolks, beaten
1 tsp. vanilla

In a saucepan, combine buttermilk, sugar, flour, and salt. Cook 6 to 8 minutes, then pour over egg yolks, a little at a time. (Be careful not to lump the egg yolks.) Cook this mixture about 4 minutes or until thick. Add vanilla and set aside to cool.

CHOCOLATE FLUFF ICING:
4 Tbsp. butter
3/4 c. powdered sugar
1-1/2 squares chocolate, melted
1 tsp. vanilla
1/8 tsp. salt
2 egg whites
3/4 c. powdered sugar

Cream butter, then add sugar, chocolate, vanilla, and salt. Beat egg whites until stiff and add powdered sugar. Mix with chocolate mixture and cover top and sides of cake. Add more powdered sugar if necessary.

Milky Way Cake

1/2 tsp. soda
1 c. buttermilk
2 sticks oleo
8 Milky Way bars, regular
   size
2 c. sugar
4 eggs
2-1/2 c. flour
1 tsp. vanilla
1 c. chopped pecans

Dissolve soda in buttermilk. Melt 1 stick oleo with candy bars. Cool. Cream sugar with remaining oleo. Add eggs, one at a time, beating well after each. Add flour alternately with buttermilk mixture and follow with vanilla, pecans, and candy mixture. Bake in sheet pan for 1 hour at 325°.

 ICING:
2 c. sugar
1 c. canned milk
1/2 stick oleo
1 (8 oz.) pkg. chocolate
   chips
1 pint marshmallow cream
1 tsp. vanilla

In a saucepan, mix sugar, milk, and oleo. Cook 4 minutes. Add chocolate chips, marshmallow cream, and vanilla. Stir well and spread on cake.

Mollie Shofner's Coconut Cake

Most famous cake in Lamesa!

1 box Duncan Hines white
   cake mix
3 eggs
1-1/4 c. water
1/3 c. oil

Mix above ingredients and bake in 3 layers.

 ICING:
1-1/2 c. water
2-1/2 c. sugar
8 egg whites, beaten stiff
Coconut

Boil water, then add sugar. Boil until this makes a thread when it runs off a spoon. Pour over the egg whites. Put between layers and add plenty of coconut. Cover top and sides of cake and sprinkle with coconut.

Pineapple-Coconut (7-Up) Cake

We've enjoyed Bertha Gardenhire's recipe for years.

1 box Duncan Hines
　Lemon Supreme cake
　mix
1 (5-1/2 oz.) box lemon
　instant pudding mix
3/4 c. Crisco oil
4 eggs
1 (10 oz.) bottle 7-Up

Mix and pour into a 9″ × 13″ pan that has been sprayed with Baker's Joy. Bake at 350° until done, about 35 minutes. This may fall in the middle.

ICING:
1-1/2 c. sugar
2 Tbsp. flour
1 small can crushed
　pineapple
1 stick butter
3 egg yolks, beaten
1 small can coconut
1/2 c. chopped pecans

Mix sugar and flour, then add pineapple, butter, and egg yolks. Cook together until thick. Add coconut and pecans. Spread on cake while hot.

Pineapple Sheet Cake

One of Patsy Sanders' recipes and one of Bryan's favorites

1-1/2 c. sugar
1 (15-1/4 oz.) can crushed
　pineapple, drained and
　liquid reserved
2 eggs
2 c. flour
1 tsp. soda
1/2 tsp. salt
2 tsp. vanilla

Mix sugar and liquid from pineapple, add eggs. Add dry ingredients, pineapple, and vanilla. Bake in a sheet pan 25 to 30 minutes at 350°.

ICING:
1 c. sugar
1 stick butter
1 small can milk
2 tsp. vanilla
3/4 c. pecans, chopped
1/2 can coconut

In a saucepan, mix sugar, butter, and milk. Boil for 2 minutes. Add vanilla. Sprinkle coconut and pecans over cake, then pour icing over cake.

Pineapple Upside-Down Cake
Little Mother's version of a traditional dessert

TOPPING:
1/2 c. brown sugar
3 Tbsp. butter
6 or 7 pineapple rings,
    reserve juice
6 or 7 Maraschino cherries
1/2 c. pecans, chopped

Use large iron skillet. Heat sugar and butter until they melt. Place pineapple rings in bottom of mixture and put one cherry in center of each pineapple. Sprinkle pecans over mixture.

PINEAPPLE CAKE:
3/4 c. butter
1 c. sugar
2 eggs
2 c. flour
1 tsp. baking powder
1 tsp. soda
1/8 tsp. salt
3/4 c. pineapple juice

Beat butter and sugar well, add slightly beaten eggs. Sift together flour, baking powder, soda, and salt. Alternately add flour and pineapple juice. Mix well. Pour over pineapples in iron skillet. Bake in preheated oven at 350° for 45 minutes to 1 hour.

Poppyseed Cake
A Fort Stockton delicacy from Nancy Askew Warren

1 yellow cake mix
1 pkg. instant butter pecan
    pudding mix
4 eggs
3/4 c. oil
1 c. water
1/4 c. poppyseeds

Beat all ingredients for 2 minutes at medium speed. Bake in well-greased and floured bundt pan at 350° for 1 hour.

Six Egg Cake
Ronnie Askew's favorite cake

1 c. Crisco (or 2 sticks
    oleo)
2 c. sugar
6 eggs
1 tsp. vanilla
Dash salt
2 c. flour (sifted)

Cream Crisco and sugar. Add eggs one at a time and beat at least one minute after each egg. Add vanilla, salt, and flour. Blend well. Bake in a greased and floured bundt pan for 1 hour at 325°.

Pound Nut Cake

A lovely lady, Mrs. Elsie Brewer, served this cake to family and friends.

2 c. sugar
2 sticks butter
5 eggs
2 c. flour
1 Tbsp. vanilla
1 tsp. almond extract
2 c. pecans, chopped

Cream sugar and butter. Add eggs, one at a time. Add flour, saving small amount to go over pecans. Add flavorings and nuts. Bake in a greased and floured tube cake pan for 1 hour and 15 minutes at 300°.

Prism Cake

This is a beautiful, colorful dessert.

1 pkg. orange Jello
1 pkg. strawberry Jello
1 pkg. lime Jello
4-1/2 c. water
1/2 c. sugar
1 c. pineapple juice
1 pkg. lemon Jello
1/2 c. whipped cream
1/2 Tbsp. vanilla
1 box vanilla wafers

Separately dissolve each of the first three packages of Jello in 1-1/2 cups boiling water. Keep separate and congeal in flat pans. Cut into small squares. Mix sugar, pineapple juice, and lemon Jello. Heat until Jello is completely dissolved. Refrigerate until slightly congealed. Fold in whipped cream and add vanilla. Then fold in the diced Jello squares. Line a Pyrex dish with vanilla wafers and pour the Jello mixture over the wafers. Let this congeal.

Rum Cake

One of Sirita's specialties

1/2 lb. oleo
1-3/4 c. sugar
1 tsp. vanilla
5 eggs
2 c. flour

Cream oleo and sugar. Add vanilla then add eggs, one at a time. Add flour and mix well. Bake in a tube pan at 325° for 1 hour.

ICING:
1/2 c. water
1/2 c. sugar
1/2 c. white Karo
1 tsp. rum extract

Bring water, sugar, and Karo to a good boil. Cool and add rum extract. Make holes in top of cake with a knife. Pour icing over cake slowly and let the icing run into the holes. Use all icing.

Prune Cake
From Virginia Goggans' Private Collection

1 c. Wesson oil
1-1/2 c. sugar
1 c. buttermilk
2 c. flour
1 tsp. salt
1 tsp. cinnamon
1 tsp. allspice
1/2 tsp. soda
1 c. pecans, chopped
1 c. cooked, mashed
   prunes or dates

Beat oil, sugar, and buttermilk. Then add remaining ingredients. Pour into loaf or tube pan and cook at 350° for 45 minutes.

ICING:
1 c. sugar
1/2 tsp. soda
1/2 c. buttermilk
1 Tbsp. butter or
   margarine

Mix ingredients and pour immediately over hot cake.

Pumpkin Cake
Bobby's request for every holiday!

2 c. sugar
4 eggs
2 c. flour
1 tsp. salt
1-1/4 c. Wesson Oil
1 can pumpkin (2 cups)
2 tsp. soda
3 tsp. cinnamon

Mix all ingredients and bake in tube pan for 1 hour at 325°.

ICING:
1 stick oleo
1 (3 oz.) pkg. cream
   cheese, softened
1 box powdered sugar (4 c.
   sifted)
1 c. finely chopped pecans
1 Tbsp. vanilla

Whip oleo and cream cheese. Add sugar, pecans, and vanilla.

Red Cocoa Cake

Sirita gets hugs from Brandie and Bryan when she bakes this cake.

4 Tbsp. cocoa
1 tsp. soda
1 c. hot water
1-1/2 c. sugar
1/2 c. Crisco
1/2 c. sour cream
2 eggs
2 c. flour
1/2 tsp. salt
1 tsp. vanilla

Dissolve cocoa and soda in hot water. Let cool. Cream sugar, Crisco, and sour cream. Add eggs, one at a time. Then mix flour, salt, and vanilla. Alternate flour with cocoa mixture. Grease and flour two 9″ layer pans or one oblong pan. Pour batter into prepared pans and bake at 350° about 25 minutes.

ICING:
1 stick butter
1/4 c. cocoa
1 box powdered sugar
1/4 c. milk

Place butter and cocoa in saucepan, and bring to a boil. Add mixture to sugar and mix well. Add milk gradually and blend. Spread over cake.

Red Velvet Cake

Linda's Christmas treat for the Caswell clan

1/2 c. shortening
1-1/2 c. sugar
2 eggs
2 oz. red food coloring
2 Tbsp. cocoa
1 tsp. salt
2-1/4 c. flour
1 c. buttermilk
1 tsp. vanilla
1 tsp. soda
1 Tbsp. vinegar

Do not beat as you mix ingredients, but blend gently. Cream shortening, sugar, and eggs. In a separate dish, blend food coloring and cocoa, then add to creamed mixture. Add salt and flour and blend. Add buttermilk and vanilla and blend. Add soda and blend completely, but do not beat. Last, add vinegar and blend. Bake in greased layer pans for 30 minutes at 350°.

BUTTER CREAM
FROSTING:
3 Tbsp. flour
1 c. milk
1 c. sugar
1 c. margarine, softened at
  room temperature
1 tsp. vanilla

It is very important that the ingredients be at the correct temperature for this recipe to be a success. Cook flour and milk over very low heat until it is thick. Let it cool completely. (It must be completely cooled.) Cream sugar, margarine, and vanilla until it is fluffy. Add completely cooled mixture to creamed mixture and beat until it is like whipped cream. HINT: Do not soften the margarine in the microwave.

Rum Cake by Lottie Walker

1 c. oleo
2 c. sugar
4 eggs (I separate and beat
  whites and add last)
3 c. flour
1/2 tsp. soda
1/2 tsp. baking powder
1/4 tsp. salt
1 c. buttermilk
1 tsp. rum flavoring
1/2 c. pecans, chopped

Cream oleo and sugar; add eggs one at a time. Sift dry ingredients together and add alternately with buttermilk. Add flavoring. Sprinkle chopped pecans in bottom of floured tube pan. Pour in batter and cook at 325° for about 1 hour. Let cool 10 minutes, then pour on sauce while still in pan.

 SAUCE:
1 c. water
2 c. sugar
1 Tbsp. butter
2 Tbsp. rum extract

Mix water, sugar, and butter and bring to boil. Let boil 1 to 2 minutes. Add rum extract. Pour around edges of cake until absorbed.

Sour Cream Pound Cake

Grandma Morgan serves this to Ben and Clay at Christmas.

2 sticks oleo, softened
3 c. sugar
6 eggs, separated
3 c. sifted flour
1/2 pt. sour cream
1/4 tsp. soda
1 tsp. vanilla
1 tsp. butter flavoring
1 tsp. almond flavoring

Cream oleo and sugar. Add egg yolks, one at a time and beat after each one. Measure flour and set aside. In a separate dish mix sour cream, soda, and flavorings.

Add flour and sour cream mixtures alternately to the first mixture. Fold in 6 stiffly beaten egg whites. Pour into a greased and floured tube pan. Bake at 325° for 1 hour and 10 minutes.

Variations: 1 cup coconut and coconut flavoring; lemon flavoring; 2 small cans crushed pineapple, drained; nuts. To add any of these, just dump in the addition on the last flour addition.

Strawberry Cake
Brandie's favorite

1 box white cake mix
1 pkg. strawberry Jello
3 eggs
1/2 c. water
1/2 c. strawberries, thawed
3/4 c. Wesson oil

Mix all ingredients and bake in two layers for 30 minutes at 350°.

ICING:
1/2 stick butter (4 Tbsp.)
1 box powdered sugar (4 c. sifted)
1/2 c. strawberries, thawed

Cream butter and sugar. Add strawberries and mix thoroughly.

The Cake That Doesn't Stay Around
A new recipe from Ruby Martin of Brownfield and sure to become a popular choice.

3 c. flour
2 c. sugar
1 tsp. soda
1 tsp. cinnamon
1 tsp. salt
3 eggs
1-1/2 c. Crisco oil
1 (8-1/2 oz.) can crushed pineapple, drained
1 c. chopped pecans
2 c. mashed bananas
1-1/2 tsp. vanilla

Mix all dry ingredients together and make a well in the bowl. Add eggs, oil, pineapple, pecans, bananas, and vanilla. Stir, but do not beat. Bake in greased and floured bundt pan at 350° for 1 hour and 10 minutes, or until done. Can be frozen.

ICING:
1 c. brown sugar, packed
1 Tbsp. cornstarch
2 Tbsp. milk
2 Tbsp. butter
1/2 c. flaked coconut

In 1-quart casserole blend together brown sugar, cornstarch, and milk. Add butter. Microwave at high 2 minutes, stirring after 1 minute. Pour over cooled cake and sprinkle with flaked coconut.

Vanilla Wafer Cake
Jean Dorman's fantabulous dessert

2 c. sugar
1/2 tsp. salt
1/2 tsp. baking powder
1/2 tsp. soda
2 sticks oleo, melted
6 eggs
1 can coconut
1 c. chopped pecans
1/2 c. sweet milk
12 oz. box vanilla wafers,
   crushed

Mix sugar, salt, baking powder, and soda. Blend with oleo. Add one egg at a time, beating after each one. Add coconut and pecans, then milk. Add vanilla wafers. Pour into a greased and floured bundt pan and bake 1-1/2 hours at 300°.

ICING:
6 Tbsp. melted butter
2/3 c. brown sugar
1/4 c. Pet milk
1 c. coconut
1/2 tsp. vanilla
1/2 c. chopped pecans

Mix all ingredients well. Spread on warm cake. Broil about 2 minutes.

Watergate Cake
Ruby Martin's St. Patrick's Day dessert for William

1 pkg. white cake mix
3/4 c. oil
3 eggs
1 c. 7-Up or Club soda
1 (3-1/2 oz.) pkg. pistachio
   instant pudding
1 c. chopped nuts
1/2 c. coconut

Mix ingredients and pour into a greased and floured 9″ × 13″ pan. Bake at 350° for 40 minutes.

ICING:
2 pkg. dry whipped
   topping mix (Dream
   Whip)
1-1/2 c. milk
1 (3-1/2 oz.) pkg. pistachio
   instant pudding
1/2 c. coconut
3/4 c. chopped pecans

Beat topping mix, milk, and pudding until thick. Spread on cake and sprinkle coconut and pecans over top.

White Chocolate Cake
Virginia Goggans' elegant and delicious cake

2 c. sugar
1 c. shortening
5 egg yolks
1 c. buttermilk
2-1/2 c. flour
1 tsp. soda
1 tsp. salt
4 oz. white chocolate
1/2 c. water
1 tsp. vanilla
5 egg whites, stiffly beaten

Cream together sugar, shortening, and egg yolks. Add buttermilk. Sift together flour, soda, and salt. Add to mixture. Melt chocolate in water and cool, and add vanilla and stir into above mixture. Fold in egg whites. Bake in 3 layers at 350° about 25 to 30 minutes.

ICING:
1 stick oleo
1 c. sugar
3 egg yolks
1 large can evaporated
   milk
2 c. coconut
1 c. chopped pecans
1 tsp. vanilla

Melt oleo. Add sugar, egg yolks, and milk. Cook over medium heat, stirring constantly until thick. Remove from heat. Add coconut, pecans, and vanilla. Cool and spread on cake.

Yum Yum Cake
Joe's birthday cake from Virginia

2 c. flour
1-1/4 tsp. soda
1/4 tsp. salt
2 c. sugar
2 eggs
1 tsp. vanilla
1 large can crushed
   pineapple, undrained

Mix together and bake at 350° for 30 minutes in 2 (8") cake pans.

FROSTING:
1 stick oleo, melted
1 can coconut
1 small can evaporative
   milk
1 c. chopped pecans
1 c. sugar mixed with 3
   Tbsp. flour

Mix and cook until thick. Put on cake while warm.

Cake of All Cakes

Mothers of young children can certainly identify with this one!

Light the oven. Get out bowl, spoons and ingredients. Grease the pan. Crack nuts. Remove 18 blocks and 7 toys from the kitchen table. Measure 2 cups of flour. Remove Kelly's hands from the flour. Wash flour off. Measure one more cup of flour to replace the flour on the floor. Put the flour, baking powder and salt in a sifter. Get the dust pan and brush up pieces of bowl which Kelly knocked on the floor. Get another bowl. Answer the doorbell. Return to the kitchen and remove Kelly's hands from the bowl. Wash Kelly. Get out egg. Answer phone. Return. Take out greased pan. Remove pinch of salt from pan. Look for Kelly. Get another pan and grease it. Answer the phone. Return to the kitchen and find Kelly. Remove the grimy hands from the bowl. Wash off shortening. Take up greased pan and find 1/2" of nutshells in it. Head for Kelly who flees, knocking bowl off the table. Wash kitchen floor, wash the table. Wash the walls, wash the dishes. (CALL THE BAKERY AND ORDER A CAKE.) Lie Down.
Anonymous

Caramel Frosting

1/2 c. butter
1 c. brown sugar
1/4 tsp. salt
1/4 c. milk
2-1/2 c. sifted powdered
   sugar
1/2 tsp. vanilla

Melt butter in a large saucepan. Blend in brown sugar and salt. Cook over low heat for 2 minutes, stirring constantly. Add milk and continue stirring until mixture comes to a boil. Remove from heat. Gradually blend in sugar. Add vanilla and mix well. Thin with cream if necessary.

Caramel Icing

1-1/2 c. brown sugar
1/4 c. Carnation milk
2 Tbsp. butter

Bring to boil and boil three minutes, stirring constantly. Beat until creamy and thick enough to spread. Add a little cream if necessary to make it easy to spread.

Chocolate Icing

2 c. sugar
2 Tbsp. cocoa
1 stick butter
1/2 c. milk
1/4 c. white Karo
1 tsp. vanilla

In a small saucepan, mix sugar and cocoa, then add butter. Cook over low heat, stirring, until butter is melted and ingredients are blended. Add milk, Karo, and vanilla and cook 3 minutes. Cool and spread on cake.

Seven Minute Frosting

2 egg whites
1-1/2 c. sugar
1-1/2 tsp. light corn syrup
  or cream of tartar
1/3 c. cold water
Dash salt
1 tsp. vanilla

Place all ingredients, except vanilla, in double boiler. Cook, beating constantly with beater, until mixture forms peaks, or about 7 minutes. Remove from heat and add vanilla. Beat until this reaches spreading consistency.

Cheesecake
Thanks to Pam Rieathbaum of San Antonio for this fantastic recipe.

CRUST:
1-2/3 c. graham cracker
   crumbs
2 Tbsp. sugar
1-1/3 tsp. cinnamon
2/3 stick butter, melted (5-
   1/3 Tbsp.)

Mix all ingredients and press on bottom and sides of Pyrex dish. Chill for at least 30 minutes.

FILLING:
3 (8 oz.) pkg. cream
   cheese, softened
1 c. sugar
3 eggs
1 pint sour cream (2 c.)
3 Tbsp. sugar
1 tsp. vanilla

Beat cream cheese and 1 cup sugar. The longer you beat it, the creamier, richer, and higher it will be. Add eggs one at a time and beat well after each one. Put in crumb crust and bake 20 minutes at 375°. Remove and let cool completely. Mix sour cream, 3 tablespoons sugar, and vanilla. Spread on cake and bake at 500° for 5 to 10 minutes. It is best if made the day before, but is good anytime. Serve with topping of your choice.

Cheesecake
A favorite of Frances Ray of Lubbock

1 c. graham cracker
   crumbs
1/4 c. sugar
1/2 c. melted butter
2 (8 oz.) pkg. cream
   cheese, softened
1/2 c. sugar
3 whole eggs
2 c. sour cream
1-1/4 c. sugar
1 tsp. vanilla
Almonds (opt.)

Combine graham crackers, sugar, and melted butter. Pour into a 10" pie pan, press to shape pie shell. Bake 5 minutes at 300° and cool. Beat softened cream cheese until smooth, add sugar and eggs, continue beating until well blended. Pour into baked crust and bake for 20 minutes at 300°. Remove from oven and let cool to room temperature. When pie has cooled, combine sour cream, sugar, and vanilla. Pour gently over cheesecake. Sprinkle with almonds if desired. Bake 10 minutes more at 300°. Cool to room temperature. Chill 24 hours.

Cheesecake

CRUST:
1/4 lb. butter or margarine
1-1/2 c. graham cracker
  crumbs
1/3 c. powdered sugar

Melt butter and add to graham cracker crumbs and sugar. Line the bottom of a spring form pan, packing firmly.

FILLING::
1 c. sugar
3 (8 oz.) pkg. cream cheese
1 generous tsp. vanilla
  flavoring
4 eggs
1 pt. sour cream
1 (21 oz.) can pie filling

Blend sugar, cream cheese, vanilla, and eggs. Pour into spring form pan (the crust is as yet unbaked) and bake in preheated oven at 350° for 50 minutes. Remove from oven and top with sour cream and return to oven for another 5 minutes. Let cake cool. Top with pie filling. Chill overnight.

Individual Cheesecakes

1 box vanilla wafers
2 (8 oz.) pkg. cream cheese
2 eggs
3/4 c. sugar
1 tsp. vanilla
1 can cherry pie filling

Place 1 wafer in a cupcake liner in a muffin pan. Beat cream cheese, eggs, sugar, and vanilla. Fill each cup half full. Bake at 350° for 12 minutes. Let cool and chill. Put cherry pie filling on top of each cheesecake after completely chilled.

Mini-Tart Cheesecakes

The ultimate in elegance and taste

3/4 c. milk
2 tsp. vanilla
2 eggs
1 c. sugar
1/2 c. Bisquick
2 (8 oz.) pkg. cream cheese
1 can pie filling

Mix milk, vanilla, eggs, sugar, and Bisquick in food processor or blender, then add cream cheese and re-blend. Spray mini-muffin tins with Baker's Joy and fill 3/4 full. Bake at 350° for 20 minutes or until slightly brown around the edges. COOL COMPLETELY IN PANS. Can freeze these before topping with pie filling. Makes about 72.

Almond Bark Clusters
Quick, easy, and delicious!

1 (24 oz.) pkg. white
    almond bark
2 c. chopped pecans
2 c. pretzels
2 c. Rice Krispies cereal
2 c. Captain Crunch cereal

Melt almond bark in microwave in a large bowl. Add other ingredients and mix until well coated. Drop by spoonfuls onto wax paper.

Apricot Coconut Balls
A very tart dessert

2 lb. dried apricots
3 cans coconut
1 can Eagle Brand milk
2 c. powdered sugar

Run apricots through a food chopper. Add coconut and Eagle Brand milk. Blend thoroughly. Refrigerate overnight. Form into 1″ balls. Roll in powdered sugar. DO NOT COOK.

Chocolate Spiders
A Halloween treat that Ben and Clay love

1/2 pkg. chocolate bark
1 pkg. chow mein noodles
1 c. salted peanuts

Melt chocolate bark in microwave on medium setting about 1-1/2 minutes. Melt completely. Add noodles and nuts. Stir until well-coated. Drop by spoonfuls on wax paper.

Chocolate Covered Coconut Candy

1 stick oleo
2 cans coconut
4 c. chopped pecans
1 can Eagle Brand milk
3 tsp. vanilla
2 boxes sifted powdered
  sugar
1-1/2 squares parafin
2 pkg. chocolate chips
  (small size)

Melt oleo and pour over coconut. Add pecans, Eagle Brand milk, and vanilla. Mix well. Add sugar and continue mixing. Shape into balls, dip in chocolate coating, and put on wax paper.

CHOCOLATE COATING:
Melt parafin in microwave in a large butter dish and then add chocolate chips. Watch the parafin closely as it burns easily. The nice thing about using the butter dish is throwing the dish away when you are through.

Chocolate Oatmeal Fudge

2nd Place Howard County Fair 1986 submitted by Linda Womack of Lubbock

2 c. sugar
3 Tbsp. cocoa
1/2 c. milk
1/2 c. butter (1 stick)
1/2 c. crunchy peanut
  butter
1 Tbsp. vanilla
3 c. Quick oatmeal

Combine sugar, cocoa, milk, and butter in saucepan and bring to a boil. Boil 1 minute. Remove from heat and add peanut butter, vanilla, and oatmeal. Work fast and drop by teaspoonfuls onto wax paper. Let cool.

Cocoa Fudge

The old-fashioned, great-tasting kind

2/3 c. cocoa
3 c. sugar
1/8 tsp. salt
1-1/2 c. milk
4-1/2 Tbsp. butter
1 tsp. vanilla
3/4 c. chopped pecans

Mix cocoa, sugar, and salt. Add milk. Bring to a boil, stirring frequently. Cook to soft ball stage. Remove from heat and add butter and vanilla. Add chopped pecans and pour into a buttered dish and let set until firm.

HINT:
To test for soft ball stage, drop a small amount into a cup of cold water and it should form a soft ball.

"Creamy" Pecan Pralines

Dr. Jim Vick serves this at Christmas bridge parties in Waco.

2 lb. light brown sugar
2 small cans of evaporated
  milk
4 Tbsp. Karo Syrup, light
4 Tbsp. water
1 stick butter or oleo,
  (1/4 lb.)
2 tsp. vanilla, can't beat
  Adams Extract
3 c. shelled pecans

Boil together sugar, milk, Karo syrup, and water until the soft ball stage (I use a candy thermometer). Usually go a degree or two past soft ball. Remove from heat and add butter or oleo. Then let it cool some and add the vanilla. Stir some and let it cool some more, then add the pecans. Drop by spoonfuls onto wax paper, about the size of a silver dollar. Will make 50 to 60 pralines of this size. If the candy cools down too much and you can't pour it onto the wax paper, simply reheat the mixture until it flows again. Also at the end you may have candy and no pecans left. I usually have a few extra pecans and I add them to the candy to come out even.

Date Chews

1 c. dates
1 c. dried apricots
1 c. pecans
1/2 c. coconut
2 tsp. cream
3 tsp. vanilla
1/2 c. brown sugar
1/2 c. powdered sugar

Put dates, apricots, pecans, and coconut through food chopper, using medium blade. Add cream and vanilla and blend together. Roll into small balls between palms of hands until firm and smooth. Coat each ball with brown sugar, then with powdered sugar. Yields about 2 dozen.

Orange Pralines

Yummy, yummy!

2 c. white sugar
3 Tbsp. white Karo
3 Tbsp. grated orange peel
3/4 c. fresh orange juice
1-1/2 c. pecans, chopped

Boil first 4 ingredients until a soft ball stage, 230°. Add pecans and beat until creamy. Drop by spoonfuls on waxed paper. Makes about 4 dozen. If mixture becomes too stiff to drop, add orange juice, 1 teaspoon at a time until soft enough.

Divinity

Betty Askew has made this for lots of family gatherings.

2 c. sugar
1/2 c. water
1/2 c. white Karo
2 egg whites
1/2 tsp. vanilla
1/2 to 3/4 c. pecans,
    chopped

Cook sugar, water, and Karo until it will thread. Beat egg whites until they peak. Gradually add cooked mixture to beaten egg whites. Pour about 1/2 mixture into eggs and cook the remaining 1/2 about 3 minutes more. Gradually add remaining mixture to eggs. Add vanilla and pecans. Beat well. Let set in bowl until it completely cools and place on wax paper with teaspoon to form a ball.

Date Nut Candy

Aunt Sister's treat — Arlys' favorite

2 c. milk
1/8 tsp. salt
4 c. sugar
1 small pkg. chopped dates
1 stick butter
2 c. chopped pecans
2 tsp. vanilla

Cook milk, salt, and sugar to a soft ball, then add dates. Cook until thick. Add butter and let set until melted. Then add pecans and vanilla and stir thoroughly. Let cool in pan. While cooling, wet a cheesecloth about 12" × 24". Pour mixture in dampened cheesecloth and form into a long roll about 1" in diameter. Wrap in cheesecloth and refrigerate for 3 hours. Remove and slice in 1/4" slices to serve.

HINT:
A lightweight cotton cloth can be substituted for the cheesecloth.

Easter Treats

A delightful and tasty treat for children's parties

1 (1 lb.) pkg. white
    almond bark
1 (5 oz.) can chow mein
    noodles
1 pkg. M & M peanut
    candies

Melt almond bark in microwave for 1 minute and stir. If necessary, heat again for 15 seconds. Add noodles and stir gently until noodles are coated. Drop by tablespoonfuls onto wax paper and press 1 M & M into the center of each. These should resemble a little bird's nest. Makes 40 to 45 treats.

White Confetti Fudge

A Christmas treat from Grandma Morgan

1-1/2 lb. white almond
   bark
1 can Eagle Brand milk
1/8 tsp. salt
1 tsp. vanilla
1 c. chopped candied
   cherries
1 c. chopped candied
   pineapple

In heavy sauce pan melt almond bark with Eagle Brand milk and add salt, vanilla, and fruit. Spread evenly into 8″ square pan lined with wax paper. Chill 2 to 3 hours, or until firm. Turn fudge onto cutting board and peel off paper and cut into squares. Store loosely covered at room temperature.

Krispie Date Balls

A crunchy, chewy snack from Virginia Goggans

3/4 c. sugar
1 stick oleo
1 c. chopped dates
1 egg, beaten
1/2 c. pecans, chopped
2 c. Rice Krispies
1 tsp. vanilla
1-1/2 c. coconut

Combine sugar, oleo, dates, egg, and pecans. Boil 3 minutes, stirring constantly. Remove from heat and add Rice Krispies and vanilla. Stir until well-coated. Cool and form into small balls. Roll in coconut. Makes about 3 dozen.

Peanut Brittle

This version of a candy classic is from Sue Elrod of Brownfield.

3 c. sugar
1/2 c. water
1 c. white Karo
1 tsp. salt
3 Tbsp. butter
3 c. peanuts
2 tsp. soda

Cook sugar, water, and Karo until it spins a tread. Add salt, butter, and peanuts. Cook until golden color and turn off heat. Add soda and mix well, pour into buttered pans. Better when thin.

Peanut Brittle by Granddaddy Martin

1/4 c. white Karo
1/4 c. water
1 c. sugar
1 Tbsp. butter
1 c. raw peanuts
1 tsp. soda

In an iron skillet, cook Karo, water, sugar, and butter until it comes to a boil. Add peanuts. Cook about 6 or 7 minutes. (This will turn a light brown color.) Remove from burner. Add soda and mix well. Pour into a greased cookie sheet and spread as thin as possible.

Fire Stick Candy

4 c. sugar
1 c. water
1 c. white Karo
5 drops red food coloring
3/4 tsp. oil of cinnamon

Mix sugar, water, and Karo in heavy saucepan. Bring to a boil over medium heat, stirring constantly. Stir in food coloring and continue to cook without stirring until mixture reaches hard crack stage, or 300° on a candy thermometer. Remove from heat, stir in oil of cinnamon, and spread on an oiled pan. Cool and break into pieces.

Peanut Butter Fudge
From the kitchen of Linda Givens

4 c. sugar
1/2 tsp. salt
2 c. milk
1 tsp. vanilla
1 Tbsp. butter
1 (12 oz.) jar smooth
   peanut butter

In a sauce pan mix sugar, salt, and milk and boil until soft ball stage. Add vanilla, butter, and peanut butter. Beat until smooth and turn out on buttered dish. Let fudge cool and cut into squares.

Peanut Clusters

1 (8 oz.) pkg. sweet
   chocolate chips
2/3 c. Eagle Brand milk
1 c. parched peanuts

Melt chocolate chips. Add Eagle Brand milk and blend. Add peanuts and stir until well coated and mixture begins to thicken. Drop on wax paper.

Peanut Patties

Willie Mae Caswell gave this recipe to Debbie soon after she and Bobby married.

2 c. sugar
1/2 c. white Karo
1-1/2 c. water
3 c. raw peanuts
1 c. powdered sugar
Red food coloring

Mix sugar, Karo, water, and peanuts and cook to 225° on candy thermometer. Remove pan from burner and add powdered sugar and a few drops food coloring. Mix thoroughly. Spoon into patties on wax paper.

Peanut Patties by Pat

3 c. sugar
1 c. white Karo
1 c. water
1 lb. raw peanuts (about 3 cups)
1/2 stick butter
1/2 tsp. red food color

In a saucepan, mix sugar, Karo syrup, and water and bring to a rolling boil; one that can't be stirred down. Add peanuts and cook to hard boil. Remove from heat and add butter and food coloring. Beat just a little and put on buttered plate, or drop by spoonfuls into patties.

Pecan Coconut Clusters

Virginia's quick treat for Ginny and Katrina

1-1/2 c. pecan pieces
8 oz. almond bark
1 c. coconut

Spread pecans in glass dish and microwave on slow for 5 or 6 minutes, or until lightly toasted. Stir at 2 minute intervals. Set aside. Place almond bark in a 2-quart microwave bowl and microwave on medium for 3 or 4 minutes, or until melted. Stir until smooth and cool for 2 minutes. Stir in coconut and pecans. Drop by rounded teaspoonfuls onto wax paper. Form into a round ball. Makes 4 dozen.

Pecan Goodies
A delicious snack from Vivian Broyles of Lamesa

1 egg white
1 c. brown sugar
1/8 tsp. salt
1/4 tsp. cinnamon
1/4 tsp. cream of tartar
1 c. pecan halves

Beat egg white until stiff and gradually add sugar. Add salt, cinnamon, and cream of tartar. Continue beating until very stiff. Drop in pecan halves, stir until coated. Bake on ungreased cookie sheet at 200° for one hour.

Razzle Dazzles
These are great to serve at showers and parties.

1 pkg. caramel candies
1 tsp. milk
1 (1 lb.) pkg. miniature
  marshmallows
1 can shredded coconut

Melt candy and milk. Dip marshmallows individually in candy mixture using toothpicks. Roll in coconut. Set on wax paper to cool.

Rice Krispie Balls
A fast and tasty snack from Margaret Hartman

1 c. sugar
1 c. white Karo
1/2 c. peanut butter
1/2 pkg. butterscotch
  morsels
6 c. Rice Krispies

Mix sugar and Karo and bring to a good rolling boil. Add peanut butter and butterscotch morsels. Pour over Rice Krispies. Mix. When cool, roll into small balls.

Sour Cream Candy
This is an old recipe, but one of our favorites.

3 c. brown sugar
1 c. sour cream
2 Tbsp. butter
1 c. chopped pecans
1 tsp. vanilla

Cook sugar and sour cream until it first forms a soft ball when dropped in cold water. Add butter and remove from heat. Add pecans and vanilla. Beat vigorously until it thickens. Pour into greased platter and let cool.

Toffee

Lynn McCraw gives this as a very elegant and appreciated gift.

1 pkg. slivered almonds
  (about 2 oz.)
1 tsp. vanilla
1 c. sugar
2 sticks oleo
3 Tbsp. water
1 (8 oz.) pkg. milk
  chocolate chips

Grease flat pan (about 9″ × 13″) with oleo. Sprinkle almonds on pan. Put vanilla aside to be ready to use.

Melt sugar, oleo, and water in saucepan. Stir and cook fast over high burner to hard crack stage (about 149° on a candy thermometer.) It will look light brown or burlap color when done. Take off burner quickly and add vanilla and stir. Pour hot mixture over almonds. You may have to drizzle it because it will be hard to spread. Sprinkle chocolate chips over mixture. As they begin to melt, spread evenly. Let harden. You may need to refrigerate candy before cracking.

Wonderful Pralines

Waymouth McNeil's taste-tempting candy

10 egg whites
4 c. brown sugar (2 lbs.)
3-1/3 oz. honey (8-1/2
  Tbsp.)
1/4 tsp. salt
9 c. pecan pieces
2 tsp. vanilla extract
6-1/2 oz. shredded coconut

Combine all ingredients in mixing bowl. Mix at medium speed for 2 minutes. Spoon heaping tablespoons of batter on lightly greased baking pan about 2″ apart. Bake at 325° for 17 to 20 minutes. Let cool in pan for 10 minutes. Will be very soft when removed.

Fudge

Jeanne makes this for Richard, Alan, Brian, and Jon Mark and also for the church bake sales.

4-1/2 c. sugar
1 large can evaporative
  milk
1 (8 oz.) pkg. miniature
  marshmallows
1 (18 oz.) pkg. milk
  chocolate chips
1 stick margarine
2 c. chopped pecans
1 tsp. vanilla

In a large sauce pan, combine sugar and milk. Stir and bring to a rolling boil. Boil over medium heat for 8 minutes, stirring constantly. Remove from heat and add marshmallows and chocolate chips. Stir and then add margarine. Stir until everything is melted and well-blended. Then add pecans and vanilla. Mix well. Pour into a buttered 9″ × 13″ pan. Cool and cut into squares.

HINT:
This freezes well. Cut into squares first and freeze with wax paper between layers.

Cake Mix Cookies

These are quick, easy, and you'll love the taste and texture.

1 pkg. Dream Whip
1/2 c. cold milk
1/2 tsp. vanilla
1 cake mix (your favorite
  flavor)
1 egg
1/2 c. powdered sugar

Blend the Dream Whip, milk, and vanilla in a deep, narrow-bottom bowl. Beat at high speed with electric mixer about 4 minutes, or until topping thickens and forms peaks. Pour Dream Whip into a large mixing bowl, add cake mix and egg. Stir until well blended, using a spoon. If you use a mixer, these cookies will not be as good. Drop by teaspoonfuls into powdered sugar and coat completely. Place on greased cookie sheet and bake at 350° for 10 to 15 minutes. Makes about 4 dozen. Hint: The flavor of cake mix will determine the color and flavor of the cookies. A lemon cake mix makes a terrific tasting cookie.

Cake Mix Oatmeal Cookies

1 pkg. Spice cake mix
2 c. oatmeal
2 eggs
1/2 c. oil
1/2 c. milk
2 c. raisins
1 c. chopped pecans
1/4 c. brown sugar

Mix all ingredients well. Drop by spoonfuls on ungreased cookie sheet and bake at 350° for 10 to 12 minutes.

Chocolate Chip Cookies a la Debbie

Get ready for lots for compliments!

2-3/4 c. flour
1 tsp. soda
1 tsp. salt
1/2 c. butter, softened
3/4 c. sugar
3/4 c. brown sugar
1 tsp. vanilla
2 eggs
1 (6 oz.) pkg. chocolate
   chips
1 c. chopped pecans

Preheat oven to 375°. Combine flour, baking soda, and salt and set aside. Combine butter, sugar, brown sugar, and vanilla in large bowl. Beat well. Add eggs and continue beating. Gradually add flour mixture. Stir in chocolate chips and nuts. Drop by spoonfuls and bake for 8 to 10 minutes, being careful not to overbake.

Cinnamon Cookies

These are great to serve with coffee.

1-1/2 sticks margarine
1 c. sugar
1 egg, separated
2 c. flour
2 Tbsp. cinnamon
1/2 tsp. salt
1 c. chopped pecans

Mix margarine and sugar together with a spoon. Add egg yolk and stir well. Sift flour, cinnamon, and salt together. Add to creamed mixture. Mix well and knead with hands. Pat out on cookie sheet or oblong cake pan. Beat egg white slightly and spread over dough. Sprinkle nuts over top and press lightly into dough. Bake at 325° for 30 minutes. Cut into oblong strips while still warm.

Cinnamon-Sugar Tortillas
An authentic Mexican recipe

1/4 c. sugar
1/2 tsp. cinnamon
4 (8") flour tortillas
Vegetable oil

Mix sugar and cinnamon, set aside. Cut each tortilla into 4 wedges. Heat 1/2" oil in large skillet. Fry tortillas a few at a time for 1 minute or until browned. Drain on paper towels, and sprinkle with sugar mixture.

Corn Flake Cookies
Maw-Maw Bailey has delighted family and friends with her cookies for years.

1/2 c. oleo, melted
1/2 c. brown sugar
1/2 c. white sugar
1 egg
1-1/4 c. flour
1/2 tsp. baking powder
1/2 tsp. soda
1/4 tsp. salt
1/2 tsp. vanilla
1 can coconut
2 c. Corn Flakes

Mix all ingredients and drop by spoonfuls on greased cookie sheet. Bake at 375° for 10 minutes or until lightly browned.

Date Cookies

1 (8 oz.) box chopped
  dates
1 c. chopped pecans
1/2 c. white Karo
1/2 c. water
1 lb. brown sugar
2 sticks butter
2 eggs
4 c. flour
1 tsp. cream of tartar
1 tsp. soda
1 tsp. vanilla

Cook dates, pecans, Karo, and water until thick and then cool. This is the filling.

Mix brown sugar, butter, eggs, flour, and seasonings. Roll on wax paper making a large rectangle, then spread with filling. Roll up like a jelly roll. Put in refrigerator overnight. Then slice and bake at 350° until lightly browned.

Dishpan Cookies
Mama Mia! What a cookie!

2 tsp. soda
2 c. brown sugar
2 c. white sugar
2 c. oil
4 eggs
1/2 tsp. cinnamon
1/2 tsp. cloves
1/2 tsp. nutmeg
2 tsp. vanilla
5 c. flour
1-1/2 c. instant oats
4 c. Corn Flakes, Wheat
   Chex, OR Rice Krispies

Mix all ingredients thoroughly. Drop by spoonfuls on cookie sheet. Bake for 12 to 15 minutes in a 350°oven. Makes 12 to 15 dozen. These freeze well.

Drop Sugar Cookies

1 c. oleo
2/3 c. brown sugar,
   packed
2/3 c. sugar
2-1/4 c. flour
2 tsp. soda
1 egg
1/2 tsp. salt
2 Tbsp. hot water
1 tsp. vanilla

Mix well and drop on greased cookie sheet. Bake at 350° until golden brown.

Drop Sugar Cookies
These are soft like old-timey tea cakes.

1/2 c. shortening
1 c. sugar
2 eggs
1/2 tsp. vanilla
1/4 tsp. salt
1/2 tsp. soda
1 tsp. baking powder
1/3 c. milk
2 c. flour

Mix all ingredients and drop by spoonfuls on cookie sheet sprayed with Pam. Bake at 350° for 10 minutes.

Hersheys Chocolate Cookies

2nd Place Howard County Fair 1984 submitted by Linda Womack of Lubbock

1-1/4 c. butter, softened
2 c. sugar
2 eggs
2 tsp. vanilla
2 c. unsifted flour
3/4 c. cocoa
1 tsp. soda
1/2 tsp. salt
1 c. chopped pecans

Cream butter and sugar in large bowl. Add eggs and vanilla, blend well. Combine flour, cocoa, soda, and salt. Blend into creamed mixture. Stir in pecans. Drop by teaspoonfuls onto ungreased cookie sheet. Bake in 350° oven for 8 to 9 minutes. Cool 1 minute on cookie sheet before removing to cooling rack.

Holiday Fruit Drop

1 c. shortening
2 c. brown sugar
2 eggs
1/2 c. buttermilk
3-1/2 c. flour
1 tsp. soda
1 tsp. salt
1-1/2 c. broken pecans
2 c. candied cherries
2 c. dates, diced

Pre-heat oven to 400°. Mix shortening, sugar, and eggs. Stir in buttermilk. In separate bowl, blend 3 cups flour, soda and salt. Add to first mixture. Mix pecans, cherries, and dates with remaining 1/2 cup flour, then add to other mixture. Chill at least 1 hour. Drop 2″ apart on greased cookie sheet. Bake 8 to 10 minutes.

Ice Box Oatmeal Cookies

1 c. shortening
1 c. brown sugar
1 c. white sugar
2 eggs
1-1/2 c. flour
1 tsp. soda
1 tsp. salt
1/2 c. coconut
1/2 c. chopped pecans
3 c. oatmeal
1 tsp. vanilla

Mix and form into two rolls and chill before slicing to bake. You may even freeze before baking if you like. Bake at 350°, but do not brown.

Mrs. Mac's Sugar Cookies
Bea Russell's mother's recipe

3/4 c. Crisco
1-1/2 c. sugar
2 eggs
1 tsp. salt
1 tsp. soda
1/2 c. buttermilk
1 tsp. vanilla
3-1/2 c. flour

Mix all ingredients. Knead, roll out thin, and cut. Sprinkle with sugar, if you like. Bake at 375°. (Do not over bake).

Neiman Cookies
This wonderful recipe was given to us by a good friend who asked to remain unnamed.

2 c. butter
2 c. sugar
2 c. brown sugar
4 eggs
2 tsp. vanilla
4 c. flour
5 c. blended oatmeal*
1 tsp. salt
2 tsp. baking powder
2 tsp. baking soda
24 oz. chocolate chips
1 (8-oz.) grated Hershey
   bar
3 c. chopped pecans

Cream butter and both sugars. Add eggs and vanilla. Mix together with flour, oatmeal, salt, baking powder, and baking soda. Add chips, candy, and pecans. Roll into balls and place 2″ apart on a cookie sheet. Bake for 6 to 10 minutes at 375°. Makes 112 cookies, but the recipe can easily be divided in half.

*Blended oatmeal: Measure and blend in a blender to a fine powder.

Pecan Crispies
Bertha Gardenhire's good, good recipe

1/2 c. shortening
1/2 c. butter
2-1/2 c. brown sugar
2 eggs, beaten
1/4 tsp. salt
1/2 tsp. soda
2-1/2 c. flour
1 c. chopped pecans

Cream shortening, butter, and sugar. Add eggs and beat. Add sifted dry ingredients then nuts. Drop by spoonfuls about 2″ apart on greased cookie sheet. Bake at 350° for 12 to 15 minutes. To make crispy cookies, mash flat with a spatula after baking for 5 minutes, then finish baking.

Oatmeal Cookies

2 sticks oleo, softened
1 box brown sugar (2-1/4
   c. packed)
2 eggs, beaten
2 c. flour
2 tsp. vanilla
1 tsp. baking powder
1 tsp. soda
4 c. instant oats
1-1/4 c. coconut
1 c. chopped pecans

Mix all ingredients and drop on cookie sheet by spoonfuls 2″ apart. Bake at 350° until lightly browned.

Oatmeal Hermits

A great recipe from Terry Scott of Crawford

1 c. margarine, melted
1 c. packed brown sugar
1 egg
1/4 c. milk
1 tsp. cinnamon (heaping)
1 tsp. vanilla
3/4 tsp. salt
1/2 tsp. baking soda
1-1/2 c. uncooked oats
   (quick or old fashioned)
1 c. flour
1/2 c. wheat flour
1/2 c. oat bran
1 c. raisins

Preheat oven to 350°. Combine all ingredients in large bowl, mixing well. Drop batter by rounded tablespoonfuls onto cookie sheets. Bake 8 to 10 minutes, or until light golden brown. Cool on cookie sheets. Makes 5 dozen.

Peanut Butter Cookies

1 c. shortening
1 c. peanut butter
1 c. brown sugar
1 c. white sugar
2 eggs
2-1/2 c. flour
2 tsp. soda

Cream shortening and peanut butter. Add sugar, eggs, and dry ingredients. Form dough into small balls and press flat. Bake at 350° until lightly browned.

Oatmeal Scotchies

1 c. flour
1 tsp. baking soda
1/2 tsp. salt
1/2 tsp. cinnamon
1 c. oleo, softened
3/4 c. sugar
3/4 c. brown sugar
2 eggs
1 tsp. vanilla
3 c. uncooked oats (quick
   or old fashioned)
1 (12 oz.) pkg. butterscotch
   morsels

Preheat oven to 375°. In small bowl, combine flour, baking soda, salt, and cinnamon; set aside. In large bowl, combine oleo, sugar, brown sugar, eggs, and vanilla. Beat until creamy. Gradually add flour mixture. Stir in oats and butterscotch morsels. Drop by tablespoonfuls onto ungreased cookie sheets. Bake at 375° for 7 to 8 minutes. Makes about 4 dozen cookies.

Orange Slice Cookies

Margaret Hartman makes these colorful little cookies for her sweet sister, May Jean.

2 c. Crisco
1 c. white sugar
2 c. brown sugar
3 eggs
1-1/2 tsp. soda
3 Tbsp. water
3 c. flour
1-1/2 tsp. baking powder
1-1/2 c. chopped pecans
3 c. oats
2 c. orange slices (candy
   slices cut in small
   pieces)
1 can Angle Flake coconut

Cream Crisco and sugars, add eggs. Dissolve soda in water and add to creamed mixture. Add other ingredients. Chill. Make a small ball and put on greased cookie sheet. Bake 10 to 15 minutes at 325°.

Peanut Butter Cookies

3/4 c. butter or margarine
1-1/4 c. sugar
3/4 c. packed light brown
   sugar
2 large eggs
1 tsp. vanilla
1-1/2 c. peanut butter
2-1/2 c. sifted flour
2 tsp. baking soda
1/2 tsp. salt

Preheat oven to 350°. In a mixing bowl cream butter and gradually add sugars and beat until light and fluffy. Beat in eggs and vanilla. Blend in peanut butter. Sift together flour, baking soda, and salt. Gradually add to creamed mixture. Roll into balls and put on baking sheet. Press with back of floured fork to make crisscross. Bake 10 to 12 minutes. Cool on wire rack. Makes 8 dozen.

Pineapple Cookies

1 c. soft shortening
1-1/2 c. sugar
1 egg
1 (9 oz.) can crushed
   pineapple, undrained
   (1 c.)
3-1/2 c. sifted flour
1 tsp. soda
1/2 tsp. salt
1/4 tsp. nutmeg
1/2 c. chopped pecans

Mix shortening, sugar, and egg. Stir in pineapple. Sift together dry ingredients and add to mixture. Stir in pecans. Chill at least 1 hour. Drop by rounded teaspoonfuls on lightly greased cookie sheet. Bake 8 to 10 minutes at 400°. Makes about 5 dozen.

Sandies

We love for Shirley Draper to make these for our parties.

1 c. butter
1/3 c. sugar
2 tsp. water
2 tsp. vanilla
2 c. sifted flour
1 c. chopped pecans
Powdered sugar

Cream butter and sugar, then add water and vanilla. Blend in flour and pecans. Chill dough 4 hours. Shape into small balls. Bake on ungreased cookie sheets at 325° for about 20 minutes. If desired, roll in powdered sugar when slightly cooled. Makes 3 dozen.

Pink Cookies

McMurry students swarmed Mack Eplen's for these.

1-3/4 c. powdered sugar
2 c. shortening
2 tsp. salt
1/2 c. finely chopped
   pecans
2 eggs
1/2 c. milk
1-1/2 tsp. vanilla
3/4 tsp. lemon extract
7 c. flour

Mix all ingredients into smooth dough. (This will be very stiff.) Divide and roll into lengths until it reaches 1″ diameter. Cut into 1″ pieces. Make indentions with thumb or spoon in center of each cookie. Bake at 400° for 10 minutes. Makes about 7 dozen.

ICING:
1/2 c. oil
1/2 c. white Karo
2 Tbsp. water
1/4 tsp. red color
Dash salt
3/4 tsp. vanilla
1/2 tsp. cherry flavoring
1 c. powdered sugar
1-1/2 tsp. milk

Bring oil, Karo, and water to a boil. Transfer to mixing bowl and add red color, flavorings and sugar. Beat until it becomes a thick paste. (You may need to add a little extra powdered sugar. The humidity will affect this.) Continue mixing until smooth, then add milk to reach desired consistency.

Snickerdoodles

1 c. soft shortening
1-1/2 c. sugar
2 eggs
2-3/4 c. sifted flour
2 tsp. cream of tartar
1 tsp. soda
1/4 tsp. salt

Preheat oven to 400°. Mix shortening, sugar, and eggs thoroughly. Sift together flour, cream of tartar, soda, and salt; stir into first mixture. Form dough into balls about the size of a walnut. Roll in mixture of sugar and cinnamon. Place about 2″ apart on ungreased cookie sheet. Bake 8 to 10 minutes.

TOPPING:
1/4 c. sugar
4 tsp. cinnamon

Mix ingredients in a small bowl or plastic butter dish. This makes it easy to coat each ball formed by the cookie dough.

Pistachio Cookies

Warning: These little cookies are addictive.

1 c. oleo, slightly melted
1/4 c. white sugar
3/4 c. brown sugar
1/4 tsp. almond flavoring
1 tsp. vanilla
1/8 tsp. green food
 coloring (opt.)
1 (4 oz.) pkg. pistachio
 instant pudding mix
2 eggs
2-1/4 c. flour
1 tsp. baking soda
1 (12 oz.) pkg. butterscotch
 morsels

In a large mixing bowl, cream oleo and sugar. Add almond flavoring, vanilla, food coloring, and instant pudding mix. Beat until smooth. Add eggs and beat well. In a small bowl, mix flour and soda, then gradually add to first mixture. Stir in morsels with a wooden spoon. Cover and chill overnight. Form into smooth balls by teaspoonfuls. Place 2" apart on ungreased cookie sheets. Bake at 375°for 8 to 10 minutes.

GLAZE:
1 c. powdered sugar
Milk
Green food coloring

Mix powdered sugar and enough milk to make it spreadable. Add food coloring as desired. Drizzle on cookies.

Sugar Cookies

1 c. shortening
2 c. sugar
3 eggs
1 tsp. vanilla, lemon, OR
 almond flavoring
1 tsp. soda
1 tsp. salt
3-1/2 c. flour

Cream shortening, sugar, eggs, flavoring, soda, and salt. Add flour and shape dough into an oval roll, and place in plastic bag. Chill at least two hours. Then roll out dough and cut in desired shapes with cookie cutters. Bake cookies at 350° being careful not to brown.

Tea Cakes a la Joyce Bailey

Maw-Maw Bailey has spoiled children, grandchildren, and great-grandchildren with these.

1-1/2 c. sugar
3/4 c. oleo
2 eggs
2 Tbsp. milk
2 tsp. baking powder
3 c. flour
1 tsp. vanilla
Dash salt (opt.)

Cream sugar and oleo. Add eggs and blend. Add remaining ingredients and mix until completely blended. Chill dough before rolling out to cut into cookies. Bake at 375° until very lightly browned.

Blonde Brownies

1 c. sifted flour
1/2 tsp. baking powder
1/8 tsp. soda
1/2 tsp. salt
1/2 c. chopped pecans
1/3 c. shortening
1 c. brown sugar
1 egg
1 tsp. vanilla
1/2 pkg. chocolate chips

Sift together flour, baking powder, soda, and salt. Add pecans and mix well. Set aside. Melt shortening in saucepan. Remove from heat, add sugar, and mix well. After cooling, add egg and vanilla. Then add flour mixture a small amount at a time. Pour into square baking dish and sprinkle chocolate chips on top. Bake at 350° for 25 to 30 minutes.

Brownies

Best ever!

3 sticks butter, melted
3 c. sugar
6 eggs
2 tsp. vanilla
2-1/4 c. sifted flour
3 Tbsp. cocoa
1 c. chopped pecans

Preheat oven to 350°. Mix ingredients and place in greased and floured 9″ × 13″ pan. Bake 35 minutes.

Brownies by Margaret Hartman

4 eggs
2 c. sugar
5 Tbsp. cocoa
1 c. melted Crisco
1 c. flour
1 c. pecans, chopped
1 tsp. vanilla

Beat eggs lightly, add sugar. Melt cocoa and Crisco together and add to mixture. Add flour, pecans, and vanilla. Bake 30 minutes at 350°. Cut in squares while warm.

Butterscotch Brownies

One of Mac's bridge surprises!

1 (12 oz.) pkg. butterscotch
   flavored morsels
1/3 c. margarine or butter
2 c. graham cracker
   crumbs
1 c. pecans, chopped
1 (8 oz.) pkg. cream
   cheese, softened
1 (14 oz.) can Eagle Brand
   milk
1 tsp. vanilla extract
1 egg

Preheat oven to 350° or 325° for glass dish. In medium saucepan melt morsels and butter. Stir in crumbs and pecans. Press half the mixture firmly into bottom of greased 9″ × 13″ baking dish. In large bowl beat cream cheese until fluffy, then beat in Eagle Brand milk, vanilla, and egg. Mix well. Pour into prepared dish. Top with remaining crumb mixture. Bake 25 to 30 minutes. Chill before cutting. Refrigerate leftovers.

Cheesecake Bars

Easy and absolutely delicious!

1 box butter cake mix
2 eggs
1 stick oleo, softened
1 c. chopped pecans
1 (8 oz.) pkg. cream cheese
1 box powdered sugar
1 egg

Mix cake mix, 2 eggs, oleo, and pecans and press into a 9″ × 13″ Pyrex dish. Mix cream cheese, powdered sugar, and 1 egg. Spread this on top of the first mixture. Bake at 350° for 30 to 45 minutes. After cooling, cut into small squares. Freezes well.

Cherry-Walnut Bars

2-1/2 c. flour
1/2 c. sugar
1 c. butter, softened
2 eggs
1 c. brown sugar
1/2 tsp. salt
1/2 tsp. baking powder
1/2 tsp. vanilla
1 small jar Maraschino
    cherries
1/2 c. chopped walnuts

Mix flour, sugar, and butter until crumbly. Press into a 9" × 13" pan. Bake at 350° for 20 minutes or until lightly brown. Blend eggs, brown sugar, salt, baking powder, and vanilla. Drain and chop cherries, reserving liquid. Stir cherries and nuts into egg and sugar mixture. Spread mixture on top of baked crust. Return to oven and bake 25 minutes. Remove from oven and cool.

FROSTING:
1 Tbsp. butter, softened
1 c. powdered sugar
Cherry liquid
1/2 c. flaked coconut
    (opt.)

Combine butter and sugar and enough cherry liquid to spread. Frost bars. Sprinkle with coconut. When icing has set, cut into bars.

Chocodiles

Marina Martin from Monahans entered this in a cooking contest.

3 c. flour
1/2 c. butter or margarine
1/2 c. shortening
1/3 c. crunchy peanut
    butter
1/4 tsp. salt
1 egg yolk, beaten
1 tsp. vanilla

Combine flour, butter, shortening, peanut butter, and salt. Mix with low speed of mixer until mixture is like coarse crumbs. Add egg yolk and vanilla and mix well. Press mixture firmly into ungreased jelly-roll pan. Bake at 350° for 25 to 30 minutes. Cool slightly and spread with Chocolate Crunch while warm, then cut into squares.

CHOCOLATE CRUNCH:
1 c. (6 oz.) semi-sweet
    chocolate pieces
1/2 c. crunchy peanut
    butter
1-1/2 c. corn soya cereal

Melt chocolate pieces in top of double boiler. Stir in peanut butter and soya cereal.

Date Nut Dream Bars

A quick and delicious recipe from Beverly Womack

1 small pkg. chopped dates
1 c. pecans, chopped
1 c. water
1 pkg. white cake mix
1/3 c. oleo, softened
1 egg

Preheat oven to 350°. Mix dates, pecans, and water and cook on low heat until thick. Set aside. Mix cake mix, and oleo until crumbly. Reserve 1/2 cup for topping. Add egg to remaining mixture and beat. Press into a greased 9″ × 13″ pan, spread on date mixture, and top with reserved crumbs. Bake for 30 to 40 minutes. Cool completely and slice.

Graham Cracker Bars

Leta Warren's finger-lickin', good cookies

Cinnamon graham
   crackers
2 sticks oleo
1 c. brown sugar
1-1/2 c. chopped pecans

Place 1 layer of cinnamon graham crackers on jelly roll pan. Boil oleo, brown sugar, and pecans for 2 to 4 minutes. Pour over crackers and spread with fork. Bake at 350° for 10 minutes.

Holiday Fruit Bars

Lynna Rash won first place with these at the Lynn County Bake Show.

3 c. all-purpose flour
1 tsp. ground cinnamon
1 tsp. ground nutmeg
1/4 tsp. ground cloves
Dash salt
2 c. sugar
1 c. margarine, softened
3 large eggs
1 c. chopped dates
1 tsp. baking soda
   dissolved in 2 tsp. water
1 c. chopped walnuts
Additional sugar

Mix flour, cinnamon, nutmeg, cloves, and salt. Set aside. Beat sugar and margarine in a large bowl with electric mixer until light and fluffy. Beat in eggs, one at a time; add dates and dissolved baking soda. On low speed, gradually beat in flour mixture. By hand, stir in nuts. Chill several hours until firm. Heat oven to 350°. Grease baking sheets. Form dough into six rolls, about 10″ long, on a lightly floured surface. Place two rolls 5″ apart on each prepared baking sheet. Flatten to 1/2″ thickness. Sprinkle with sugar. Bake 15 to 18 minutes, until golden brown. While hot, cut diagonally into 1″ slices. Cool on baking sheets for 5 minutes.

Honey Bars

This quick dish comes from Clarene Chambers.

1 pkg. spice cake mix
2 Tbsp. melted butter
1 c. chopped pecans
1 c. packed brown sugar
2 Tbsp. honey
2 eggs

Combine all but eggs in large bowl. Break eggs in measuring cup and add water to make 2/3 cup. Add to other mixture and mix just until blended. Do not use mixer. Spread in greased 9″ × 13″ pan. Bake at 350° for 40 minutes. Sprinkle with powdered sugar. Cool and cut into squares.

Lemon Squares

CRUST:
1/2 c. real butter
1/2 c. sifted powdered
   sugar
1/4 tsp. salt
2 c. flour

Melt butter in baking pan, add other ingredients. Press evenly in 9″ × 13″ pan and up the sides. Bake at 350° for 25 minutes.

FILLING:
4 slightly beaten eggs
2 c. sugar
4 Tbsp. flour
5 Tbsp. lemon juice
Rind of one lemon, grated

Mix and pour over crust. Bake 25 minutes at 325°.

Mississippi Mud Bars
A chocolate lover's dream!

2 sticks oleo
1/3 c. cocoa
1 c. flaked coconut
1 c. chopped pecans
4 eggs
2 c. sugar
1-1/2 c. flour
1 jar marshmallow cream

ICING:
1 lb. powdered sugar
1 stick melted oleo
1/3 c. cocoa
1/2 to 2/3 c. canned milk
1 tsp. vanilla

Melt oleo; stir in cocoa, coconut, pecans, eggs, sugar, and flour. Spread batter in $10'' \times 15''$ greased and floured pan. Bake 20 minutes at 350°. While hot spread with 1 jar of marshmallow cream. Let cool before icing.

Blend all ingredients until smooth. Pour over cake. Cut into bars.

Orange Gumdrop Chews

3 eggs
1 Tbsp. water
2 c. brown sugar
1/2 tsp. salt
1-1/2 c. candy gumdrops
   (orange slices) cut up
1 (3-1/2 oz.) can flaked
   coconut (about 1-1/4 c.)
1/2 c. chopped walnuts
2 c. flour, sifted

Beat eggs with water until foamy. Gradually add sugar and salt, beating until light and fluffy. Thoroughly mix candy, coconut, walnuts, and flour, then stir into egg mixture. Spread in greased large jelly roll pan. Bake at 375° for 18 to 20 minutes, or until done. Cool and cut into bars or squares. Makes about 4 dozen.

Pies, Puddings & Ice Cream

Osgood Pie
Lucille Smith's oh-so-good pie

2 eggs, separated
1 c. sugar
1 Tbsp. butter
1-1/2 tsp. vinegar
1/2 c. white Karo
1/4 tsp. cinnamon
1/4 tsp. cloves
1/2 c. chopped pecans
1/2 c. raisins
1 unbaked pie shell

Beat egg whites and set aside. Beat egg yolks; add sugar, butter, vinegar, Karo, and spices. Mix and add egg whites, pecans, and raisins. Pour into unbaked pie shell. Bake at 350° for 35 to 45 minutes. Makes 1 pie.

Buttermilk Pies

3 c. sugar
4 Tbsp. flour
1/8 tsp. salt
1/4 lb. butter
6 eggs
1 c. buttermilk
1 Tbsp. vanilla
2 unbaked pie shells

Mix sugar, flour, and salt, then add butter. Beat well. Add eggs one at a time, beating after each egg. Add buttermilk gradually, then add vanilla. Bake in two 9" unbaked shells at 300° to 325° for 40 minutes.

Pecan Pie
Ruby Martin's holiday favorite for her family

3 eggs, well-beaten
2/3 c. sugar
1 c. light Karo
Dash of salt
3 Tbsp. butter, melted
1 tsp. vanilla
1 c. chopped pecans
1 unbaked pie shell

Mix and pour into an unbaked pie shell. Cook 15 minutes at 400°, then lower oven to 350° for about 30 more minutes. Makes one pie.

Lemon Chess Pie

Aunt Madeline's wonderful recipe

2 c. sugar
1/4 c. melted butter
4 eggs, slightly beaten
1/4 c. lemon juice
1 Tbsp. cornmeal
1 unbaked pie shell

Mix and pour into unbaked pie shell. Cook 35 to 40 minutes at 375°. Makes one pie.

Fruit Salad Pie by Pat Spradling

2 cans cherry pie filling
1 small can crushed
   pineapple, undrained
1 c. sugar
1/4 c. flour
1 (6 oz.) pkg. cherry Jello
3 mashed bananas
1/3 c. chopped pecans
1 small carton Cool Whip
2 baked pie shells

Cook pie filling, pineapple, sugar, and flour about 7 minutes and let cool. Stir in Jello, bananas, and pecans. Pour in pie shells and chill. Top with Cool Whip.

East Texas Sweet Potato Pie

Clarene Chambers from Tahoka sent this one to us.

2 sweet potatoes, baked
   and mashed
1 stick oleo
3 eggs
1 tsp. nutmeg
1 c. sugar
1 tsp. vanilla
1/2 c. milk
1/8 tsp. salt
1 large or 2 small pie shells

Mix all together and pour into unbaked pie shells. Bake at 325° for 45 minutes to 1 hour, or until firm. (Makes 1 large or 2 small pies)

Apple Crumb Pie

This belonged to Mrs. Claude Schooler.

4 to 6 tart apples
1 unbaked pie shell
1/2 c. sugar
1 tsp. cinnamon
1/2 c. sugar
1/2 c. flour
1/3 c. butter

Peel apples, slice thin, and arrange in shell. Sprinkle with 1/2 cup sugar mixed with cinnamon. Sift remaining 1/2 cup sugar with flour, cut in butter until crumbly. Sprinkle over apples. Bake at 450° for 10 minutes, then lower heat to 350° and bake about 40 minutes.

French Apple Pie

One of Kathy Martin's exceptional recipes

5 or 6 c. apples, peeled and diced
2/3 c. white sugar or brown sugar
1/8 tsp. salt
1-1/2 Tbsp. cornstarch
1/4 tsp. cinnamon
1/8 tsp. nutmeg
1 Tbsp. lemon juice
1 tsp. vanilla
1 (9″) unbaked pie shell

Mix apples with next 7 ingredients and put in uncooked pie shell.

TOPPING:
3/4 c. flour
1 c. white sugar
1 tsp. cinnamon
1/2 tsp. salt
1/2 c. softened margarine

In another bowl mix flour, sugar, cinnamon, salt. Cut in margarine until it resembles coarse crumbs. Put on top of apples, covering them completely. Bake at 350° for 30 to 40 minutes or until brown.

Apple Cream Pie

1/3 c. pecans, chopped fine
1 unbaked pie shell
3/4 c. sugar
2 Tbsp. flour
1/4 tsp. cinnamon
7 c. peeled, sliced apples
1/3 c. half-and-half

Place pecans on bottom and sides of lightly greased pie plate. Place unbaked pie shell on top of pecans. Mix sugar, flour, and cinnamon, and sprinkle half of mixture in bottom of pie shell. Arrange apple slices on top. Sprinkle apples with remaining sugar mixture. Drizzle with half-and-half. Bake at 450° for 15 minutes, reduce heat to 350° and bake 45 minutes longer.

Ice Box Pies

4 eggs, separated
1 c. sugar
1 small can crushed
 pineapple
1/2 pkg. strawberry Jello
1 tsp. vanilla
1 vanilla wafer crust

Beat egg yolks and add 1/2 cup sugar and pineapple. Cook until thick. Remove from heat and add 1/2 package Jello. While this is cooling, beat egg whites until stiff. Add remaining 1/2 cup sugar and vanilla. Blend the two mixtures together. Pour into crust and sprinkle vanilla wafer crumbs on top.

Fresh Fruit Crisp

1 c. instant oats
1/4 c. firmly packed
 brown sugar
1/4 c. oleo, melted
1/4 tsp. cinnamon
1/4 c. firmly packed
 brown sugar
2 Tbsp. flour
1/2 tsp. cinnamon
1/4 c. water
6 c. apples, peaches, or
 pears, peeled and sliced

Preheat oven to 350°. Combine oats, 1/4 cup brown sugar, oleo, and cinnamon and set aside. Combine remaining ingredients except fruit. Add fruit slices, tossing to coat. Spoon into 8″ square glass baking dish. Top with oats mixture. Bake 40 to 45 minutes or until fruit is tender.

Custard Pie

Many thanks to Beverly Womack for this!

3 eggs
1 (13 oz.) can evaporated
 milk
1 c. sugar
3 Tbsp. flour
3 Tbsp. oleo, melted
Nutmeg to taste

Grease and flour a 9″ square baking dish. Combine all ingredients in blender for 30 seconds. Pour into pan. Bake at 350° for 40 to 45 minutes, or until a knife comes out clean.

Millionaire Pie

2 c. powdered sugar
1 stick margarine, softened
1 large egg
1/4 tsp. salt
1/4 tsp. vanilla
2 (8″) pie shells, baked
1 c. whipping cream
1 c. crushed pineapple,
    drained
1/2 c. chopped pecans

Cream together powdered sugar and margarine. Add egg, salt, and vanilla. Mix until light and fluffy. Spoon mixture evenly into pie shells; chill. Whip cream until stiff. Blend in pineapple and pecans. Spoon on top of egg mixture and chill thoroughly. Makes 2 pies.

Best Strawberry Pie

Leta Warren and Mary Brandon make this pie for their families.

1 can Eagle Brand milk
1/4 c. lemon juice
1 (16 oz.) pkg. frozen
    strawberries, thawed
    and drained
1 c. pecans, chopped
1 med. carton Cool Whip
2 vanilla wafer or graham
    cracker crusts

Mix and pour into 2 vanilla wafer or graham cracker crusts. May be frozen indefinitely. Take from freezer 20 to 25 minutes before serving.

Strawberry Pie

A refreshing summertime dessert

1 c. sugar
2 Tbsp. cornstarch
1 c. water
4 Tbsp. dry strawberry
    Jello
Red food color
1 qt. fresh strawberries
1 baked pie shell
1 small carton Cool Whip

Mix sugar, cornstarch, and water in a small saucepan. Boil 3 to 4 minutes. Remove from heat and stir in Jello until dissolved. Add a few drops of red food coloring. Fold in strawberries. Pour into pie shell. Cover generously with Cool Whip. Store in refrigerator until served.

Key Lime Pie
One of Little Mother's best pies

3 large limes
1 pkg. unflavored gelatin
1/2 c. sugar
1/4 tsp. salt
1/4 c. water
4 eggs, separated
2 drops green food
  coloring
1/2 c. sugar
1 tsp. cream of tartar
1 c. Cool Whip
1 graham cracker pie shell

Cut and squeeze limes, using pulp, to get approximately 1/2 cup juice. Set this aside. In a saucepan, mix gelatin, sugar, and salt. Add water and mix well. Add beaten egg yolks and lime juice. Cook over low heat until it boils. Immediately remove from heat and add food coloring. Chill until slightly set. Beat egg whites until stiff, then add sugar and cream of tartar. Fold into gelatin mixture. Gently blend in Cool Whip. Pour into pie shell and chill.

German Chocolate Pie
1st Place Howard County Fair 1984 submitted by Linda Womack of Lubbock

2 c. sugar
2 eggs
1 c. coconut
3-1/2 tsp. cornstarch
1/4 c. cocoa
1/4 c. water
1/4 c. flour
1 (12 oz.) can milk
1/4 c. soft butter
2 unbaked pie shells
1 c. chopped pecans

Mix all ingredients, except pecans, with electric mixer. Blend in pecans. Pour into two 8″ unbaked pie shells. Bake 1 hour at 350° or until knife inserted in center comes out clean.

Baked Apricot Pies
Genny Park serves these at Christmas bridge parties.

1 (8 oz.) cream cheese
2 sticks butter
2 c. flour
1/4 tsp. salt
1 tsp. cooked apricots for
  each pie
1 egg white, slightly beaten
1/4 c. sugar

Mix cream cheese, butter, flour, and salt. Roll dough thin, cut into 4″ circles. Place 1 teaspoonful cooked apricot in each circle. Fold in half. Press around edge with fork to seal. Brush top with slightly beaten egg white and sprinkle lightly with sugar. Place on greased cookie sheet. Bake at 400° until slightly browned, about 15 minutes.

Grandmother Askew's Lemon Pie

1-1/2 c. sugar
3 Tbsp. flour
2 c. water
5 eggs, separated
1/2 c. lemon juice
2 Tbsp. butter
1/2 tsp. vanilla
1/2 c. sugar (for meringue)
1 tsp. cream of tartar
2 baked pie shells

Mix sugar and flour, and add 1/2 cup water. Mix thoroughly. Add egg yolks and mix well. Add lemon juice and remaining water. Add butter and vanilla and cook until thick. Pour in cooked pie shells. Makes two pies.

Add cream of tartar to egg whites and beat until stiff. Add 1/2 cup sugar. Pour on pies and brown in hot oven.

Old-fashioned Lemon Meringue Pie

Waco Dan thinks this is one of Wey's best.

1 c. all purpose flour
2-1/2 c. sugar
Dash of salt
2-1/2 c. water
6 eggs, separated
2 Tbsp. butter or
    margarine
1 c. lemon juice
Grated rind of 2 lemons
1 (11″) baked pie shell,
    cooled
1 tsp. cream of tartar
12 Tbsp. sugar

Combine flour, sugar, and salt in top of double boiler. Add water and slightly beaten egg yolks, stirring until well mixed. Place over hot water and cook 12 to 13 minutes, stirring constantly. (Should be thick). Cover and cook 8 minutes longer. Remove from heat. Add butter and stir until melted. Stir in lemon juice and rind, cool slightly. Spoon into pie shell. Beat egg whites until foamy, add cream of tartar and 12 tablespoons of sugar, 2 tablespoons at a time, beating well after each addition. Continue to beat until mixture stands in stiff peaks. Pile meringue on pie filling, spread to edge of crust to seal. Bake at 375° about 10 minutes, or until meringue is slightly browned.

Mollie Shofner's Lemon Pie

4 c. water
4 c. sugar
3 Tbsp. flour
3 Tbsp. lemon juice
6 eggs, separated
2 Tbsp. butter
2 baked pie shells

Boil the water. Mix sugar, flour, lemon juice, and beaten egg yolks. Mix well, then pour into boiling water. Add butter and stir until thick. Pour into pie shells. Beat egg whites and add 1/2 cup sugar. Pour on pies and brown in hot oven.

Coconut Pies
Christine's favorite pie

2 c. sugar, separated
3 Tbsp. flour
1/2 c. milk
5 eggs, separated
2 c. milk
1 tsp. vanilla
1 Tbsp. butter
1 can coconut
1 tsp. cream of tartar
2 baked pie shells

Combine 1-1/2 cups sugar, flour, and 1/2 cup milk, and mix well. Add 5 beaten egg yolks to mixture. Mix well, then add remaining milk, vanilla, and butter. Cook until thick and fold in 1/2 can coconut. Pour into baked pie shells. Beat 5 egg whites to a stiff peak and add cream of tartar. Add 1/2 cup sugar gradually to beaten egg whites. Pour over cooked mixture, and sprinkle 1/2 can coconut over egg whites. Place in hot oven and brown lightly. Makes 2 pies.

Chocolate Cream Pies
Mayme Martin's original recipe

2 c. sugar, separated
3 Tbsp. flour
1/3 c. cocoa
1/2 c. milk
5 eggs, separated
2 c. milk
1 tsp. vanilla
1 Tbsp. butter
1 tsp. cream of tartar
2 baked pie shells

Mix 1-1/2 cups sugar, flour, and cocoa with 1/2 cup milk. Add 5 beaten egg yolks to mixture and mix well. Add remaining milk, vanilla, and butter. Cook until thick, then pour into pie shells and set aside. Beat 5 egg whites to a stiff peak and add cream of tartar. Add 1/2 cup sugar gradually to beaten egg whites. Pour over pies. Place in hot oven and brown lightly. Makes 2 pies

Lemon Ice Box Pie
Donna Whitley says this is a real pucker-upper pie!

3 lemons
1 (8 oz.) carton Cool Whip
1 can Eagle Brand milk
1 graham cracker crust

Squeeze juice from lemons and set aside. Reserve 1 rind for garnish. Mix Cool Whip and Eagle Brand milk. Add lemon juice slowly and mix well. Pour into graham cracker crust and chill. Garnish with slices of rind. You may add more lemon juice if you want to really pucker-up!

Lemon Pie
Veta Ford of Tahoka puts a new twist in an old-time favorite.

8 oz. sour cream
4 eggs, separated
1 (4-3/4 oz.) vanilla
  pudding mix (not
  instant)
1-1/3 c. milk
1 (6 oz.) frozen lemonade,
  undiluted
1/3 c. sugar
2 Tbsp. cornstarch
2 Tbsp. water
1/4 c. fresh lemon juice
1 baked pie shell or
  graham cracker crust

Combine sour cream and egg yolks in saucepan, mix well. Stir in pudding mix, milk, lemonade, and sugar. In a separate dish, combine cornstarch and water, and mix well. Add to lemon mixture. Cook over medium heat, stirring constantly until thickened. Remove from heat, stir in lemon juice. Pour into baked pie shell, or graham cracker crust.

TOPPING:
4 egg whites
1/2 tsp. cream of tartar
1/2 c. sugar

Mix egg whites and cream of tartar, beat until frothy. Gradually add sugar, 1 tablespoon at a time, beating until stiff peaks form. Spread on pie, sealing well at edges. Bake at 350° for 12 to 15 minutes.

Cherry Cream Cheese Pie
Brandie's favorite

8 oz. cream cheese
1 can Eagle Brand milk
1/2 c. lemon juice
1 tsp. vanilla
1 graham cracker crust
1 can cherry pie filling

Soften and beat cream cheese until fluffy. Add milk and blend. Stir in lemon juice and vanilla. Pour in crust and chill until firm. Add pie filling on top when ready to serve.

Stir And Mix Cobbler
Sammye Middleton's quick and delicious dessert

1 c. sugar
1/4 c. shortening
1/4 tsp. salt
1 c. milk
1-1/2 c. flour
2 tsp. baking powder

Mix all ingredients well, grease baking dish, pour batter in bottom of 9"x13" dish.

 FRUIT MIXTURE:
4 c. fruit
2 c. juice or water
1/2 c. sugar
2 Tbsp. butter

Mix and pour over first mixture. Bake at 350° 1 hour if thick, 1/2 hour if thin. For peaches, add 1 teaspoon nutmeg. For apples, add 1 teaspoon cinnamon.

Apple Dumplings
Donna Forbes sure knows how to fix a great German dessert.

2 c. sugar
2 c. water
1/4 tsp. cinnamon
1/4 tsp. nutmeg
1/4 c. butter
6 apples
2 c. flour
1 tsp. salt
2 tsp. baking powder
3/4 c. shortening
1/2. milk

Combine sugar, water, cinnamon, and nutmeg. Cook 5 minutes and add butter. Pare and core apples. Sift dry ingredients, cut in shortening, and add milk all at once. Stir just until flour is moistened. Roll 1/4" thick and cut in 6" squares. Place apple on each square, sprinkle generously with additional sugar and spices. Dot with butter; fold corners of dough, pinch edges together. Place in greased baking dish 1" apart and pour sauce over the apples. Bake at 350° for 45 minutes. (Serve hot with cream, if desired.)

Pie Crust by Margaret Hartman

4 c. flour
1-1/3 c. Crisco
1 egg
1/2 c. cold water
1 Tbsp. vinegar
2 tsp. salt

Cut Crisco into flour. Beat egg, water, vinegar, and salt together. Add liquid to flour mixture. Mix well and roll out. Makes 4 crusts.

Wafer Crust For Two Pies

1 box Vanilla wafers
1 stick margarine, melted

Crush one box vanilla wafers with food processor, or place wafers in Ziploc bag and crush with rolling pin. Divide wafers into 2 Pyrex dishes. Pour half of the margarine in each pan and completely work into wafers. Press wafers firmly on sides and bottom of pan. A good way to get a smooth crust is to set an empty pie pan inside the one you are working on and gently press the pans together. This will give you a smooth, uniform crust.

Pineapple Chess Pie
Bertha Morgan bakes this often.

2 c. sugar
1/2 c. butter or margarine,
   softened
4 eggs, beaten
3 Tbsp. flour
1 (8 oz.) can crushed
   pineapple, drained
1/2 c. coconut
1 tsp. vanilla
1 unbaked 9″ pie shell

Combine sugar and butter and cream well. Add beaten eggs and flour, mix well. Stir in pineapple, coconut, and vanilla. Bake at 350° for 45 minutes, or until set.

Stir-N-Roll Pie Crust

1-1/3 c. sifted flour
1 tsp. salt
1/3 c. Wesson oil
3 Tbsp. cold milk

Heat oven to 475°. Mix flour and salt. Measure Wesson oil and milk into same cup (but don't stir). Pour all at once into flour. Stir until mixed. Press into a ball. Flatten slightly. Place between 2 sheets of waxed paper, about 12″ square. Roll out gently to edges of paper. Dampen table top to prevent slipping. Peel off top paper. If dough tears, mend it without moistening. Lift paper and crust by corners. Place paper-side-up in 8″or 9″ pie pan. Peel off paper. Ease into pan. Flute edge and prick pastry with a fork. Bake 8 to 10 minutes. Cool before filling.

Pecan Delight

4 egg whites
1 c. sugar
1 tsp. vanilla
20 white crackers,
   crumbled
1 c. pecans, chopped
1 small carton Cool Whip

Beat egg whites until stiff and fold in sugar, vanilla, cracker crumbs, and pecans. Pour into well greased pie pan and bake at 350° for 30 minutes. Top with Cool Whip.

Japanese Fruit Pie

3 eggs, beaten
1 c. sugar
1/2 c. white Karo
1/2 c. butter, melted
1 tsp. white vinegar
1/4 tsp. salt
1/2 c. raisins
1/2 c. coconut
1/2 c. pecans, chopped
1/2 c. walnuts, chopped
1 9" pie shell, unbaked

Mix first 6 ingredients, stir well. Add raisins, coconut, and nuts and pour into shell. Bake at 350° for 45 to 50 minutes.

Texas Delight

An Askew family favorite from Aunt Sister

1 c. flour
1/2 c. oleo
1/2 c. chopped pecans
1 (8 oz.) pkg. cream
   cheese, softened
1 large carton Cool Whip
1 c. powdered sugar
2 small pkg. instant
   pudding (any flavor)
2-1/2 c. milk

FIRST LAYER:
Mix flour, oleo, and pecans and press into 9" × 13" baking pan. Bake 15 minutes at 350° and cool.

SECOND LAYER:
Mix cream cheese, 1/2 carton Cool Whip, and powdered sugar and spread on cooled crust.

THIRD LAYER:
Mix pudding and milk until thick. Spread on cream cheese layer. Spread remainder of Cool Whip on top and garnish with pecans. Chill several hours.

Blueberry Yum-Yum

3 c. graham cracker
   crumbs
1/2 stick melted butter
2 envelopes Dream Whip
1 c. cold milk
1 Tbsp. vanilla
1 (8 oz.) pkg. cream cheese
3/4 c. sugar
1 can blueberry pie filling

Mix graham cracker crumbs and melted butter. Line a 9" × 13" baking dish forming a crust. Mix Dream Whip, milk, and vanilla. Fold in cream cheese, then add sugar. Blend thoroughly. Pour 1/2 mixture over crust. Add pie filling. Cover with remaining mixture. Garnish with graham cracker crumbs.

Cherry Supreme

Terri Vardeman of Levelland fixes this for Joe Bill, Justin, and Jayme.

1-1/2 c. flour
1-1/2 sticks oleo
3 Tbsp. sugar
1 c. chopped pecans
2 pkg. Dream Whip
1 (8 oz.) pkg. cream
   cheese, softened
2 c. powdered sugar
1 can cherry pie filling

Mix flour, oleo, sugar, and pecans and pat into 9" × 13" pan. Bake at 350° for 25 minutes. Prepare Dream Whip as directed. Beat cream cheese and powdered sugar until fluffy. Fold Dream Whip into cream cheese mixture. Spread over cooled crust. Top with pie filling.

Pistachio Pudding Salad

1 pkg. instant pistachio
   pudding
1/4 c. milk
1 small can crushed
   pineapple
1/2 pkg. small
   marshmallows
1 (8 oz.) carton Cool Whip

Mix all ingredients together thoroughly. Refrigerate.

Old-Fashioned Banana Pudding
Mayme Martin's treat for her children and grandchildren

1-1/2 c. sugar
2 Tbsp. flour
2-1/2 c. milk, separated
5 egg yolks, beaten well
1 tsp. vanilla
1 Tbsp. butter
5 or 6 bananas
1/2 to 3/4 box vanilla
   wafers

Blend sugar and flour with 1/2 cup milk, and mix thoroughly. Add egg yolks and mix well. Add remaining milk, a small amount at a time. Stirring constantly, cook mixture until it thickens. Remove from heat, add vanilla and butter. Stir well until butter is melted. In a pretty bowl, layer wafers and sliced bananas. Pour pudding mixture on top.

Edwardian Creme
From Luanne Klaras of Nick's Restaurant in Waco

2 sticks unsalted butter,
   softened
1 (8 oz.) pkg. cream
   cheese, softened
1-1/2 c. confectioners'
   sugar
2-1/2 Tbsp. fresh lemon
   juice
2 tsp. vanilla
1/2 c. golden raisins
10 oz. individually quick
   frozen raspberries

In bowl with electric mixer, beat together butter and cream cheese until mixture is light and fluffy. In small bowl, stir together confectioners' sugar, lemon juice, and vanilla until well combined. Beat mixture into butter mixture a little at a time. Fold in raisins. Chill creme for 1 to 6 hours. Process raspberries in blender or food processor. Divide the sauce between 6 champagne or dessert glasses. With a small ice cream scoop, put 1 scoop of creme in each glass. Makes 6 servings. For a sweeter taste, substitute frozen raspberries in syrup.

Strawberry Delight
A delightful dish from Rachel Huffaker

CRUST:
1 stick oleo
1-1/4 c. flour
1/4 c. brown sugar
1/4 c. pecans, chopped

Melt butter and pour over dry ingredients and cook. Put into long baking dish and bake at 375° for 15 minutes.

FIRST LAYER:
2 (8 oz.) pkg. cream cheese, softened
2 tsp. vanilla
1 c. sugar
4 eggs

Mix and pour over crust. Bake at 350° for 15 to 20 minutes or until firm. Let cool.

SECOND LAYER:
3 Tbsp. flour
2 large pkg. strawberries, drained (reserve juice)

Mix flour with the reserved juice and cook until it thickens. Add berries and blend well. Pour over cooled first layer.

TOPPING:
2 cartons whipping cream
1/2 c. powdered sugar

Whip the cream and add sugar. Spread over second layer. Garnish with chopped pecans and strawberries if desired.

Boiled Custard
An old family recipe given to us by Arbie Brumit

4 eggs
4 heaping Tbsp. sugar
4 c. sweet milk
1 Tbsp. vanilla
Cinnamon (opt)
Nutmeg (opt)

Beat eggs well. Add sugar and beat again. Heat milk slowly, until slightly warm. Pour over eggs and sugar. Mix well. Cook in double boiler until thickens and coats a metal spoon. Remove from heat. Add vanilla, sprinkle with cinnamon or nutmeg on top. Chill. Serve with cookies or over plain cake. This is nourishing and easy to digest.

Banana Pudding

An O'Donnell favorite from Sue Forbes

2 c. milk
4 Tbsp. flour
1-1/4 c. sugar
Pinch of salt
3 eggs, separated
1 tsp. vanilla
2 Tbsp. oleo
1/2 box vanilla wafers
3 bananas, sliced
1 carton whipping cream

Put milk in a saucepan and place on burner. While this is heating, mix together flour and sugar. Add salt. Add enough hot milk to this to make a sauce, then add the beaten egg yolks. Stir all of this into the hot milk. Continue cooking and stirring until thick. Remove from heat and add vanilla and oleo. Stir and set aside to cool. Can be cooked a day ahead of time to be used when ready to serve. In large bowl put vanilla wafers on the bottom. Cut up 3 bananas on top of the vanilla wafers. Whip whipping cream and put on top. Just before serving, fold all together. (Do not use instant pudding or Cool Whip.)

English Toffee

1 stick oleo
2 c. unsifted powdered
  sugar
2 eggs, separated
1/4 tsp. salt
3-1/2 Tbsp. cocoa
1 tsp. vanilla
1 c. pecans, chopped
1-1/2 c. vanilla wafer
  crumbs, divided in half

Cream oleo and powdered sugar. Add egg yolks, one at a time. Add salt, cocoa, vanilla, and pecans. Beat egg whites until stiff and fold into first mixture. Spread half of the vanilla wafer crumbs in a 9" square pan. Pour in chocolate mixture, and sprinkle rest of crumbs over top. Chill at least 12 hours. Top with Cool Whip if desired.

Pistachio Delight

Joey gets hugs from Rex, Lynna, and Lee when she serves this.

1-1/2 c. flour
1-1/2 sticks oleo
1/2 c. sugar
1/2 c. pecans, chopped
1 c. powdered sugar
1 (8 oz.) pkg. cream cheese
1 carton Cool Whip
1 large box pistachio
    pudding mix
1 c. chopped pecans
1 Hershey candy bar

Mix first 4 ingredients and pat into a 9″ × 13″ pan. Cook at 350° for 25 minutes. Let cool. Blend powdered sugar, cream cheese, and 1 cup Cool Whip. Spread on cooled crust. Mix pudding according to package directions and spread over cream cheese mixture. Top with Cool Whip. Garnish with chopped pecans and grated Hershey bar.

Amaretto Chocolate Silk Pudding

Frances Austin's recipe for a rich tasting dessert without the cost of lots of calories.

2 c. skimmed milk
1/2 c. sugar
1/4 c. unsweetened cocoa
1/4 c. cornstarch
1/4 c. amaretto liquer
2 Tbsp. margarine (opt.)
3/4 tsp. vanilla
1/8 tsp. almond extract

Scald milk by heating in microwave to 140°. In separate dish, mix sugar, cocoa, and cornstarch. Pour milk into blender and add amaretto. Add dry ingredients and blend. Pour in bowl and cook in microwave for 1 minute. Stir well two or three times. Cook until thick. Add margarine, vanilla, and almond extract. Stir well. Serve hot or cold with or without pecans or almonds.

Hot Fudge Sauce

A Chocoholics dream!

4 (1 oz.) squares semi-sweet
    chocolate
2 Tbsp. butter
1 (14 oz.) can Eagle Brand
    milk
1 tsp. vanilla
1/8 tsp. salt

Melt chocolate and butter. Add other ingredients and blend thoroughly. Serve over ice cream.

Oreo Cookie Ice Cream Pie

We got this from Susan McCord. Her mother-in-law, Jean, crushes the Oreos by putting them in a Ziploc bag and driving her car over them!

1 large pkg. Oreo cookies
1 stick oleo
1/2 gal. vanilla ice cream, softened
1 stick oleo
6 Tbsp. cocoa
1/2 c. sugar
1 large can Pet milk
1-1/2 tsp. vanilla
1 (8 oz.) Cool Whip
1/2 c. chopped pecans

Make crumbs of a little less than one large package of Oreo cookies. Melt 1 stick of oleo in 9"x13" Pyrex dish. Mix Oreo crumbs and melted oleo and press into bottom and sides of dish. Chill. Add softened ice cream to top of crumbs and freeze. In a double boiler, melt 1 stick of oleo over low heat. Mix cocoa and sugar then gradually add to oleo. Gradually add milk and mix well. Cook over medium heat until thickens. Remove from heat. Add vanilla. Cool completely and layer on top of frozen mixture. Cover with Cool Whip and pecans. Keep frozen until ready to serve.

Banana Nut Ice Cream

Nancy Franklin makes this for Jerry Dee, Misty, Kristy, Richie, and Tyler.

6 eggs
1 can evaporated milk
3 c. sugar
2 tsp. vanilla
1 c. chopped pecans
4 bananas
Milk

Beat eggs and evaporated milk until foamy. Add sugar and vanilla and blend well. Add nuts and sliced bananas and mix. Pour into freezer and add enough milk to fill freezer about 2" from top. Freeze according to freezer directions.

Milky Way Ice Cream

8 Milky Way bars
2 c. milk
6 eggs
2 c. sugar
2 tsp. vanilla
1 can evaporated milk
Milk

Melt Milky Ways in the 2 cups milk. Cool. While cooling, beat eggs, add sugar. Beat well. Add vanilla and evaporated milk. Fold in cooled Milky Way mixture. Mix well. Pour into 1 gallon freezer. Add milk to fill 2" from top.

Strawberry Ice Cream

This is for a 5-quart freezer.

2 baskets fresh strawberries
1/2 c. sugar
8 eggs
2-3/4 c. sugar
3 tsp. vanilla
1-1/2 pints cream
Milk

Cut strawberries ahead and prepare with sugar. Beat eggs until thick. Add sugar and beat. Add vanilla, cream, and strawberries. Mix well. Pour into freezer and finish filling with milk. Freeze according to freezer directions.

Caramel Add-A-Crunch Topping

1-1/4 c. instant oats, uncooked
1/3 c. firmly packed brown sugar
1/3 c. oleo, melted

Combine all ingredients in heavy 10″ skillet; mix well. Cook over medium heat 3 to 4 minutes or until golden brown, stirring constantly. Sprinkle onto large cookie sheet to cool. Chill. Store in tightly covered container in refrigerator. To serve, sprinkle over yogurt, ice cream, pudding, or fruit.

Tutti Frutti Ice Cream

Alisa Dollar makes this for Monty, Josh, and Jenny.

2 cans Eagle Brand milk
3 pints Coffee Rich (non-dairy creamer)
1 (1 lb.) can crushed pineapple
5 bananas, mashed
1 large box frozen strawberries, thawed
1 c. chopped pecans

Mix ingredients in order. Pour into freezer and finish filling with milk. Freeze according to freezer directions.

Frozen Chocolate Dessert
Bertha Brewer's hit at the family reunion.

1 (13 oz.) can evaporated
  milk
1 (10 oz.) pkg. miniature
  marshmallows
1 (6 oz.) pkg. semi-sweet
  chocolate chips
3/4 c. oleo
1 (3-1/2 oz.) can coconut
2 c. graham cracker
  crumbs
1/2 gal. vanilla ice cream,
  in square carton
1 c. chopped pecans

Combine first 3 ingredients in top of double boiler. Bring water to boil. Cook on low heat until all are melted. Remove from heat and cool.

Combine oleo and coconut in small pan. Lightly brown coconut. Stir in graham cracker crumbs. Press 3/4 of crumb mixture into 9" x 13" pan.

Cut ice cream into 1/2" slices. Arrange 1/2 of the slices over crust. Pour 1/2 of chocolate mixture over ice cream. Repeat layers.

Combine remaining graham cracker crumbs and pecans. Sprinkle over top of dessert. Cover and freeze until firm. This will keep for weeks.

Let stand at room temperature for 5 minutes before serving.

Banana Ice Cream
Granddaddy Martin's treat for 60 years!

6 eggs
2-1/2 c. sugar
1 large can evaporated
  milk
3 mashed bananas
1/2 c. chopped pecans
  (opt.)
1 Tbsp. vanilla
Milk

Mix eggs and sugar and beat well in mixer. Add evaporated milk, bananas, pecans, vanilla, and small amount of milk and mix well. Pour in freezer, add enough milk to fill freezer within 2" from top. You can use the same recipe for vanilla ice cream by omitting bananas and pecans. To make strawberry ice cream, substitute 1-1/2 cups of mashed strawberries for the bananas.

Oreo Dessert
Ice cream lovers beware of this tempting dessert!

1 (1 lb. 4 oz.) pkg. Oreo
   cookies, crushed
1 stick margarine, melted
1/2 gal. vanilla ice cream,
   softened

Crush Oreos with food processor or place them in Ziploc bag and use a rolling pin. Mix Oreos with margarine. Use 3/4 of mixture to form crust in a 9″ × 13″ dish. Reserve 1/4 of mixture to garnish top. Pat down well. Spread ice cream onto crust. Sprinkle reserved mixture on top of ice cream. Freeze. Cut in squares and serve.

Cherry Nut Ice Cream
Sirita's speciality for backyard parties

6 eggs
2 c. sugar
1 c. white Karo
2 tsp. vanilla
1 large can evaporated
   milk
1 can dark sweet Bing
   cherries
1 c. chopped pecans
Milk

Beat eggs, sugar, and Karo until thick. Add vanilla, evaporated milk, cherries, and pecans. Pour into freezer and finish filling with milk. Freeze according to freezer directions.

Black Cherry Sauce
Topping for ice cream, pound cake, or cheesecake

1 (2 lb.) can pitted black
   cherries
2 Tbsp. butter
1-1/2 Tbsp. cornstarch
2 Tbsp. sugar
1/2 tsp. almond extract
1/2 tsp. vanilla

Drain cherries, reserve juice. In a small saucepan, melt butter and add juice, mixing well. Add cornstarch and sugar, stirring until smooth. Heat over low heat, stirring constantly, until thickened. Remove from heat and add cherries and flavorings. Stir gently to blend.

Brown Sugar Ice Cream

5 eggs, beaten
1 (1 lb.) pkg. dark brown
  sugar
1 c. whipping cream
2 c. half and half
3 c. milk
1 c. pecans, chopped

Combine eggs and sugar, mix well. Add remaining ingredients. Stir well. Pour mixture into 1 gallon freezer. Freeze according to freezer instructions.

Potpourri

Sugar and Spice Pecans

These really make a nice gift. Joe Goggans loves them!

1 egg white
3/4 c. sugar
2-1/2 Tbsp. water
1/2 tsp. salt
1 tsp. cinnamon
1/4 tsp. allspice
1/4 tsp. cloves
1/4 tsp. nutmeg
8 c. pecan halves

Beat egg white slightly with a fork. Add other ingredients except pecans and mix well. Add pecans last and stir until evenly coated. Spread in a greased pan. Bake at 275° for 50 to 55 minutes. Remove to waxed paper to cool. Store in airtight container.

Caramel Popcorn

Polly's dish for the family reunion

1 c. real butter
1 c. sugar
1/2 c. white Karo
1 tsp. vanilla
4 - 5 qts. pop corn, popped
1 can peanuts

Mix butter, sugar, and Karo in a large bowl and cook 11 to 13 minutes in microwave until golden brown. Add vanilla. Pour over pop corn and peanuts. Mix together and pour on foil. Hint: Put the popped corn in a large rubbermaid tub or something like that, Tupperware will melt when the hot syrup is added. A large roasting pan also works.

Maple Flavored Syrup

4 c. sugar
1/2 c. brown sugar
2 c. water
1 tsp. vanilla
1 tsp. maple flavoring

In a saucepan, combine sugar and water, stirring until dissolved. Bring to a boil. Cover, then boil gently for 10 minutes. Remove from heat and cool slightly, then add vanilla and maple flavorings. Stir only until mixed.

Quick Dried Bread Crumbs

2 slices bread

Place bread slices on plastic rack in microwave and cook on high for 1 to 1-1/2 minutes, or until dry. Cool. Break each slice into several pieces. Grate in blender or crush into crumbs with rolling pin. Store in airtight container. Makes about 1/2 cup crumbs.

Bath Salts

This makes a nice gift.

3 c. Epsom salt
1 Tbsp. glycerin
2 to 4 drops food color
Perfume

Put the Epsom salt into a glass or metal bowl, as plastic may stain. In a small paper cup, mix glycerin, food color, and enough perfume to make the mixture fragrant. Then add the glycerin mixture to the Epsom salt slowly and stir until mixed completely. If the fragrance is not strong enough, you can add more perfume to the Epsom salt. Place the bath salt in a decorative container and add a bow.

Herb Croutons

1/2 loaf thin sliced white
   bread
3 Tbsp. olive oil
1/2 c. Romano cheese,
   grated
2 to 3 tsp. garlic powder
1-1/2 to 2 tsp. dried salad
   herbs, crushed

Preheat oven to 225°. Cut bread into 1/2″ cubes. Place on cookie sheet, sprinkle with olive oil. Mix cheese, garlic powder, and herbs. Sprinkle over bread. Bake for 1 hour, turning croutons twice. Cool and refrigerate in tightly covered dish.

Relish or "Chow-Chow"
Eldon Carroll has shared his relish with us for years.

8 c. shredded green
   tomatoes
8 c. shredded cabbage
4 c. chopped onions
1/2 c. pickling salt
1 tsp. mustard
1 tsp. allspice
1 tsp. celery seed
5 c. sugar
1 quart white vinegar
1-1/2 c. bell peppers,
   chopped
1-1/2 c. red bell peppers,
   chopped
3/4 c. jalapeno peppers
   with seeds

Mix well and bring to a boil and cook for 25 minutes. Seal in sterilized jars. Makes about 8 pints.

Baked Caramel Corn
Long-time favorite from Vera Etter

9 qt. popped corn
1 can mixed nuts (opt.)
1 tsp. salt
2 sticks margarine
2 c. brown sugar
1/2 c. white Karo
1 tsp. vanilla
1-1/2 c. miniature
   marshmallows
1 tsp. soda

Put corn and nuts in a large roasting pan. Boil remaining ingredients except soda for 5 minutes. Add soda to mixture and pour over corn and nuts and mix well. After mixing, spread lightly on 2 large cookie sheets and bake at 250° for 1 hour. Stir twice during baking.

Pop-Corn Balls

2 c. sugar
1 c. white Karo
1/2 tsp. cream of tartar
1 Tbsp. butter
1/2 tsp. soda
6 qt. popped corn

Cook first 4 ingredients to a hard ball stage and remove from heat. Add soda to mixture and pour over corn and form balls. (Hint, wet your hands often with water as you work with the hot mixture.)

Tortilla Conqueso

This recipe of Donna Forbes is definitely a perfect "10"!

8 to 10 tortillas
1 can Rotel
1 pt. whipping cream (do
  not whip)
Grated cheese

Fry the tortillas. Start in bottom of pie pan with tortilla, then add a tablespoon of Rotel and a tablespoon of whipping cream, then grated cheese all over top. Continue in this manner until you have used all of the tortillas. For the top, you should have a tortilla with cheese grated over it. Bake for 30 minutes at 350°. Frequently spoon sauce over tortillas while baking. Can be cut into small pieces and served with toothpicks.

Spiced Pears, Peaches, and Apples

5 c. sugar
2 c. white vinegar
2 cinnamon sticks
2 Tbsp. whole cloves
4 quarts fruit

Cook sugar, vinegar, and spices 20 minutes. Drop in fruits, a few at a time, and cook until tender. Pack into hot sterilized jars.

Mustard

A handy recipe from Polly Cord

1 (2 oz.) can Calumet dry
  mustard
1 c. vinegar
2 egg yolks
1 c. sugar

Mix mustard with vinegar and let stand overnight. Mix egg yolks and sugar in a double boiler. Add vinegar and mustard mixture. Stir and cook until thick.

Microwave Spicy Pecans

1 Tbsp. butter, melted
2 Tbsp. Worcestershire
  sauce
Dash of Tabasco sauce
1-1/2 c. pecans
Salt and pepper to taste

Mix first 3 ingredients in a microwave bowl. Add pecans and stir to coat. Microwave on high for 5 to 6 minutes, stirring twice. Season with salt and pepper.

Cranberry, Apple, Pear Sauce

This is great served in a pear half as a salad.

2 lb. fresh cranberries
3 apples, pared, cored, and
  diced
2 pears, pared, cored, and
  diced
2 Tbsp. grated orange peel
2 tsp. ground cinnamon
2 c. golden raisins
2 c. sugar
1 c. fresh orange juice
1/4 tsp. nutmeg
1/2 c. orange flavored
  liqueur

Heat all ingredients except liqueur in large saucepan to boiling. Then reduce heat. Simmer, uncovered, stirring frequently about 45 minutes, or until mixture thickens. Stir in liqueur. Refrigerate covered for 4 hours or overnight. Serve sauce slightly chilled. Will keep a month or longer if kept refrigerated, or it can be frozen. This makes about 6 cups.

Sugared Bacon Strips

Use these to spice up lots of dishes. Thanks to Terry Scott for this wonderful recipe.

1/2 to 1 lb. bacon, room
  temperature
1 c. brown sugar

Roll, shake, or pat bacon in brown sugar. Place strips in pan with sides. Bake at 350° until well done, about 30 to 40 minutes. Remove and drain on brown paper bag. These will get hard as they cool. Keep in refrigerator until ready to use. Crumble up and use in salads, vegetables, eggs, casseroles, etc.

Recipe for Celebration

Share this recipe with a friend to celebrate any special occasion — like an observation that went well, a test that is over and passed, or any accomplishment.

1 bottle of foaming bath
  oil (any fragrance)
4 to 10 candles
drink of your choice
  (anything from wine to
  milk shakes)

Take all ingredients to bathroom and lock the door. Run the tub as full as possible with warm water and use lots of bath oil. Light all candles and then turn off the light. Lie back, relax, and enjoy your drink. OPTIONAL: Give your husband the key to the door.

Hints

Hints

1 tablespoon of butter or a tablespoon of cooking oil added to water when boiling spaghetti will prevent foaming.

To keep brown sugar soft, keep in sealed container.

To remove the residue from sticky tags without scratching surfaces, clean with a soft cloth using a small amount of lemon oil.

Never use tap water on your house plants if you have a water softener, as the salt will kill your plants.

To clean an iron skillet, place skillet on a burner and turn the burner on high. Let it heat for 10 to 20 minutes. This will burn off any build up on the skillet. Put a little Crisco on a paper towel and coat the inside of the skillet with a thin film of grease. As the skillet cools, this grease will be absorbed into the skillet and will prevent the skillet from rusting.

When a recipe calls for sugar and chocolate, mix together before adding any liquid. Add a small amount of liquid first and mix well, then add remaining liquid.

When broiling in oven, always broil with oven door slightly open.

Use a hen for chicken casseroles, as they have better flavor and finer textured meat.

Stew hens with lots of celery, onion, salt, and pepper. The rich broth which is left can be used in casserole sauces.

To prevent rice from becoming gummy, boil rice with plenty of water until done. Drain rice and rinse with cold water, gently separating the grains. Steam the rice in a colander to reheat it.

Always use a baked pie crust for a cream pie.

Refrigerate chicken pieces before frying. The chicken will be tender and have a better flavor.

When frying chicken liver, use a fork or an ice pick to make holes in the liver before frying. This will prevent popping.

Fry chicken with lid on skillet. It will make it tender.

When freezing peas, fish, or chicken, cover with water before sealing packages. This helps prevent freezer burn.

When you find your favorite sausage on sale, buy several pounds. Fry all the sausage and freeze. Pop in the microwave for a quick snack.

Cover eggs in water to boil. Cook 8 to 10 minutes, then pour hot water out. Roll eggs around in pan firmly until they crack. Fill pan with cold water and let set 2 or 3 minutes. Shell will come off easily.

If bread is browned but not cooked in the center, cover top loosely with foil, but do not seal and continue cooking.

A few drops of lemon juice added to rice will keep the grains separate.

Potatoes will bake in a hurry if they are boiled in salted water for 10 minutes before placing in hot oven.

Keep dried fruits in tightly covered container.

To keep berries in best condition, store them unwashed and spread out.

Carrots and beets wilt less with tops removed.

Ripen peaches, pears, plums, avocados, and tomatoes at room temperature.

A teaspoon each of cider vinegar and sugar added to salty soup or vegetables will remedy the situation.

When making gravy, brown the flour well with the oil before adding the liquid to avoid pale or lumpy gravy.

Keep all utensils in good working order.

To tint coconut, add a few drops of food coloring and a few drops of milk.

Cut up dates and other sticky fruits with wet scissors. Dip scissors in water occasionally.

For fluffy scrambled eggs, add 1/4 cup cottage cheese for every four eggs.

Measurements and Substitutions

1 tablespoon	3 teaspoons
1 cup	16 tablespoons
1 cup	8 ounces
2 cups	1 pint
2 pints	1 quart
4 quarts	1 gallon
1 liquid ounce	2 tablespoons
2 cups sugar	1 pound
3-1/2 cups flour	1 pound
1 cup cake flour	7/8 cup all-purpose flour
1 cup honey	1 cup sugar plus 1/4 cup liquid
1 ounce chocolate	1 square
1 ounce chocolate	3 tablespoons cocoa plus 1 tablespoon shortening
1 cup sour milk	1 cup milk plus 1 tablespoon vinegar or 1 tablespoon lemon juice
1 cup sugar	1-1/2 cups powdered sugar
1 cup brown sugar	1 cup sugar plus 4 tablespoons molasses
1 stick oleo	1/2 cup oleo
1 cup sour cream	1 cup evaporated milk plus 1 tablespoon vinegar
1 cup milk	1/2 cup canned milk plus 1/2 cup water
1 clove garlic	1/4 teaspoon garlic powder
1 cup raw macaroni	2 cups cooked macaroni
1 cup raw rice	3 to 4 cups cooked rice
1 pound unshelled pecans	2-1/4 cups shelled pecans
1 pound shelled pecans	4 cups pecans
1 medium onion	1/2 cup chopped onion
1 small onion	1 tablespoon instant minced onion
1 teaspoon dry mustard	1 tablespoon prepared mustard
pinch	as much as can be taken between tip of finger and thumb

Index

Index

A

Almond Bark Clusters, 195
Alpine Appetizers, 12
Amaretto Chocolate Silk Pudding, 239
Amazin' Raisin Cake, 167
Ambrosia, 70
Angel Flake Biscuits, 43
Apple Cranberry Muffins, 56
Apple Cream Pie, 225
Apple Crumb Pie, 225
Apple Dumplings, 232
Apple Pie Cake, 167
Applesauce Cake, 168
Apricot Brandy Pound Cake, 168
Apricot Coconut Balls, 195
Apricot Frozen Salad, 77
Apricot Fruit Salad, 69
Apricot Salad, 74
Apricot Salad by Aunt Virginia, 75
Artichoke Delight, 24
Artichoke Dip, 20
Artichoke Salad, 67
Artichokes Au Gratin, 155
Au Gratin Potatoes, 148
Avocado Mold Salad, 73

B

Bacon and Cheese Surprise, 24
Bacon and Chicken Liver, 9
Bacon Crunchies, 17
Bacon-stuffed Cabbage, 109
Bake-Ahead Breakfast, 29
Baked Almond Rice, 163
Baked Apricot Pies, 228
Baked Beans, 160
Baked Caramel Corn, 249
Baked Chicken with Honey, 117
Baked Corn, 158
Baked Fish by Rachel Huffaker, 102
Baked Onions, 152
Baked Parmesan Chicken by Clarene
   Chambers, 120
Baked Squash, 145
Banana Frozen Dessert, 76
Banana Ice Cream, 242
Banana Nut Cake, 169

Banana Nut Ice Cream, 240
Banana Pudding, 238
Banana Split Cake, 168

BAR DESSERTS
   Blonde Brownies, 215
   Brownies, 215
   Brownies by Margaret Hartman, 216
   Butterscotch Brownies, 216
   Cheesecake Bars, 216
   Cherry-Walnut Bars, 217
   Chocodiles, 217
   Date Nut Dream Bars, 218
   Graham Cracker Bars, 218
   Holiday Fruit Bars, 218
   Honey Bars, 219
   Lemon Squares, 219
   Mississippi Mud Bars, 220
   Orange Gumdrop Chews, 220
Bar-B-Q Sauce by Arlys, 127
Barbeque Sauce a la Debbie, 128
Bath Salts, 248
Bean Casserole, 161
Bean Salad, 64
Bean's Ole, 108
Beef and Bean Burritos, 97
Beef Burgundy, 85
Beef Enchilada Rice, 96
Beef Jalapeno Cornbread by Mary
   Brandon, 135
Beef Jerky, 12
Beef Kabobs, 85
Beefy Baked Beans, 135
Beer Rolls, 43
Ben's Fruit Salad, 71
Best Strawberry Pie, 227

BEVERAGES
   Celebration Punch, 37
   Cranberry Perk, 37
   Frozen Fruit Punch, 37
   Fruit Punch, 38
   Golden Punch, 38
   Hot Cranberry Punch, 38
   Instant Hot Chocolate, 39
   Instant Spice Tea, 39
   Tomato Juice Cocktail, 39
   Versatile Punch, 40

Wassil Cider, 40
Bill's Tortilla Soup, 131
Black Cherry Sauce, 243
Black-Eyed Pea Dip, 21
Blonde Brownies, 215
Blueberry Muffins — Wonderful!, 57
Blueberry Salad, 72
Blueberry Yum-Yum, 235
Boiled Custard, 237
Border Patrol Special, 136
Bourbon Wieners, 9
Bran Muffins, 56

BREADS

Muffins
Apple Cranberry Muffins, 56
Blueberry Muffins —
    Wonderful!, 57
Bran Muffins, 56
Honey Bunches, 55
Pineapple Muffins, 56
Plum Muffins, 57

Quick
Angel Flake Biscuits, 43
Beer Rolls, 43
Broccoli Cornbread, 43
Cheese Biscuits Red Lobster
    Style, 44
Cornbread, 44
Cornbread Plus, 44
Flour Tortillas, 43
Fresh Apple Bread by Carolyn
    Dorning, 45
Gingerbread, 45
Lemon Bread, 45
Poppy Seed Cheese Bread, 46
Ranch Biscuits, 47
Rolls in a Flash, 46
Vegetable Bread, 47
Whole Wheat Biscuits, 47
Zucchini Bread, 46
Zucchini Bread, 48

Yeast
Bucket Bread, 48
Coffee Cake, 49
Cream Cheese Braids, 50
Dilly Bread, 51
Easy Rolls, 51
Holiday Wreath Bread, 52
Kolache, 53

Linda's Hot Rolls, 53
Onion Bread, 49
Potato Hot Rolls, 54
Refrigerator Bread Dough, 54
Refrigerator Hot Rolls, 54
Sour Dough Starter and Rolls, 55
Yeast Biscuits, 48
Yeast Biscuits, 55
Breakfast Egg and Cheese Souffle, 29
Broccoli And Corn Casserole, 156
Broccoli Casserole Abilene Style, 156
Broccoli Cornbread, 43
Broccoli Salad, 62
Broccoli Salad, 63
Broccoli-Cauliflower Salad, 63
Broccoli-Cheese Soup, 129
Broiled Ham with Sweet and Sour
    Sauce, 109
Brown Sugar Ice Cream, 244
Brownfield Hot Sauce, 153
Brownies, 215
Brownies by Margaret Hartman, 216

BRUNCH
Bake-Ahead Breakfast, 29
Breakfast Egg and Cheese Souffle, 29
Buttermilk Hot Cakes, 30
Cheese Javelina, 30
Cheese Quiche, 30
Cheeseburger Quiche, 31
Cheesy Egg Casserole, 31
Cream Cheese Breakfast Bread, 32
Fruit Pizza, 32
Grit Casserole, 33
Hot Cheese Grits, 33
Jalapeno Quiche, 33
Party Brunch, 34
Puffed Eggs, 31
Quiche, 35
Quiche Delight, 35
Super Duper Quiche, 34
Bucket Bread, 48
Buttermilk Cake, 169
Buttermilk Hot Cakes, 30
Buttermilk Pies, 223
Butterscotch Brownies, 216

C

Cabbage Casserole, 147
Cabbage Slaw by Margaret Carter, 59
Cajun Shrimp, 105

Cake Mix Cookies, 204
Cake Mix Oatmeal Cookies, 205
Cake of All Cakes, 191

CAKES
Amazin' Raisin Cake, 167
Apple Pie Cake, 167
Applesauce Cake, 168
Apricot Brandy Pound Cake, 168
Banana Nut Cake, 169
Banana Split Cake, 168
Buttermilk Cake, 169
Cake of All Cakes, 191
Caramel Frosting, 191
Caramel Icing, 192
Carrot Pecan Cake, 171
Cheesecake, 193
Cheesecake, 194
Chocolate Applesauce Cake, 170
Chocolate Cake, 171
Chocolate Chip Cake, 172
Chocolate Eclair Cake, 172
Chocolate Icing, 192
Chocolate Sheath Cake, 173
Date Nut Cake, 173
Dump Cake, 174
Five Flavor Cake, 174
Fresh Apple Cake, 175
Fresh Coconut Cake, 175
Fresh Pear Cake, 176
Fudge Cup Cakes, 167
Hell Cake, 177
Hershey Cake, 176
Hot Milk Cake, 177
Hummingbird Cake from
    Hereford, 178
Individual Cheesecakes, 194
Italian Cream Cake, 178
Lemon Cake, 179
Lemon Fruit Cake by Bertha
    Gardenhire, 175
Marble Chocolate Chip
    Cupcakes, 179
Mayonnaise Cake, 180
Milk Chocolate Cake, 180
Milky Way Cake, 181
Mini-Tart Cheesecakes, 194
Mollie Shofner's Coconut Cake, 181
Pineapple Sheet Cake, 182
Pineapple Upside-Down Cake, 183
Pineapple-Coconut (7-Up) Cake, 182

Poppyseed Cake, 183
Pound Nut Cake, 184
Prism Cake, 184
Prune Cake, 185
Pumpkin Cake, 185
Red Cocoa Cake, 186
Red Velvet Cake, 186
Rum Cake, 184
Rum Cake by Lottie Walker, 187
Seven Minute Frosting, 192
Six Egg Cake, 183
Sour Cream Pound Cake, 187
Strawberry Cake, 188
The Cake That Doesn't Stay
    Around, 188
Turtle Cake, 170
Vanilla Wafer Cake, 189
Watergate Cake, 189
White Chocolate Cake, 190
Yum Yum Cake, 190

CANDIES
Almond Bark Clusters, 195
Apricot Coconut Balls, 195
Chocolate Covered Coconut
    Candy, 196
Chocolate Oatmeal Fudge, 196
Chocolate Spiders, 195
Cocoa Fudge, 196
"Creamy" Pecan Pralines, 197
Date Chews, 197
Date Nut Candy, 198
Divinity, 198
Easter Treats, 198
Fire Stick Candy, 200
Fudge, 204
Krispie Date Balls, 199
Orange Pralines, 197
Peanut Brittle, 199
Peanut Brittle by Granddaddy
    Martin, 200
Peanut Butter Fudge, 200
Peanut Clusters, 200
Peanut Patties, 201
Peanut Patties by Pat, 201
Pecan Coconut Clusters, 201
Pecan Goodies, 202
Razzle Dazzles, 202
Rice Krispie Balls, 202
Sour Cream Candy, 202
Toffee, 203

White Confetti Fudge, 199
Wonderful Pralines, 203
Caramel Add-A-Crunch Topping, 241
Caramel Frosting, 191
Caramel Icing, 192
Caramel Popcorn, 247
Carrot Pecan Cake, 171
Carrot Ring, 158
Carrot Salad, 66
Carrot Slaw, 59
Carrots, 66
Carrots with Pizzazz, 158

CASSEROLES
Beef Jalapeno Cornbread by Mary
   Brandon, 135
Beefy Baked Beans, 135
Border Patrol Special, 136
Cheese-Sausage Cornbread, 137
Cheeseburger Pie, 136
Cherokee Casserole, 138
Chicken Casserole, 138
Chinese Tuna Casserole, 135
Enchiladas, 140
Gad-About's Casserole, 139
Green Chili Enchiladas, 141
Green Enchiladas, 140
Green Enchiladas a la Bea Russell, 141
Lasagne Casserole, 142
Lum's Casserole, 137
Mexican Casserole, 142
Mexican Cornbread Casserole, 143
Seafood And Rice Casserole, 143
Spanish Rice, 139
Tuna-Noodle Casserole, 137
Cauliflower Salad, 62
Celebration Punch, 37
Cheese Ball, 26
Cheese Ball, 27
Cheese Biscuits Red Lobster Style, 44
Cheese Cookies by John Fisher, 7
Cheese Crackers, 16
Cheese Javelina, 30
Cheese Logs, 11
Cheese Quiche, 30
Cheese Squares, 13
Cheese Straws, 17
Cheese-Sausage Cornbread, 137
Cheeseburger Pie, 136
Cheeseburger Quiche, 31
Cheesecake, 193

Cheesecake, 194
Cheesecake Bars, 216
Cheesy Egg Casserole, 31
Cherokee Casserole, 138
Cherry Cream Cheese Pie, 231
Cherry Frozen Salad, 77
Cherry Nut Ice Cream, 243
Cherry Pie Filling Salad, 68
Cherry Salad, 69
Cherry Salad, 74
Cherry Supreme, 235
Cherry-Walnut Bars, 217
Chicken And Rice, 115
Chicken and Rice, 116
Chicken And Spaghetti, 115
Chicken Casserole, 138
Chicken Chili Pie, 123
Chicken Continental, 122
Chicken Divan, 123
Chicken Enchiladas, 117
Chicken Enchiladas, 126
Chicken in Lemon Sauce, 125
Chicken Salad, 78
Chicken Salad, 79
Chicken Stuffed Potatoes, 126
Chicken With Ranch Dressing And
   Bacon, 119
Chili Con Queso, 20
Chili for a Year, 100
Chilies Rellenos, 97
Chinese Beef & Peppers, 95
Chinese Cabbage, 147
Chinese Tuna Casserole, 135
Chocodiles, 217
Chocolate Applesauce Cake, 170
Chocolate Cake, 171
Chocolate Chip Cake, 172
Chocolate Chip Cookies a la
   Debbie, 205
Chocolate Covered Coconut Candy, 196
Chocolate Cream Pies, 230
Chocolate Eclair Cake, 172
Chocolate Icing, 192
Chocolate Oatmeal Fudge, 196
Chocolate Sheath Cake, 173
Chocolate Spiders, 195
Christine's Chicken And Broccoli, 119
Christine's Hash, 89
Cinnamon Apples by Inez Stone, 68
Cinnamon Cookies, 205

Cinnamon-Sugar Tortillas, 206
Clam Chowder, 131
Cocktail Crackers, 8
Cocoa Fudge, 196
Coconut Pies, 230
Coffee Cake, 49
Coke Salad, 72
Cole Slaw, 59
Company Pork Roast, 111

COOKIES
    Cake Mix Cookies, 204
    Cake Mix Oatmeal Cookies, 205
    Chocolate Chip Cookies a la
      Debbie, 205
    Cinnamon Cookies, 205
    Cinnamon-Sugar Tortillas, 206
    Corn Flake Cookies, 206
    Date Cookies, 206
    Dishpan Cookies, 207
    Drop Sugar Cookies, 207
    Hersheys Chocolate Cookies, 208
    Holiday Fruit Drop, 208
    Ice Box Oatmeal Cookies, 208
    Mrs. Mac's Sugar Cookies, 209
    Neiman Cookies, 209
    Oatmeal Cookies, 210
    Oatmeal Hermits, 210
    Oatmeal Scotchies, 211
    Orange Slice Cookies, 211
    Peanut Butter Cookies, 210
    Peanut Butter Cookies, 212
    Pecan Crispies, 209
    Pineapple Cookies, 212
    Pink Cookies, 213
    Pistachio Cookies, 214
    Sandies, 212
    Snickerdoodles, 213
    Sugar Cookies, 214
    Tea Cakes a la Joyce Bailey, 215
Corn Casserole, 157
Corn Chowder, 133
Corn Flake Cookies, 206
Corn Pudding, 157
Cornbread, 44
Cornbread Plus, 44
Cornbread Salad, 61
Country Club Fruit Salad, 71
Country Style Stuffed Peppers, 115
Cowabunga Catfish, 106
Cowboy Stew, 132

Crab Dip Mold, 80
Crabby Mushrooms, 11
Cranberry Perk, 37
Cranberry Salad, 72
Cranberry, Apple, Pear Sauce, 251
Cream Cheese and Lime Jello, 74
Cream Cheese Braids, 50
Cream Cheese Breakfast Bread, 32
Cream Cheese Dip, 24
Creamy Ham Roll-Ups, 111
"Creamy" Pecan Pralines, 197
Creole Beans, 160
Cucumber Salad, 68
Curried Rice Salad, 79
Curried Shrimp Cheese Ball, 19
Custard Pie, 226

D
Date Chews, 197
Date Cookies, 206
Date Nut Cake, 173
Date Nut Candy, 198
Date Nut Dream Bars, 218
Deluxe Cucumbers, 159
Deviled Eggs, 161
Dilly Bread, 51

DIPS
    Artichoke Delight, 24
    Artichoke Dip, 20
    Bacon and Cheese Surprise, 24
    Black-Eyed Pea Dip, 21
    Chili Con Queso, 20
    Cream Cheese Dip, 24
    Curried Shrimp Cheese Ball, 19
    Flamboyant Fondue, 26
    Fresh Vegetable Dip, 22
    Fruit Dip, 25
    Fruit Dressing, 25
    Ham Spread, 19
    Hot Broccoli Dip, 23
    Layer Dip, 21
    Mexican Dip, 19
    Mozzarella Cheese Dip, 23
    Olive and Pimiento Cheese Ball, 27
    Pineapple-Cheese Spread, 18
    Potato Dip, 24
    Prairie Fire Dip, 18
    Quick and Easy Dip, 19
    Russian Sauce, 22
    Sausage Cheese Dip, 22

Seafood Spread, 20
Shoepeg Dip, 23
Shrimp Dip, 17
Shrimp Spread, 21
Spinach Dip, 25
Tuna Ball, 27
Zesty Meatballs And Dip, 18
Dishpan Cookies, 207
Divinity, 198
Drop Sugar Cookies, 207
Dump Cake, 174

E

East Texas Sweet Potato Pie, 224
Easter Treats, 198
Easy Pineapple Baked Ham, 113
Easy Pork Chops, 108
Easy Rolls, 51
Edwardian Creme, 236
Elegant Ham and Asparagus, 110
Enchiladas, 140
English Toffee, 238

ENTREES

Beef

Beef and Bean Burritos, 97
Beef Burgundy, 85
Beef Enchilada Rice, 96
Beef Kabobs, 85
Chili for a Year, 100
Chilies Rellenos, 97
Chinese Beef & Peppers, 95
Christine's Hash, 89
Cowboy Stew, 132
Fabulous Brisket, 83
Fried Steak And Gravy, 93
Hawaiian Meatballs, 87
Jambalaya, 120
Lasagna, 92
Meatloaf, 99
Mexicali Boat, 94
Mexican Beef and Chip, 87
Mexican Beef Hash, 86
Mexican Dish in a Hat, 84
Mexican Good Stuff, 100
Pepper Steak Deluxe, 90
Ring Meat Loaf, 98
Rolled Roast, 94
Rump Roast, 92
Runzas (Yeast dough filled with
    hamburger & cabbage), 99

Snazzy Individual Meatcups, 91
Spaghetti Pie, 89
Spaghetti Sauce by Nadine
    Rogers, 88
Spaghetti with Meatballs, 88
Spanish Noodles, 95
Stuffed Peppers, 93
Swedish Meat Balls in Curry
    Sauce, 96
Swiss Meat Loaf, 98
Swiss Steak, 90
Swiss Steak Deluxe, 91
Terrific Pizza, 91
Texas Red Chili, 86
Three Day Brisket, 83

Fish

Baked Fish by Rachel Huffaker, 102
Cajun Shrimp, 105
Cowabunga Catfish, 106
Fish Batter, 102
Indonesian Fried Rice, 104
Jambalaya, 120
Marinated Salmon Steaks, 104
Onion-Baked Catfish, 106
Salmon Croquettes, 101
Seafood Cacciatore, 106
Shrimp and Rice a la Bobby, 101
Shrimp Scampi, 105
Spicy Grilled Catfish, 101
Tuna and Rice Supreme, 103
Tuna Casserole, 103
Tuna Delight, 102
Tuna Fish Rolls a la Virginia, 103

Pork

Bacon-stuffed Cabbage, 109
Bean's Ole, 108
Broiled Ham with Sweet and Sour
    Sauce, 109
Company Pork Roast, 111
Country Style Stuffed Peppers, 115
Creamy Ham Roll-Ups, 111
Easy Pineapple Baked Ham, 113
Easy Pork Chops, 108
Elegant Ham and Asparagus, 110
Grilled Brown-Sugar Pork
    Chops, 107
Ham and Potato Casserole, 109
Ham Loaf by Wanda Henson, 113
Holiday Ham, 114

Hot Ham and Cheese
Sandwiches, 110
Pizza Rye, 112
Pork and Noodles, 113
Pork Chops, 107
Pork Chops, Potato, and Onion
Casserole, 107
Pork Tenderloin With Orange
Sauce, 114
Spareribs With Apples And
Squash, 112

Poultry
Baked Chicken with Honey, 117
Baked Parmesan Chicken by
Clarene Chambers, 120
Chicken And Rice, 115
Chicken and Rice, 116
Chicken And Spaghetti, 115
Chicken Chili Pie, 123
Chicken Continental, 122
Chicken Divan, 123
Chicken Enchiladas, 117
Chicken Enchiladas, 126
Chicken in Lemon Sauce, 125
Chicken Stuffed Potatoes, 126
Chicken With Ranch Dressing And
Bacon, 119
Christine's Chicken And
Broccoli, 119
French Chicken, 126
Hot Chicken Salad Sandwiches, 127
Italian Chicken and Rice, 116
Jambalaya, 120
Lum's Turkey, 121
Mexican Chicken, 118
Mom's Chicken Enchiladas, 117
Old-Fashion Chicken Pie, 121
Polynesian Chicken, 118
Sweet and Sour Chicken, 119
Sweet and Sour Chicken with
Pineapple, 122
Turkey And Dressing, 124
Turkey or Chicken and
Dressing, 125
Zesty Chicken, 124

Sauces
Bar-B-Q Sauce by Arlys, 127
Barbeque Sauce a la Debbie, 128
Gravy, 129

Marinade For Chicken Or
Pork, 128
Roast Gravy, 128

F
Fabulous Brisket, 83
FINGER FOODS
Alpine Appetizers, 12
Bacon and Chicken Liver, 9
Bacon Crunchies, 17
Beef Jerky, 12
Bourbon Wieners, 9
Cheese Ball, 26
Cheese Ball, 27
Cheese Cookies by John Fisher, 7
Cheese Crackers, 16
Cheese Logs, 11
Cheese Squares, 13
Cheese Straws, 17
Cocktail Crackers, 8
Crabby Mushrooms, 11
Fried Cheese, 15
Ham And Cheese Appetizers, 16
Little Smokies in a Blanket, 10
Olive Nut Sandwiches, 7
Party Sandwiches, 14
Prize Mushrooms, 15
Sandwich Spread, 8
Sausage Pinwheels, 17
Sausage-Cheese Balls, 15
Sausage-Onion Squares, 16
Spinach Cheese Triangles, 13
Spinach Quiche, 10
Stillwater, Oklahoma Beef Jerky, 12
T V Trash, 9
Tortilla Rollups, 8
Water Chestnut Appetizers, 13
Fire Stick Candy, 200
Fish Batter, 102
Five Flavor Cake, 174
Flamboyant Fondue, 26
Florentine Rice, 163
Flour Tortillas, 43
Frank's Okra, 155
French Apple Pie, 225
French Chicken, 126
Fresh Apple Bread by Carolyn
Dorning, 45
Fresh Apple Cake, 175
Fresh Coconut Cake, 175

Fresh Fruit Crisp, 226
Fresh Pear Cake, 176
Fresh Vegetable Dip, 22
Fried Cheese, 15
Fried Steak And Gravy, 93
Frozen Chocolate Dessert, 242
Frozen Fruit Punch, 37
Fruit Dip, 25
Fruit Dressing, 25
Fruit Pizza, 32
Fruit Punch, 38
Fruit Salad Pie by Pat Spradling, 224
Fudge, 204
Fudge Cup Cakes, 167

G

Gad-About's Casserole, 139
German Chocolate Pie, 228
German Cole Slaw by Clarene
    Chambers, 65
Gingerbread, 45
Glazed Carrots, 159
Golden Crisp Onion Rings, 152
Golden Hominy, 159
Golden Punch, 38
Graham Cracker Bars, 218
Grandmother Askew's Lemon Pie, 229
Gravy, 129
Green Bean and Broccoli Salad, 63
Green Bean Casserole, 160
Green Beans Deluxe, 161
Green Chili Enchiladas, 141
Green Enchiladas, 140
Green Enchiladas a la Bea Russell, 141
Green Rice, 164
Grilled Brown-Sugar Pork Chops, 107
Grilled Corn-On-The-Cob, 157
Grilled Fancy Potatoes, 150
Grit Casserole, 33

H

Ham And Cheese Appetizers, 16
Ham and Potato Casserole, 109
Ham Loaf by Wanda Henson, 113
Ham Spread, 19
Hawaiian Meatballs, 87
Heavenly Hash, 69
Hell Cake, 177
Herb Croutons, 248
Hershey Cake, 176

Hersheys Chocolate Cookies, 208
Holiday Fruit Bars, 218
Holiday Fruit Drop, 208
Holiday Ham, 114
Holiday Wreath Bread, 52
Hominy a la Wessie Carroll, 159
Honey Bars, 219
Honey Bunches, 55

HORS D'OEUVRES
    Alpine Appetizers, 12
    Artichoke Delight, 24
    Artichoke Dip, 20
    Bacon and Cheese Surprise, 24
    Bacon and Chicken Liver, 9
    Bacon Crunchies, 17
    Beef Jerky, 12
    Black-Eyed Pea Dip, 21
    Bourbon Wieners, 9
    Cheese Ball, 26
    Cheese Ball, 27
    Cheese Cookies by John Fisher, 7
    Cheese Crackers, 16
    Cheese Logs, 11
    Cheese Squares, 13
    Cheese Straws, 17
    Chili Con Queso, 20
    Cocktail Crackers, 8
    Crabby Mushrooms, 11
    Cream Cheese Dip, 24
    Curried Shrimp Cheese Ball, 19
    Flamboyant Fondue, 26
    Fresh Vegetable Dip, 22
    Fried Cheese, 15
    Fruit Dip, 25
    Fruit Dressing, 25
    Ham And Cheese Appetizers, 16
    Ham Spread, 19
    Hot Broccoli Dip, 23
    Layer Dip, 21
    Little Smokies in a Blanket, 10
    Mexican Dip, 19
    Mozzarella Cheese Dip, 23
    Olive and Pimiento Cheese Ball, 27
    Olive Nut Sandwiches, 7
    Party Sandwiches, 14
    Pineapple-Cheese Spread, 18
    Potato Dip, 24
    Prairie Fire Dip, 18
    Prize Mushrooms, 15
    Quick and Easy Dip, 19

Russian Sauce, 22
Sandwich Spread, 8
Sausage Cheese Dip, 22
Sausage Pinwheels, 17
Sausage-Cheese Balls, 15
Sausage-Onion Squares, 16
Seafood Spread, 20
Shoepeg Dip, 23
Shrimp Dip, 17
Shrimp Spread, 21
Spinach Cheese Triangles, 13
Spinach Dip, 25
Spinach Quiche, 10
Stillwater, Oklahoma Beef Jerky, 12
T V Trash, 9
Tortilla Rollups, 8
Tuna Ball, 27
Water Chestnut Appetizers, 13
Zesty Meatballs And Dip, 18
Hot Broccoli Dip, 23
Hot Cheese Grits, 33
Hot Chicken Salad Sandwiches, 127
Hot Cranberry Punch, 38
Hot Fudge Sauce, 239
Hot Ham and Cheese Sandwiches, 110
Hot Milk Cake, 177
Hot Sauce, 153
Hot Sauce Olé, 153
Hummingbird Cake from Hereford, 178

I

Ice Box Oatmeal Cookies, 208
Ice Box Pies, 226
ICE CREAM
Banana Ice Cream, 242
Banana Nut Ice Cream, 240
Black Cherry Sauce, 243
Brown Sugar Ice Cream, 244
Caramel Add-A-Crunch Topping, 241
Cherry Nut Ice Cream, 243
Frozen Chocolate Dessert, 242
Hot Fudge Sauce, 239
Milky Way Ice Cream, 240
Oreo Cookie Ice Cream Pie, 240
Oreo Dessert, 243
Strawberry Ice Cream, 241
Tutti Frutti Ice Cream, 241
ICINGS
Caramel Frosting, 191
Caramel Icing, 192

Chocolate Icing, 192
Red Cocoa Cake, 186
Seven Minute Frosting, 192
Individual Cheesecakes, 194
Indonesian Fried Rice, 104
Instant Hot Chocolate, 39
Instant Spice Tea, 39
Italian Chicken and Rice, 116
Italian Cream Cake, 178

J

Jalapeno and Potato Casserole, 149
Jalapeno Quiche, 33
Jambalaya, 120
Japanese Fruit Pie, 234

K

Key Lime Pie, 228
Kolache, 53
Krispie Date Balls, 199

L

Lasagna, 92
Lasagne Casserole, 142
Layer Dip, 21
Layered Potato Salad, 66
Lemon Bread, 45
Lemon Cake, 179
Lemon Chess Pie, 224
Lemon Fruit Cake by Bertha
    Gardenhire, 175
Lemon Ice Box Pie, 230
Lemon Pie, 231
Lemon Squares, 219
Lena's Relish, 61
Lime Jello Salad, 76
Lime Salad Dressing, 81
Linda's Hot Rolls, 53
Little Smokies in a Blanket, 10
Liz's Frozen Okra Dish, 155
Lum's Casserole, 137
Lum's Turkey, 121

M

Macaroni and Cheese, 162
Macaroni Salad, 61
Maple Flavored Syrup, 247
Marble Chocolate Chip Cupcakes, 179
Marinade For Chicken Or Pork, 128
Marinated Salmon Steaks, 104

Mayonnaise Cake, 180
Meatloaf, 99
Melon Salad, 70
Mexicali Boat, 94
Mexican Beef and Chip, 87
Mexican Beef Hash, 86
Mexican Casserole, 142
Mexican Chicken, 118
Mexican Cornbread Casserole, 143
Mexican Dip, 19
Mexican Dish in a Hat, 84
Mexican Good Stuff, 100
Microwave Spicy Pecans, 250
Milk Chocolate Cake, 180
Milky Way Cake, 181
Milky Way Ice Cream, 240
Millionaire Pie, 227
Mini-Tart Cheesecakes, 194
Mississippi Mud Bars, 220
Mollie Shofner's Coconut Cake, 181
Mollie Shofner's Lemon Pie, 229
Mom's Chicken Enchiladas, 117
Mozzarella Cheese Dip, 23
Mrs. Mac's Sugar Cookies, 209
Mustard, 250

N

Neiman Cookies, 209

O

Oatmeal Cookies, 210
Oatmeal Hermits, 210
Oatmeal Scotchies, 211
Old-Fashion Chicken Pie, 121
Old-Fashioned Banana Pudding, 236
Old-fashioned Lemon Meringue Pie, 229
Olive and Pimiento Cheese Ball, 27
Olive Nut Sandwiches, 7
Onion Bread, 49
Onion-Baked Catfish, 106
Orange Apricot Ring, 75
Orange Gumdrop Chews, 220
Orange Jello Salad, 75
Orange Pralines, 197
Orange Slice Cookies, 211
Oreo Cookie Ice Cream Pie, 240
Oreo Dessert, 243
Oriental Seafood Salad, 81
Osgood Pie, 223

P

Party Brunch, 34
Party Sandwiches, 14
Patio Corn Salad, 60
Peanut Brittle, 199
Peanut Brittle by Granddaddy
   Martin, 200
Peanut Butter Cookies, 210
Peanut Butter Cookies, 212
Peanut Butter Fudge, 200
Peanut Clusters, 200
Peanut Patties, 201
Peanut Patties by Pat, 201
Pecan Coconut Clusters, 201
Pecan Crispies, 209
Pecan Delight, 234
Pecan Goodies, 202
Pecan Pie, 223
Pepper Steak Deluxe, 90
Pie Crust by Margaret Hartman, 232

PIES
   Apple Cream Pie, 225
   Apple Crumb Pie, 225
   Apple Dumplings, 232
   Baked Apricot Pies, 228
   Best Strawberry Pie, 227
   Buttermilk Pies, 223
   Cherry Cream Cheese Pie, 231
   Chocolate Cream Pies, 230
   Coconut Pies, 230
   Custard Pie, 226
   East Texas Sweet Potato Pie, 224
   French Apple Pie, 225
   Fresh Fruit Crisp, 226
   Fruit Salad Pie by Pat Spradling, 224
   German Chocolate Pie, 228
   Grandmother Askew's Lemon
      Pie, 229
   Ice Box Pies, 226
   Japanese Fruit Pie, 234
   Key Lime Pie, 228
   Lemon Chess Pie, 224
   Lemon Ice Box Pie, 230
   Lemon Pie, 231
   Millionaire Pie, 227
   Mollie Shofner's Lemon Pie, 229
   Old-fashioned Lemon Meringue
      Pie, 229
   Osgood Pie, 223

Pecan Delight, 234
Pecan Pie, 223
Pie Crust by Margaret Hartman, 232
Pineapple Chess Pie, 233
Stir And Mix Cobbler, 232
Stir-N-Roll Pie Crust, 233
Strawberry Pie, 227
Wafer Crust For Two Pies, 233
Pineapple Chess Pie, 233
Pineapple Cookies, 212
Pineapple Muffins, 56
Pineapple Sheet Cake, 182
Pineapple Upside-Down Cake, 183
Pineapple-Cheese Spread, 18
Pineapple-Coconut (7-Up) Cake, 182
Pink Cookies, 213
Pinto Beans, 154
Pistachio Cookies, 214
Pistachio Delight, 239
Pistachio Pudding Salad, 235
Pizza Rye, 112
Plum Muffins, 57
Polynesian Chicken, 118
Pop-Corn Balls, 249
Poppy Seed Cheese Bread, 46
Poppy Seed Dressing, 81
Poppyseed Cake, 183
Pork and Noodles, 113
Pork Chops, 107
Pork Chops, Potato, and Onion
    Casserole, 107
Pork Tenderloin With Orange
    Sauce, 114
Potato Boats, 149
Potato Casserole, 149
Potato Casserole, 150
Potato Dip, 24
Potato Hot Rolls, 54
Potato Patties, 150
Potato Soup, 132

POTPOURRI
    Baked Caramel Corn, 249
    Bath Salts, 248
    Caramel Popcorn, 247
    Cranberry, Apple, Pear Sauce, 251
    Herb Croutons, 248
    Maple Flavored Syrup, 247
    Microwave Spicy Pecans, 250
    Mustard, 250
    Pop-Corn Balls, 249
    Quick Dried Bread Crumbs, 248
    Recipe for Celebration, 251
    Relish or "Chow-Chow", 249
    Spiced Pears, Peaches, and
        Apples, 250
    Sugar and Spice Pecans, 247
    Sugared Bacon Strips, 251
    Tortilla Conqueso, 250
Pound Nut Cake, 184
Prairie Fire Dip, 18
Prism Cake, 184
Prize Mushrooms, 15
Prune Cake, 185

PUDDINGS
    Amaretto Chocolate Silk Pudding, 239
    Banana Pudding, 238
    Blueberry Yum-Yum, 235
    Boiled Custard, 237
    Cherry Supreme, 235
    Edwardian Creme, 236
    English Toffee, 238
    Old-Fashioned Banana Pudding, 236
    Pistachio Delight, 239
    Pistachio Pudding Salad, 235
    Strawberry Delight, 237
    Texas Delight, 234
Puffed Eggs, 31
Pumpkin Cake, 185

Q

Quiche, 35
Quiche Delight, 35
Quick and Easy Dip, 19
Quick Dried Bread Crumbs, 248

R

Ranch Biscuits, 47
Raspberry Jello Salad, 73
Raw Broccoli Salad, 62
Razzle Dazzles, 202
Recipe for Celebration, 251
Red Beans And Rice, 154
Red Cocoa Cake, 186
Red Velvet Cake, 186
Refrigerator Bread Dough, 54
Refrigerator Hot Rolls, 54
Relish or "Chow-Chow", 249
Rice Casserole, 162
Rice Dressing, 163
Rice Krispie Balls, 202

Ring Meat Loaf, 98
Roast Gravy, 128
Rolled Roast, 94
Rolls in a Flash, 46
Rum Cake, 184
Rum Cake by Lottie Walker, 187
Rump Roast, 92
Runzas (Yeast dough filled with
    hamburger & cabbage), 99
Russian Sauce, 22

S

Salad Fruit, 70

SALADS

Congealed
Apricot Salad, 74
Apricot Salad by Aunt Virginia, 75
Avocado Mold Salad, 73
Blueberry Salad, 72
Cherry Salad, 74
Coke Salad, 72
Cranberry Salad, 72
Cream Cheese and Lime Jello, 74
Lime Jello Salad, 76
Orange Apricot Ring, 75
Orange Jello Salad, 75
Raspberry Jello Salad, 73
Strawberry Salad, 73
Zing Salad, 76

Dressing
Lime Salad Dressing, 81
Poppy Seed Dressing, 81

Frozen
Apricot Frozen Salad, 77
Banana Frozen Dessert, 76
Cherry Frozen Salad, 77
Strawberry-Banana Frozen Salad, 77

Fruit
Ambrosia, 70
Apricot Fruit Salad, 69
Ben's Fruit Salad, 71
Cherry Pie Filling Salad, 68
Cherry Salad, 69
Cinnamon Apples by Inez Stone, 68
Country Club Fruit Salad, 71
Heavenly Hash, 69
Melon Salad, 70
Salad Fruit, 70
Watermelon Sparkle, 70

Meat
Chicken Salad, 78
Chicken Salad, 79
Crab Dip Mold, 80
Curried Rice Salad, 79
Oriental Seafood Salad, 81
Shrimp Salad, 80
Shrimp-Rice Salad, 80
Tuna Salad I, 78
Tuna Salad II, 78

Vegetable
Artichoke Salad, 67
Bean Salad, 64
Broccoli Salad, 62
Broccoli Salad, 63
Broccoli-Cauliflower Salad, 63
Cabbage Slaw by Margaret
    Carter, 59
Carrots, 66
Carrot Salad, 66
Carrot Slaw, 59
Cauliflower Salad, 62
Cole Slaw, 59
Cornbread Salad, 61
Cucumber Salad, 68
German Cole Slaw by Clarene
    Chambers, 65
Green Bean and Broccoli Salad, 63
Layered Potato Salad, 66
Lena's Relish, 61
Macaroni Salad, 61
Patio Corn Salad, 60
Raw Broccoli Salad, 62
7 Layer Salad, 64
Shoe Peg Corn Salad, 60
Spinach Supreme Salad, 67
Tossed Vegetable Salad, 65
Salmon Croquettes, 101
Sandies, 212
Sandwich Spread, 8
Sauerkraut a la Wessie, 147
Sausage Cheese Dip, 22
Sausage Pinwheels, 17
Sausage-Cheese Balls, 15
Sausage-Onion Squares, 16
Seafood And Rice Casserole, 143
Seafood Cacciatore, 106
Seafood Spread, 20
7 Bean Soup, 130
7 Layer Salad, 64

Seven Minute Frosting, 192
Shoe Peg Corn Salad, 60
Shoepeg Dip, 23
Shrimp and Rice a la Bobby, 101
Shrimp Dip, 17
Shrimp Salad, 80
Shrimp Scampi, 105
Shrimp Spread, 21
Shrimp-Rice Salad, 80
SIDE DISHES
   Baked Almond Rice, 163
   Deviled Eggs, 161
   Florentine Rice, 163
   Green Rice, 164
   Macaroni and Cheese, 162
   Rice Casserole, 162
   Rice Dressing, 163
   Sour Cream Rice, 162
Six Egg Cake, 183
Snazzy Individual Meatcups, 91
Snickerdoodles, 213
SOUPS
   Bill's Tortilla Soup, 131
   Broccoli-Cheese Soup, 129
   Clam Chowder, 131
   Corn Chowder, 133
   Potato Soup, 132
   7 Bean Soup, 130
   Spinach Florentine Soup, 130
   Taco Soup, 129
Sour Cream Candy, 202
Sour Cream Potatoes, 148
Sour Cream Pound Cake, 187
Sour Cream Rice, 162
Sour Dough Starter and Rolls, 55
Spaghetti Pie, 89
Spaghetti Sauce by Nadine Rogers, 88
Spaghetti with Meatballs, 88
Spanish Noodles, 95
Spanish Rice, 139
Spareribs With Apples And Squash, 112
Spiced Pears, Peaches, and Apples, 250
Spicy Grilled Catfish, 101
Spinach Cheese Triangles, 13
Spinach Dip, 25
Spinach Florentine Soup, 130
Spinach Madaline, 148
Spinach Quiche, 10
Spinach Supreme Salad, 67
Squash Dressing, 146

Squash Supreme Casserole, 145
Stillwater, Oklahoma Beef Jerky, 12
Stir And Mix Cobbler, 232
Stir-N-Roll Pie Crust, 233
Strawberry Cake, 188
Strawberry Delight, 237
Strawberry Ice Cream, 241
Strawberry Pie, 227
Strawberry Salad, 73
Strawberry-Banana Frozen Salad, 77
Stuffed Peppers, 93
Sugar and Spice Pecans, 247
Sugar Cookies, 214
Sugared Bacon Strips, 251
Super Duper Quiche, 34
Swedish Meat Balls in Curry Sauce, 96
Sweet and Sour Chicken, 119
Sweet and Sour Chicken with
   Pineapple, 122
Sweet Potato Casserole, 152
Sweet Potato Surprise, 151
Sweet Potatoes, 151
Swiss Meat Loaf, 98
Swiss Steak, 90
Swiss Steak Deluxe, 91

T

T V Trash, 9
Taco Soup, 129
Tea Cakes a la Joyce Bailey, 215
Terrific Pizza, 91
Texas Delight, 234
Texas Red Chili, 86
The Cake That Doesn't Stay
   Around, 188
Three Day Brisket, 83
Toffee, 203
Tomato Juice Cocktail, 39
Tortilla Conqueso, 250
Tortilla Rollups, 8
Tossed Vegetable Salad, 65
Tuna and Rice Supreme, 103
Tuna Ball, 27
Tuna Casserole, 103
Tuna Delight, 102
Tuna Fish Rolls a la Virginia, 103
Tuna Salad I, 78
Tuna Salad II, 78
Tuna-Noodle Casserole, 137
Turkey And Dressing, 124

Turkey or Chicken and Dressing, 125
Turtle Cake, 170
Tutti Frutti Ice Cream, 241

V

Vanilla Wafer Cake, 189
Vegetable Bread, 47
Vegetable Casserole, 146
VEGETABLES
　Au Gratin Potatoes, 148
　Artichokes Au Gratin, 155
　Baked Beans, 160
　Baked Corn, 158
　Baked Onions, 152
　Baked Squash, 145
　Bean Casserole, 161
　Bean's Ole, 108
　Broccoli And Corn Casserole, 156
　Broccoli Casserole Abilene Style, 156
　Brownfield Hot Sauce, 153
　Cabbage Casserole, 147
　Carrots, 66
　Carrot Ring, 158
　Carrots with Pizzazz, 158
　Chinese Cabbage, 147
　Corn Casserole, 157
　Corn Pudding, 157
　Creole Beans, 160
　Deluxe Cucumbers, 159
　Frank's Okra, 155
　Glazed Carrots, 159
　Golden Crisp Onion Rings, 152
　Golden Hominy, 159
　Green Bean Casserole, 160
　Green Beans Deluxe, 161
　Grilled Corn-On-The-Cob, 157
　Grilled Fancy Potatoes, 150
　Hominy a la Wessie Carroll, 159
　Hot Sauce, 153
　Hot Sauce Olé, 153
　Jalapeno and Potato Casserole, 149
　Liz's Frozen Okra Dish, 155
　Pinto Beans, 154
　Potato Boats, 149
　Potato Casserole, 149
　Potato Casserole, 150
　Potato Patties, 150
　Red Beans And Rice, 154
　Sauerkraut a la Wessie, 147
　Sour Cream Potatoes, 148
　Spinach Madaline, 148
　Squash Dressing, 146
　Squash Supreme Casserole, 145
　Sweet Potato Casserole, 152
　Sweet Potato Surprise, 151
　Sweet Potatoes, 151
　Vegetable Casserole, 146
　Yellow Squash Casserole, 145
　Zucchini Casserole, 146
Versatile Punch, 40

W

Wafer Crust For Two Pies, 233
Wassil Cider, 40
Water Chestnut Appetizers, 13
Watergate Cake, 189
Watermelon Sparkle, 70
White Chocolate Cake, 190
White Confetti Fudge, 199
Whole Wheat Biscuits, 47
Wonderful Pralines, 203

Y

Yeast Biscuits, 48
Yeast Biscuits, 55
Yellow Squash Casserole, 145
Yum Yum Cake, 190

Z

Zesty Chicken, 124
Zesty Meatballs And Dip, 18
Zing Salad, 76
Zucchini Bread, 46
Zucchini Bread, 48
Zucchini Casserole, 146

SIR DEB
Box 485
Tahoka, Texas 79373

Please send ________ copies of *Symphony of Flavors* at $14.95 plus $2.50 postage and handling per book. For Texas Delivery, add $1.08 sales tax per book. Make checks payable to Sir Deb. No C.O.D. orders.

Name ____

Address ____

City ____

State _______________________________________ Zip ________

- -

SIR DEB
Box 485
Tahoka, Texas 79373

Please send ________ copies of *Symphony of Flavors* at $14.95 plus $2.50 postage and handling per book. For Texas Delivery, add $1.08 sales tax per book. Make checks payable to Sir Deb. No C.O.D. orders.

Name ____

Address ____

City ____

State _______________________________________ Zip ________

- -

SIR DEB
Box 485
Tahoka, Texas 79373

Please send ________ copies of *Symphony of Flavors* at $14.95 plus $2.50 postage and handling per book. For Texas Delivery, add $1.08 sales tax per book. Make checks payable to Sir Deb. No C.O.D. orders.

Name ____

Address ____

City ____

State _______________________________________ Zip ________